TO EVERY NATION, TRIBE, LANGUAGE, AND PEOPLE

A Century of WELS World Missions

Scripture taken from the HOLY BIBLE, NEW INTERNATIONAL VERSION. Copyright © 1973, 1978, 1984 International Bible Society. Used by permission of Zondervan Bible Publishers.

All rights reserved. No part of this publication may be reproduced, stored in a retrieval system, or transmitted in any form or by any means — electronic, mechanical, photocopy, recording, or otherwise — except for brief quotations in reviews, without prior permission from the publisher.

Library of Congress Card 91-68507
Northwestern Publishing House
1250 N. 113th St., Milwaukee, WI 53226-3284
© 1992 by Northwestern Publishing House.
Published 1992
Printed in the United States of America
ISBN 0-8100-0424-0

*Dedicated to
the Rev. Edgar H. Hoenecke
and to the many others:
men, women, and their families
who have been instruments
in the Lord's hands
to carry his gospel
to the ends of the earth*

CONTENTS

Foreword		7
Preface		9
Acknowledgments		11
Beginnings	**A GRADUAL AWAKENING**	13
Apache Mission	A century of patience and persistence	23
Mission Currents One	**STRENGTHENING THE STAKES**	63
Missions in Europe	A battle for confessionalism	67
Mission Currents Two	**POSTWAR INTERNAL PROBLEMS**	111
West Africa	Answering West African appeals	117
Mission Currents Three	**THE HAPPY CONVENTION**	141
Japan	To the islands of Japan	147

Mission Currents Four	THE HOOK OF THE KAFUE	169
Central Africa	Blessings beyond expectations	175
Mission Currents Five	MISSION GOALS, POLICIES, STRATEGIES	222
Latin America (I)	A growing awareness of Latin America	227
Mission Currents Six	ORIENTAL OVERTURES	241
Southeast Asia	Opening doors to the Far East	245
Mission Currents Seven	CHANGING SCENES	279
Latin America (II)	The sleeping giant to the south	284
Conclusion	LOOKING TO THE PAST, PRESENT, AND FUTURE	299
Chronological Chart		310
Bibliography		322
Index		326

FOREWORD

"Like a mighty army, moves the Church of God"! We sing these famous words with great gusto, but the humdrum of daily life tends to blur their meaning. The hectic daily schedules that so many of us follow leave precious little time to "put our feet up" and reflect on the forward march of Christian soldiers. Other obstacles also hinder our reflecting. So much of what passes as history is either dull and lifeless, or else it is humanistic and man-centered. Distances continue to be great and distant places remote, even in the shrinking world of the 1990s. Information is often sketchy at best.

What you are about to read is guaranteed to change all that! You'll find the words of the above battle hymn taking on new meaning as you read this centennial history of Wisconsin Evangelical Lutheran Synod world missions. You will thrill to see the ever-present and all-powerful hand of God in our history. You will be spellbound at each demonstration of the grace of God at work. You will be startled to see the unfailing faithfulness of our God in the face of so many currents and cross-currents of the past century.

Christ is the force behind this history. Not only did Jesus come personally into human history, but he changed history for time and eternity by his innocent death on Calvary's cross for all people. Not only did he rise from the dead in conquering the three great enemies in history (the devil, the world, and our sinful flesh), but he sent out his disciples on a world-wide mission to carry his word of salvation "TO EVERY NATION, TRIBE, LANGUAGE, AND PEOPLE."

On the following pages you will find written the names of some of those who have gone in our place and in our name to far-flung locations on God's earth. His saving message is the only word they bring and spread. Only our gracious God can see fully what blessings are multiplying!

Some would suggest that this world is near its final destruction. Others are preoccupied with predicting God's infinite timetable. This book encourages us to work as though this book were only the first chapter of WELS missions. All else we are happy to leave to God, to whom be all glory.

William A. Meier, Chairman
Board for World Missions

PREFACE

Writing a history of 100 years of world mission outreach is a monumental task by any measure. In some ways, it is an impossible task. This history will be complete only when we take into account the hearts of countless individuals from all over the world who have come to faith in the Savior. Their names do not appear in our history book, but they do appear in the Book of Life. Indeed, we in this life can never fully know the joy our Wisconsin Synod (WELS) mission efforts have brought to the many souls touched by our gospel preaching.

At the same time, we do have a story to tell, a story of the wonders God works when his faithful people share his gospel with other people everywhere. In the WELS, this story leads us in many directions and takes many unexpected turns. It is a mission story, but it includes an account of a battle in Europe for confessionalism and our mission to bring support. It is a world-wide story, but its important beginnings were in the Southwest among the Apaches of our own country.

To show the several distinct ways the Lord has blessed this century of world missions, the writers and compilers of this book have identified seven "mission currents" that have carried us to the far reaches of the world since the humble beginnings in Apacheland. The picture of mission currents serves well to illustrate the work as it seems to flow in one direction and then another and in several directions at once. Currents, too, suggest the hand of God guiding and keeping us in the work. Finally, currents continually progress and reshape their surroundings, even as the world mission work is expanding and reshaping while you are reading this book, and new chapters are being added.

Do not, therefore, read this history as the final word on this one hundred years of missions, but as a tribute to our Savior who has given us the privilege of following the mission currents and proclaiming his gospel.

Gary P. Baumler

ACKNOWLEDGMENTS

The writing of this book has involved a number of persons. It was authorized by the Board for World Missions to commemorate the 1993 centennial of WELS World Missions. Writers of the various sections were professors Richard D. Balge, Harold R. Johne and Ernst H. Wendland, and pastors or retired pastors Howard H. Festerling, Winfred A. Koelpin, Richard E. Lauersdorf, Loren A. Schaller, and Stephen P. Valleskey. Professors Johne and Wendland were co-editors. Theodore A. Sauer served as coordinator.

Editors and staff of Northwestern Publishing House offered much help, with valuable suggestions coming particularly from chief editors Mentor E. Kujath and Gary P. Baumler. Pastors Edgar Hoenecke, William A. Meier, and Duane Tomhave and Mr. Irving Langfield of St. Paul, Minnesota, reviewed the preliminary manuscript and offered much constructive help. Original map work was done by Dr. John C. Lawrenz. A grant from the Aid Association for Lutherans helped fund the project.

To all, sincere thanks for helping bring the following story into the reader's hands.

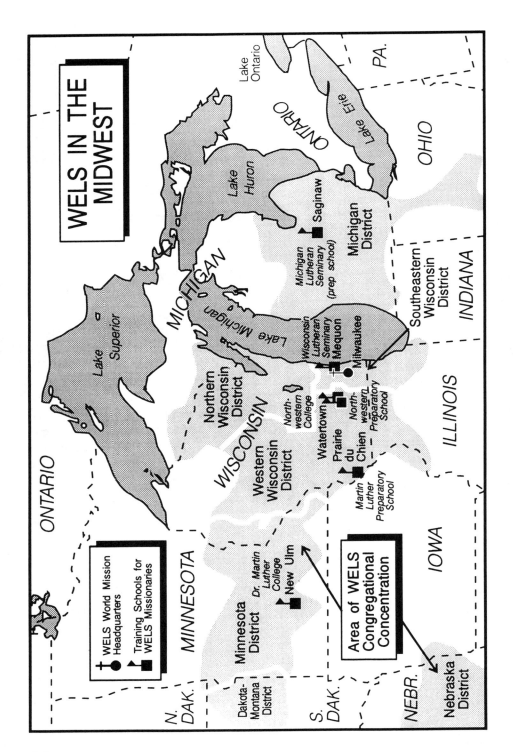

INTRODUCTION
A GRADUAL AWAKENING

A thrilling scene is described in Revelation, chapter seven. John could see large numbers of people, so many that no one could count them. They had come from every nation, tribe, language, and people and were standing before the throne of the Lamb. Dressed in white, they had just heard the 24 elders sing to the Lamb:

> You are worthy to take the scroll
> and to open its seals,
> because you were slain
> and with your blood you purchased men for God
> from every tribe and language
> and people and nation (Revelation 5:9).

In the gathering of these people, the Wisconsin Evangelical Lutheran Synod has had a growing part during the past one hundred years. From a small beginning a century ago, its mission outreach has grown until it today involves work on five continents and in fifteen countries around the world. Over 200 mission and national workers are serving some 32,000 people. This world mission program now costs over five million dollars per year.

These statistics show a marked difference from the situation a century ago when the synod sent two seminary graduates to Apacheland, U.S.A., in its first outreach into an area where no gospel work of any kind had ever been done. Even that initial, modest effort took over four decades to come into being. The Wisconsin Synod was only gradually awakening to worldwide mission activity. A number of factors played into this, factors that have to do with overall world mission development as well as with the peculiar background of the synod itself.

One might think that the fathers of the Wisconsin Synod would have held a worldwide vision of mission work from the very outset. After all, most of them had been sent to the United States by an overseas mission society. The three founders of the synod—Pastors John Muehlhaeuser, John Weinmann, and H. Wrede—all came from the Langenberg Mission Society in Germany and met in Granville, Wisconsin, on May 26, 1850, to organize "The German Evangelical Lutheran Ministerium of Wisconsin."

John Muehlhaeuser was one of the three pastors who founded the Wisconsin Synod.

In the meantime other synods were forming that later merged with the Wisconsin group to create a joint synod. These, too, grew out of the work of mission societies in Europe.

The Michigan Synod was one of these. It had its roots in the Basel Missionary Society of Switzerland. Basel's first missionary to Michigan, Friedrich Schmid, arrived there in 1833. His call included work among the Ojibway Indians. The men with whom he later brought the Michigan Synod into being in 1860, namely, Christoph Eberhardt and Stephen Klingmann, also were Basel graduates.

The Minnesota Synod, another constituent body of the Wisconsin Synod, also was organized in the year 1860. Its leader, Johann C. F. Heyer, came out of a Lutheran background in East Pennsylvania and had for many years served as a missionary to India before coming to Minnesota. For quite some time the main supply of pastors in the Minnesota Synod came from St. Chrischona, a mission society near Basel in Switzerland.

Thus we see how the mission societies of Germany and Switzerland were the chief source of pastors for the Wisconsin Synod during its formative period. Most of those who pioneered during the following years also came out of mission society backgrounds. The roster of pastors in those first decades included names such as C. J. Albrecht, C. Gausewitz, J. Bading, and G. Reim, who, as well as many others, came out of one or the other European mission society. They had a vision that extended beyond provincial boundaries. They were unafraid to undertake something new and different. By virtue of their coming to America, they were already, in a sense, "world missionaries."

World mission work during those years, however, was still going through a period of development. Until the early 1800s, the Christian religion was still largely identified with Europe and the Europeans. World mission activity took place chiefly among fellow countrymen living on other continents. The British Society for the Propagation of the Gospel, for example, was until then primarily active among English colonists. There were exceptions, of course, such as William Carey, the English Baptist who brought the gospel to India; Bartholomaeus Ziegenbalg, the German Lutheran pietist; and the Moravian Brethren from Herrnhut who labored so unselfishly among people of other parts of the world. For the most part, however, the mission societies of Europe that arose during the first half of the nineteenth century still thought first of mission work among their own countrymen overseas.

Perhaps this explains to some extent the "gradual awakening" among the fathers of the Wisconsin Synod to a worldwide mission responsibility that included people of other nations. They were both mission-minded and adventuresome, but they came out of German-speaking mission societies that regarded it their chief assignment to provide pastoral service to German immigrants.

With this assignment, they had their hands more than full in the beginning. In the midwestern part of the United States, immigrants from Germany found a climate and a countryside similar to that of their homeland. They also found a new territory, offering an opportunity to escape from an overcrowded Europe to make a living on land that a person could call his very own. Over 100,000 settlers streamed into Wisconsin from 1840 to 1850. Milwaukee has been described as "the large end of a

Many of the early settlers entered Wisconsin through the port of Milwaukee.

funnel" into which German immigrants "were poured out of the boats, and from which they traveled inland or north along the shore of Lake Michigan." German communities were established in various parts of midwestern America. They were made up chiefly of farmers and laborers ready to do anything that offered a livelihood.

There were very few pastors and teachers, however, to serve these people with the gospel. The mere task of seeking out and organizing these immigrants into congregations and then serving them with pastoral care was monumental. During these early years, many of the available pastors who came from Germany and Switzerland were like circuit riders, exploring the countryside to determine where pastoral services were most needed. One can readily see why, during these early decades, the synod gave little thought to venturing into faraway places.

These early years of the synod's history were also years of searching for a confessional identity. Coming out of a German

Protestant background did not by any means insure that one was confessionally Lutheran. This applied to pastors as well as to lay people. Thus mission societies, which served as the chief source of pastoral workers, did not always distinguish between Lutheran teaching and what was called "Evangelical" but was really a combination of Lutheran and Reformed theology. Even John Muehlhaeuser, the Wisconsin Synod's first president, had such unionistic tendencies. Under John Bading, who succeeded Muehlhaeuser in 1860, the gradual trend toward a more confessional Lutheran stance came about.

It is not our purpose here to give a detailed account of the Wisconsin Synod's move toward sound confessionalism. The following historical events, however, may help trace the progress of this development.

In 1863 a Lutheran seminary was started and in 1864 a college, both in Watertown, Wisconsin. Although the beginnings of both institutions were modest and at times managed under extremely tenuous circumstances, their gradual development was essential toward training a clergy with a united confession. Prof. Adolf Hoenecke, one of the seminary's first instructors, had much to do with the steps toward sound Lutheranism.

In 1865 the *Gemeinde Blatt,* the synod's first official church paper, began its publication. It offered a forum for expressing the confessional tone that was developing.

It was under John Bading that a gradual trend toward a more confessional Lutheran stance in the synod came about.

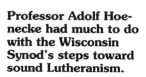

Professor Adolf Hoenecke had much to do with the Wisconsin Synod's steps toward sound Lutheranism.

17

The year 1868 saw the synod break off its relations with the unionistic mission societies of Europe, which did not consider unity of doctrine a necessity. With this break, of course, the supply of workers from Europe came to a halt.

The following year, 1869, marked the end of the synod's rather short-lived ties with the General Council of the Evangelical Lutheran Church in North America. Disagreements on the teaching of millennialism, altar and pulpit fellowship, and lodge membership led to this step, with the Wisconsin Synod taking the conservative positions.

In the meantime ties between the Wisconsin and Missouri Synods became ever closer. The two synods had been cooperating in the use of their worker-training institutions. Then their mutual leanings toward a conservative brand of Lutheranism led to the founding of the Synodical Conference in 1872, in which both synods became charter members.

Early issues of the *Gemeinde Blatt* brought reports of joint mission festivals as a regular feature.

The late Dr. Hermann Sasse, a widely respected Lutheran theologian, once declared that a church body's confessional position will largely determine its theology of missions. In other words, once we know what we want to say, we will be compelled to say it. Basing his words on those of the psalmist in Psalm 116:10, the Apostle Paul says much the same thing in 2 Corinthians 4:13: "We also believe and therefore speak." The Wisconsin Synod was steadily reaching that point in its development.

While gradually taking shape as an organized Lutheran body in America and at the same time strengthening its confessional stakes, the Wisconsin Synod by no means lost sight of the Lord's injunction to enlarge the place of its tent and to lengthen its cords (cf. Isaiah 54:2,3).

Evidence of world mission awareness in these formative years abounds in the early issues of the *Gemeinde Blatt*, the synod's official voice. These brought reports of joint mission festivals as a regular feature. According to these reports neighboring congregations would come together for an entire weekend of mission festivities. Women often worked together through the night in what was referred to as "Martha-service" to prepare meals for the guests. Churches were decorated with wreaths, garlands, and flowers. Sunday morning services called attention to the need for intensifying home mission work. Afternoon services were devoted to the task of reaching out to the heathen. Joint choirs participated. Overflowing crowds were reported. Special mission offerings were collected and duly acknowledged. Sometimes the services were held outdoors in some convenient wooded lot especially set aside for the occasion.

As fellowship ties with the German mission societies began to deteriorate, an outlet for "foreign" mission activity became available through membership in the Synodical Conference, which in 1877 began its outreach to a growing Afro-American population. Although this work was carried on within the United States, it offered opportunity to extend the gospel ministry to people of another cultural background and from a foreign environment. Eventually, under God's direction, this venture led to work on the African continent itself.

Another opportunity for "foreign" work within the boundaries of the United States arose among the various neighboring Indian tribes. While some of the men sent by European mission societies came to America specifically to convert the Indians, the urgent need to work among German-speaking people seemed to take precedence. Pastor Bading's presidential report to the synod in 1876, for example, mentions that a former mission inspector by the name of Dreves from the Hermannsburg Mission Society of Germany was to be subsidized with $500.00 annually so that he could acquaint himself with the Indian situation along the Union Pacific Railroad system to the west. Again these good intentions toward preaching to the American Indians were aborted when Dreves bypassed the Indians on his trip to California and ended up working there among unchurched Germans.

President Bading and the synod, however, did not lose sight of a real concern for worldwide mission work. As the synod observed the 400th birth year of Martin Luther in 1883, it was resolved "to seek out a mission society that was both orthodox and zealous in its outreach and to channel the synodical mission offerings into its coffers." Bading appointed a prestigious committee of five synodical leaders to engage in this search. The committee reported in the following year that it could not find a mission society that met the recommended specifications.

The committee was then instructed in 1884 "to look for young men of piety, willing and according to human judgment able to devote themselves to the service of the mission among the heathen." These men were to be trained in the synod's own educational institutions for mission service, and the synodical mission offerings were to be devoted to that purpose. By 1889 three young men were enlisted, namely, John Plocher, G. Adascheck, and Paul Mayerhoff.

Various foreign fields were considered, including Japan. The American Indians, however, received first consideration. That this interest in foreign work coincided with the forming of the federation of "The Joint Synod of Wisconsin, Minnesota, Michigan, and other States" may have had something to do with the "America first" selection. In any case, Pastors Theodore Hartwig and O. H. Koch were selected to reconnoiter for a field somewhere in the southwestern part of the United States.

Following the advice of a Presbyterian missionary by the name of Dr. Cook, the committee decided to recommend Apacheland as the place to begin. On October 3, 1893, candidates John Plocher and George Adascheck were on their way to San Carlos, Arizona, the site of the agency that administered the tribal affairs of the Apache Indians.

One might wish that the synod would have been more solidly behind this first real venture into world mission work. Such was not the case. Those who promoted it were disparagingly labeled by some as "mission brethren," an expression that put them in the same camp with the pietistic enthusiasts of some of the European mission societies. Included among the critics were synodical leaders. WELS historian and seminary professor J. P. Koehler, referring to this venture in his *History of the Wisconsin Synod*, observed: "There was something not entirely sound about Synod's heathen-mission endeavor, the idea that a church is not living up to its mission unless it engages in heathen-mission work. . . . That idea is dogmatism, with a streak of pietism, and it provoked the criticism of Prof. [Adolf] Hoenecke."

Prof. Koehler expressed his own views on this matter elsewhere when he wrote: "In outward matters the church is subject to natural developments like the rest of the world, under God. Not all groups or organizations have the same tasks. There are organizations, like people, that remain small in number and in that case have a token of their mission to do intensive rather than extensive work, by which the world may even profit more." Koehler applied this thinking to a church body that concentrates its gifts in educational work within its own midst rather than to extend its work outside its constituency.

Some within our synod already then, however, felt very strongly that a church body was not fully committed to its God-given mission unless it actively engaged in carrying out Christ's commission to preach the gospel in all the world and to every creature. This tension that arises when balancing priorities between internal church activity and the need to reach out with the gospel has ever since that time occupied the attention of Wisconsin Synod leaders when planning synodical programs. The question of meeting the synodical budget usually enters into the picture. Some maintain that a viable church body ought to be able to work aggressively in both directions, and that the one area needn't suffer at the expense of the other. The matter will almost certainly be debated as long as the synod exists.

That the synod was at this time extremely inexperienced in its mission thinking, even naive as to what world mission work really involved, became obvious very soon. Without question, those who went to Apacheland were inadequately prepared for their task. Practical as well as theological issues relating to mission work among people of a different culture needed to be clarified.

One does learn by doing, however. At least a beginning had been made. What follows is the story of the work itself.

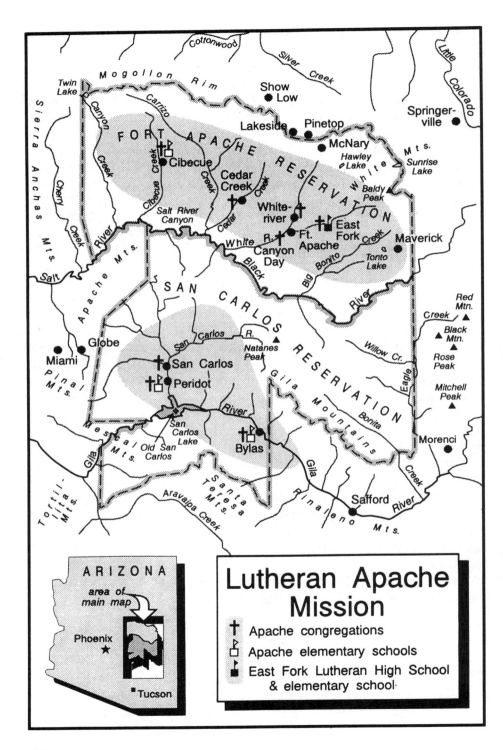

A CENTURY OF PATIENCE AND PERSISTENCE
Apache Mission

Sacaton, Arizona, was little more than a whistle stop on the Southern Pacific in 1892. For that matter, it hasn't changed much today. But Dr. Cook (Koch), Presbyterian missionary to the Pima Indians in and about Sacaton, had given our mission "scouts," Pastors Theo. Hartwig and O. H. Koch, some sage advice. They were seeking "a tribe where no missionary of any denomination had as yet set foot." No doubt they were echoing St. Paul's mission principle expressed in Romans 15:20: "It has always been my ambition to preach the gospel where Christ was not known." Dr. Cook advised them, "Try Apacheland!"

Thus began a congenial mission arrangement between Presbyterians and Lutherans in the Arizona Territory. Each respected the mission efforts of the other without interference. In an unusual way, the Apaches many years later would be able to help their Pima brothers. But we're getting ahead of our story. The genial Dr. Cook undoubtedly bubbled with words of enthusiasm and encouragement. One doubts he made much of the fact that he himself had labored nine years before winning his first convert, and nineteen years before organizing his first congregation with sixteen members. With the benefit of hindsight, one could safely conclude that if it took such an effort to win the docile Pimas, a gospel campaign to win the suspicious, warlike Apaches would have to proceed with patience and persistence. And so it was.

The Apache

To understand and appreciate an event or series of events, you have to understand a bit of history. This certainly is true when trying to understand the Apache. Back in 1541 the Spanish conquistador Coronado described the Apaches as "gentle people, not cruel, faithful in their friendship and skilled in the use of signs." What happened that the name "Apache" became synonymous for many with "ruthlessness and savage barbarism"?

In the 16th and 17th centuries the Spanish-Mexican government's policy of dealing with the Indian population was quite simple: conquer the tribes, killing as many warriors as possible and converting the women and children (by force, if necessary) to the Catholic faith. Many of the survivors were sold into slavery and prostitution. Obviously, most Indian tribes were unable to resist the superior Spanish forces and the relentless slave hunters. There was one tribe the Spanish could not subdue, however, the Apache. Once the Apaches had horses, they became a mobile, marauding force that defied Mexican control for over three centuries. No doubt this fact contributed heavily in the eventual American takeover of the Southwest. In desperation the Mexican military even attempted using Indian tribes hostile to the Apaches, such as the Pimas and Papagos. Although rich bounty was offered for Apache scalps, this method had limited success because the Papagos and the Pimas often hated the Mexicans even more than the Apaches.

The American military also had its problems with the Apache tribes. In fact, during the Civil War, when U. S. soldiers were called to action back East, the Apaches cleared all the white settlers out of the Arizona Territory except the few who took refuge in Tucson. After the war the official American policy was to contain all Indian tribes on permanent reservations. Some Apaches willingly surrendered. The majority reacted quite pre-

An Apache chief at night camp

dictably with all-out warfare. Some leaders of hostile Apache bands, such as Cochise and Geronimo, were of the caliber of which legends are made. Although both whites and Apaches committed atrocities, an overzealous press exploited only the Indian brutalities. Consequently, many of the more peaceful reservation Apaches feared retaliation by government troops and joined their hostile brothers.

General Crook, who had subdued the restive Sioux nation on the northern plains, was placed in charge of the Southwest in 1882. He quickly realized that it would take a long time for his regular army troopers to defeat the elusive Apache rebels. His daring solution was to enlist and train Apache scouts from the reservation and incorporate them into the U. S. Army, a strategy that was hotly debated in the Congress. But the general's hunch paid off. With their own people tracking them down and fighting them, the renegade Apaches became disenchanted and demoralized. By 1886 it was all over. Finally, even the fearless Geronimo and his followers surrendered to Gen. Nelson Miles, who later commanded the American forces in the war with

Spain. Simple arithmetic tells us that this was a scant seven years before the first Lutheran missionaries appeared on the scene. Later on we will meet some of these Apache "scouts."

The Apaches were accustomed to roaming about at will throughout what is now Arizona, New Mexico, and Northern Mexico. Reservation life must have been most restrictive and humiliating. They also lost some of the "guaranteed" reservation land to white speculators (sometimes to mining companies). Their rations were usually grossly inadequate. Agents who were in charge of reservations were at times out of touch with Indian culture, and even corrupt. It was during this grim episode in Apache history that our first two missionaries, John Plocher and George Adascheck, came to Apacheland in 1893.

Apacheland

To understand our Apache mission is to know some geography. If we could just take you on a personal tour of beautiful Apacheland, we have no doubt you would fall in love with it, as so many Arizonans have. The next best thing is to look at the map we have provided for you. There you will immediately notice that Fort Apache in the north and San Carlos in the south are reservations quite equal in size: each about fifty miles wide and a hundred miles long. The two reservations are separated by the Black River, which you will notice changes its name to the Salt River at the point where the White River joins it. In the early days, the missionaries from both reservations would sometimes hold conferences where the "road" came down to the Black River. Nowadays, as you can see by the map, state highway 60 crosses the Salt. What a map can't tell you is that the Salt River gorge has some of the most spectacular scenery in the Grand Canyon State.

Both reservations are "peppered" with endless ridges and valleys, covered with cedar, pine, and fir in the higher elevations and with cactus and other desert growth in the lower regions. The Fort Apache Reservation to the north has an average altitude of 5,000 to 6,000 feet, while the elevation at Coolidge Dam on the San Carlos Reservation measures only 2,500 feet above sea level. In the north are rushing mountain rivers: East Fork, North Fork, White River, plus many lesser streams. On the San Carlos Reservation, the San Carlos and the Gila rivers flow placidly toward San Carlos Lake. In Arizona, water is a precious commodity. The Apaches understood this. They needed water for drinking and irrigating the soil for corn, their staff of life.

What they needed even more was Jesus, the water of life. Our missionaries were soon to satisfy that need—so well, in fact, that within a few decades every Apache on both reservations would have had a chance to hear about Jesus. On the map you should easily find Peridot, San Carlos, Bylas, Cibecue, Whiteriver, Canyon Day, East Fork. All would soon have the gospel regularly preached and taught in them.

The Inashoods

This strange name was coined by the inventive Apache to describe the missionaries, who usually dressed in plain clothing but on Sundays appeared for the simple worship service in long, black gowns. The Apache word *inashood* can be translated, "men in the long black robes," or simply, "long gown."

The two young missionaries, Plocher and Adascheck, lost no time in bringing the good news of Christ to the Apache. By October 1893 they were on their way to San Carlos. As they had expected, conditions were quite primitive. Only a rutted wagon road and the military telegraph line connected the military post (Old San Carlos on the map) with the outside world. A ten-acre tract was assigned to them about nine miles north of the military post and Indian agency. It was named Peridot. Here a house and a small school were built. Plocher gave religious instructions twice a week to the children at the government school near the fort. The instruction was in English to 110 children. The rest of the week he taught about 20 children in his own school at Peridot.

At first, communication between missionaries and Apaches was almost impossible. Gradually, a few Indians who spoke English well enough to act as interpreters turned up. With their help the young missionaries visited the Apaches in their camps. Plocher began using his interpreter to fashion short, simple sermons in Apache, which he then could deliver on his camp visits. He was acquiring a familiarity with the difficult Apache tongue.

By 1894 our two enterprising missionaries had journeyed north as far as East Fork on the Fort Apache Reservation. They pitched their tent in the shade of "Old Cedar," a venerable tree that is still standing. Recently, Missionary Arthur Guenther told us he would "for sure" put a picket fence around "Old Cedar" some time soon. Perhaps it would last another century.

So the work had begun on both Apache reservations. Adascheck returned to Wisconsin later in 1894. His German was good, but his knowledge of English was deficient, and, as you might expect, he had little aptitude for Apache. Pastor Paul Mayerhoff had been one of the original volunteers with Plocher and Adascheck for Indian service already while in college. He was sent to the Fort Apache Reservation in 1896 and made his camp at East Fork.

Mayerhoff was a gifted man and soon mastered the Apache language. It is said he knew more Apache than the Apaches, for he could speak the dialects of both reservations with ease. Even the Smithsonian Institute in Washington considered him an authority on Apache language and culture. How eloquently he must have presented Christ crucified to his Apache hearers! What a resource person he could be for new men sent to the field!

One would like to follow each of these early pioneers to all the places where they went and tell in detail what they did. One would like to do the same for the dozens of missionaries who followed them. In a brief mission history this is quite impossible. Besides, many of the early records are sketchy and the frequent turnover of mission workers has not been fully documented. We, therefore, will take a topical approach in telling the Apache mission story, knowing in advance that many a faithful missionary or teacher will not be mentioned by name.

Tepee-to-Tepee

> The courage of these mostly German-speaking missionaries; horse-mounted; dressed in long, black frock coats with Bible in hand; venturing into the Apache camps attests to a most remarkable dedication.

This grudging compliment comes from a non-WELS Lutheran periodical. It neatly sums up the work ethic of those pioneer missionaries. Mission work among the Apaches today hasn't changed all that much. It's still primarily a "one-on-one" effort that succeeds only with the Holy Spirit's blessing.

Because the early Apache was a nomad, it was often difficult for the missionary to find his people. His best way of doing this was to follow campfire smoke that rose from this canyon or that draw. The Apaches didn't call their movable dwellings "tepees," but rather "wickiups." They were tents about twelve feet in diameter, made of beargrass cactus and animal hides over a framework of lodgepoles. The grass gave the wickiup the sweet smell of home. If you've done some camping, and years later longed for the smell of your old tent, you can appreciate

One of the last Apache wickiups, San Carlos

the nostalgia of the Apache for his wickiup. Of course today the Apaches live in modern homes as we do, and there's no longer a wickiup to be found.

When a missionary found a friendly wickiup, the family gathered about him for a brief devotion. As an earlier observer states: "It was the kindly attitude, the helpful hand, the gentle call to repentance, and the faith and love of the missionaries which finally broke down the barrier between the white man and the red man." Missionary Arthur Guenther, talking about his mother, Minnie, said that she and Missionaries Alfred Uplegger and Gustav Harders had one quality in common: an unshakable faith and love for the Apache. Minnie Guenther often accompanied her husband, E. Edgar, as he went from camp to camp. Sometimes she energetically pumped a portable reed organ and led the singing. E. Edgar Guenther had taught his Apaches some of the fine old gospel hymns. The Apache women's choir from the Whiteriver congregation is a big favorite to this day at meetings, conventions, and services— singing in their native Apache, of course. What moving, God-pleasing services they must have been in those early days, outside with only the azure Arizona sky above!

Cattle ranching and lumbering provide much of the employment on the reservations. The Apaches developed a fine strain of cattle. Those who cared for them were typical cowboys. During roundup the missionary made it a special point to turn up because it was one of those few times during the year when he could be sure of an audience. Around the campfire, after the small talk about the day's events was finished, the missionary found the Apache in a receptive mood to listen to the good news. Some of the missionaries were accomplished horsemen, which didn't hurt their standing with the Apache cowboy! It is said Missionary Henry Rosin of Peridot could rope and bulldog calves for branding with the best of them. He declined to perform before a friend's movie camera "lest it would present a wrong impression of him back east."

Pastor Francis Uplegger, who labored for years in the large San Carlos field, had learned how to ride in Germany. He was admired and considered a superb horseman. He also knew the names of the myriad desert plants that dotted the southern reservation. Through it all, "patience and persistence" were having a blessed effect: the Lord was adding daily to his church, one believer at a time. We should add that these faithful mission workers were winning the respect and allegiance of the Apaches.

The Harders Era

Prof. J. P. Koehler in his *History of the Wisconsin Synod* states that the work of Pastor Gustav Harders in Apacheland marked a new stage of development in our Apache mission. Koehler was probably the foremost Lutheran historian of his time and not given to snap judgments.

Gustav Harders—popular, highly respected pastor of a large congregation in Milwaukee and deeply involved in founding a Lutheran high school there—whatever brought him to the wilds of Apacheland? The Lord once told St. Paul that his strength was made perfect in Paul's weakness. Paul suffered from a physical problem. So did Gustav Harders. He had a degenerative throat problem (some suspect that it was really tuberculosis) that forced him in 1905 to take a year's leave of absence from his beloved Jerusalem congregation in Milwaukee. Perhaps Arizona's dry climate would cure the problem. Harders chose Peridot for his retreat. Here he gave much needed assistance to Missionary Carl Guenther (no relation to E. Edgar or Arthur), bunking in the new, vacant adobe school house. The year passed quickly. When Harders attempted to resume his duties in Milwaukee, however, it soon became obvious he would have to return to Arizona. It was now 1907, and this time the General Mission Board called him to be superintendent of our Apache Mission and also do mission work in and around Globe.

The Indians on the San Carlos Reservation had been hit with a devastating flood that ruined many of their farms. At this time large copper mines were opening in nearby Globe and the neighboring town of Miami. Many Apaches were lured there by the prospect of good wages. Some traveled even farther west to work on the irrigation projects on the Salt River.

Harders followed them. In 1907 Globe was a booming mining town, boasting a population of about 10,000. It's not nearly that large today, but the mines are still operating. House rentals were bringing ridiculous sums in 1907, but Harders was able to purchase a sizable lot with a house. With private funds he managed to build a small church and another building that served as a school. His older daughter, Irmgard, proved to be a devoted teacher. Hilda, the other daughter, prepared noon meals for the school. She also conducted a weekly evening class for some appreciative young Chinese, instructing them in the basics of English and our Christian faith.

Prosperous mining towns, much like the construction sites of our transcontinental railroads, attracted "men from every nation under heaven, from Wales to China." Mission work in Globe continued until the 1929 depression when the economy ground to a halt, and the Apaches began drifting back to the reservation.

A philanthropist is literally "one who loves people." Harders loved people because he loved his Savior. Philanthropists are famous because they give away large sums of money. Harders was driven by a passion to share the good news of Jesus with everyone. He loved people, but above all he passionately sought to bring all he met to a knowledge of the truth. He could and did talk to anyone. And this, mind you, even though he couldn't handle the English language very well! No matter. He spoke freely of God's love in Christ as best he could in English, without embarrassment. And he made himself understood!

Believe it or not, Harders somehow communicated even with a group of Chinese laborers and was in the process of instructing them. If their employers had not moved them to another job out of Harders' reach, the WELS would probably have had its first successful Chinese mission here.

Gustav Harders,
pastor, author, missionary

If you would really want to get the flavor of his linguistic gifts and the punch of his emotional appeal, you'd have to read his popular Indian novels (*Jaalahn, La Paloma,* and *Wille Wider Wille*) in the original German.

Despite his fragile health, Harders covered a good share of Arizona with horse and buggy, sowing the good seed of the gospel as he went. He might well be called the "father" of all our congregations in Arizona. The WELS centennial book, *Continuing in His Word,* concludes:

> His sermons came from the heart of a man who loved to sit at the feet of his Savior and were ever so designed as to penetrate to the very heart and soul of his hearers. They were gems of simplicity and intentionally of such design that any stranger in the audience who had never seen the inside of a church before might take home with him a picture of God's great plan of salvation for him, a sinful and lost man.

Pastor Harders died on April 13, 1917. Missionary E. Edgar Guenther of East Fork was called to succeed Harders as superintendent.

The Uplegger/Rosin Era

Perhaps no one admired Harders more than Missionary Alfred Uplegger. In the middle of his senior year at Wisconsin Lutheran Seminary, Uplegger responded to an urgent request for help from Harders at the Indian mission in Globe. Harders' health was failing. Not only was the work at Globe demanding, but there were also the frequent exploratory visits throughout Arizona in the interest of opening new missions. Besides, as superintendent of the entire Apache mission field he was expected to visit all the mission stations and fill out lengthy reports on them.

Uplegger came to Globe in January 1917 and worked with Pastor Harders until the latter's death in April. The responsibility of the church and school in Globe now rested on Uplegger's inexperienced shoulders. However, his best friend and classmate, Henry Rosin, was also assigned to Apacheland after his graduation from the seminary. "Harders' example of loving devotion and warm concern for the Indians left a life-long impression on young Uplegger and, through him, also on Henry Rosin." So wrote Pastor Edgar Hoenecke in the fall 1984 issue of the *WELS Historical Institute Journal*. For nearly two decades Hoenecke headed the Executive Committee for the Apache Indian Mission. He later became chairman and then executive secretary of the WELS Board for World Missions.

As we shall see, the relationship between Missionaries A. Uplegger and H. Rosin was close indeed, even as to important events in their lives. Both were born in 1892, the year before Plocher and Adascheck pitched their tents in Arizona. Both spent almost their entire ministries on the San Carlos Reservation, Rosin fifty years at Peridot and Uplegger over fifty years at San Carlos (Rice), less than five miles away. They died within two years of each other, Uplegger in 1984 and Rosin in 1982. Henry Rosin married Alfred Uplegger's sister, Johanna Uplegger, so they also became brothers-in-law. That same year, 1922, Alfred brought his bride, Irma née Ruge, to Arizona.

It is time to introduce Pastor Francis J. Uplegger, Alfred's and Johanna's father. Born in Rostock, Germany, the elder Uplegger came to this country in 1886 and, at the age of nineteen, entered Concordia Theological Seminary. He became a theologian of depth, having sat at the feet of such solid churchmen as C. F. W. Walther, Franz Pieper, and George Stoeckhardt.

After serving parishes in four midwestern states, in Denmark, and in Germany, he was called in 1916 as director of the Lutheran High School in Milwaukee, Wisconsin, which Harders had helped found. Then, in November 1919 at the age of 52, when many begin to think of retirement, Francis Uplegger entered upon his longest and most productive ministry: in Apacheland. Here he labored faithfully and ably until a few years before his death at age 97. For twenty of these years he served as superintendent of the entire Apache mission field.

From the beginning his Apache friends gave him the title *Inashood Hastihn*, "The Venerable Missionary." Hoenecke described him well when he wrote:

"The Venerable Missionary"—Dr. Francis Uplegger

The Apaches knew him to be a gentleman and a gentle man of God who gave them understanding, hope, and life. His manners and appearance were courtly, his speech and gesturing dramatic, his carriage stately, whether he sat ahorse or sat beside them on the red earth of the San Carlos desert, urging them with earnest, kindly, and vivid words to bethink them of their sinful mortal lot and of their high destiny as the sons and daughters of God, the Lord of Life through Christ Jesus.

As superintendent, Francis Uplegger realized that Apache language courses for missionaries were a real "must." Even though the interpreters were well-meaning, most of them did not speak a correct English and were often at a loss how to translate words and statements they did not themselves understand. New missionaries were required to spend six months learning the Apache language under Uplegger's tutelage before beginning their practical field work.

But there was no written Apache language, not even a guide for the proper pronunciation of the very difficult sounds. So Uplegger spent countless hours visiting camps, listening, jotting down words phonetically in his notebooks with the help of certain diacritical marks. Gradually a crude written Apache language appeared that could be taught to others. An Apache grammar followed soon after. Then he began to translate Bible texts and stories, a catechism, Scripture lessons, a Lutheran liturgy, even a hymnbook into Apache that included twenty-five hymns he himself had composed. In recognition of his labors, Concordia Seminary conferred on him an honorary Doctor of Divinity degree in 1957.

Obviously, Francis Uplegger was a gifted linguist. Besides German, he mastered English (without an accent), Norwegian,

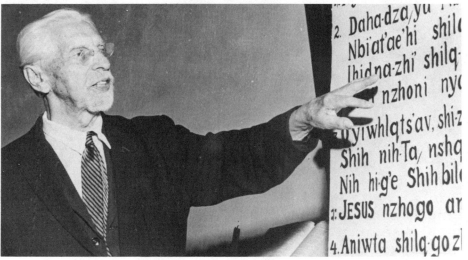

Dr. Francis Uplegger with Apache language hymn card, teaching Apache Lutheran hymns

Danish, and now Apache. Of course he was schooled in the original languages of the Scriptures, Hebrew and Greek. He was also conversant in Latin, French, and Navajo, and had picked up a smattering of Spanish. How gratifying it must have been for the Apache to hear sermons delivered in purest, classical Apache! According to former Missionary Paul Behn, Dr. Uplegger was really the only missionary who had so thoroughly mastered the Apache language. Like Mayerhoff many years before him, he knew more about the Apache language than the Apaches themselves. Francis and his son Alfred faithfully taught their congregations, leading them in group reading from charts posted at the front of the San Carlos church.

When Dr. Francis came to Apacheland to join his son, Alfred, he was accompanied by his wife, Emma, and three daughters:

The Uplegger family. Pastor and Mrs. Henry Rosin, Dr. Francis Uplegger with daughters Gertrude and Dorothea, Pastor and Mrs. Alfred Uplegger

Johanna (Mrs. Henry Rosin), Dorothea (Mrs. Paul Behn), and Gertrude. A few months prior to this writing we were visiting with Gertrude Uplegger. During the many years she looked after her father in his old age, she became, she said with wry humor, a "Jane of all trades." This apparently included everything from keeping house and clerical chores to chauffeuring the old gentleman when necessary. When he died, his tired mortal remains were laid to rest in the small cemetery on the southern slope of the Peridot mesa. It's an easy walk from the Peridot church property. His headstone is the largest in the enclosure.

The reverse side of it is inscribed with a passage in the Apache language he worked so hard to develop.

Buried in that same cemetery is Karl, only son of Alfred and Irma Uplegger. Fighting as a sergeant with the 78th or Lightning Division in Germany in World War II, he became a casualty in the Battle of the Bulge and died of his wounds on Pentecost Sunday, May 20, 1945, at Denver, Colorado.

Alfred and Irma accepted this great loss with Christian resignation, but the sorrow over Karl was always in the back of their minds. Since, due to surgery, Irma could not have more children, she found comfort taking care of babies, especially abandoned Apache babies. When one of these little ones had to be taken to the East Fork Nursery near Whiteriver, she and Alfred would take blankets and pillows and set out on the long drive through the mountains and the Salt River Canyon. Alfred wrote, "We began to do this at the time of the old Model T Fords with only isinglass curtains." Sometimes it was a nighttime trip in the Model T on gravel roads through the switchbacks of the Salt River Canyon, and a nightmare for sure when the weather didn't cooperate. Happily, there was always a warm welcome waiting at East Fork.

"Aunt Irma," as she became known everywhere in Apacheland, was sorely missed when the Lord suddenly took her home to himself in 1972. Alfred Uplegger's life went on for another twelve lonely years. In 1977 at the age of 85, he retired from active duty. Except for Karl's death, he and Irma had lived a long, happy life. Together they had served God's people at Old San Carlos, Globe, and New San Carlos. Alfred's remarkable memory remained sharp to the end of his life, and he kept faithful records, even of the weather. He died on February 25, 1984, at the grand old age of 92. His body was laid to rest in the tiny cemetery, in the words of Edgar Hoenecke, "where his dear Irma, his father Dr. Francis, his son Karl, his sister Johanna and her husband Henry Rosin, Al's lifelong friend and co-worker on the San Carlos Reservation, and a number of other colleagues all lie awaiting the sound of the last trumpet and their resurrection to life everlasting."

We don't mean to appear to be ignoring Henry Rosin. This could happen—with Rosin, that is. He was a quiet, unassuming man. In his younger years Rosin was a bundle of energy. We've already mentioned his skill as a cowboy. He was sometimes called the Peridot "sheriff," really a term of endearment, because of his straight-forward, law-abiding personality and vigor. Rosin was also eminently practical. Few building projects on the reservation were undertaken without his advice. Way back in 1941 he actually designed and built a solar system for heating water both for the parsonage and teacherage. And it worked!

Above all, Henry Rosin was proud of his Peridot mission. Under his calm, evangelical leadership both church and school enjoyed the Lord's blessing. He also was happy to send guests on their way with beautiful mementos of their visit: pieces of rock called peridot. They were lovely, deep yellowish green crystals of chrysolite. Ed Guenther wrote in 1930:

> A peridot is a stone found scattered here and there among the malpais (dark gray to black lava rock) on the rocky mesa behind the mission. When cut, it makes a beautiful gem. That will explain why it has been used so extensively for engagement rings by missionaries past and present.

It was indeed a singular blessing of the Lord that permitted the Rosins and Upleggers to remain together on neighboring mission stations for fifty years, sharing the Lord's work and also the days of joy and sorrow.

Rosin was always full of concern for his "Schatz" (Treasure), as he fondly called his wife Johanna, and she for him. In 1968 they retired to Globe and, in their last few years, lived in San Carlos until the Lord called him home in 1982.

The Guenther Era

It was not an auspicious beginning. After a whirlwind courtship and marriage in December 1910, Edgar Guenther and his bride, Minnie, had reached Globe, Arizona Territory, only to find the roads through the Nantan Mountains blocked by heavy snows. A good snowmelt solved nothing: the swollen waters washed out the plank ferry at Black River Crossing. How were they to get to East Fork on the Fort Apache Reservation? In desperation they finally used what was left of their "nest egg" and boarded the train again. Seven hundred miles later they arrived at Holbrook, Arizona, via Deming and Albuquerque, New Mexico, and still 90 miles from East Fork, no closer than when they were in Globe. But now, at least, getting there was possible. After a trip (a three-dayer) aboard a freight wagon, they finally arrived at their new home. Once the weather cooperated, Guenther was ordained and installed by Superintendent Harders. So began fifty years of dedicated service to the Apaches by E. Edgar and Minnie Guenther.

One should be aware that the disproportionately large number of pages in this section is the direct result of the disproportionately large amount of source material on the Guenthers. For example, if you're ever in Tucson and in the vicinity of the University of Arizona, you should visit the Arizona State Museum and view the permanent Guenther Apache display of some 275 valuable artifacts collected during their long stay in Apacheland. Consider also the many volumes of *The Apache Scout,* begun and edited by E. Edgar Guenther and recognized by the federal government as historical documents. Finally, as sources, remember that seven of the nine Guenther children are still alive as of this writing, including son Arthur who succeeded his father at the Whiteriver mission, and whom we have already mentioned.

The Guenther saga all began one November evening in 1910 while the students at the Wisconsin Lutheran Seminary were eating supper. Someone read a letter from the Executive of Indian Missions asking for a volunteer to help fill a pastoral vacancy among the Apache Indians. Edgar Guenther was a senior at the time. We quote from his autobiography:

> Here was my call! I rushed over to Professor Schaller . . . [and] eagerly told him I was set to go to Arizona. The next day I went down to Pritzlaff's hardware store and purchased a cook stove and two guns: a 351 Winchester rifle for keeping distant enemies at bay and a 38 Colt Army pistol for close-range encounters!

Grandson William Kessel continues:

> Guenther could never have imagined that on the basis of this split-second decision he would be required to marry within a month and move to Arizona only weeks later. There he would embark on a life-long adventure in which he would establish a school and the first orphanage in the Southwest, risk his life on numerous occasions, become somewhat of a doctor, form a close friendship with a famous Apache chief, become the first white man to be adopted into the White Mountain Apache Tribe, and be responsible for no less than six mission congregations among the Indians. Meanwhile, his wife Minnie would raise their nine children and several Apaches, be church organist, nurse, school teacher, community leader, and one day be honored

as the American Mother of the Year! Under God, it all really happened!

The first months were difficult ones as the Guenthers worked hard to earn the trust and respect of the Apaches. One of their tasks was to reopen the East Fork mission school, which had been closed for six years. This would take some doing since there were no buildings, furnishings, books, or money. The local government school in contrast provided clothing for the pupils and a noon meal. The problem of a building was quickly solved by remodeling the little "church" into a classroom. The matter of furnishings took a bit more doing, but Guenther picked up a load of scrap lumber donated by a nearby sawmill and went to work fashioning the rough lumber into desks and chairs. Meanwhile, Minnie was pounding away on the old Oliver typewriter, cranking out school lessons with applications and illustrations Apache youngsters could understand. She also volunteered to prepare the noon lunch in one of the four rooms of the parsonage. Now all that was needed was pupils.

They proved a little more difficult to come by. As they canvassed for students, one Apache responded, "Why don't you let us take more than one wife? Then there will soon be plenty of children for your school." This wasn't much help. Finally, a handsome older Apache man named Y-24 came with his two grandchildren. It was a beginning. By September, sixteen youngsters were registered.

The name "Y-24" needs some explanation. When General Crook took over the reservation back in the 1880s, he found it difficult to keep track of the nomadic Apaches. So he gave them numbers that roughly corresponded to the geographical area and clan in which they lived. Later we will meet the great chief, Alchesay. His government designation was A-1.

The winter of 1914-1915 brought a paralyzing epidemic of whooping cough and pneumonia. Hardly any children came when the school bell rang. Families had moved to hiding places in the foothills to escape the epidemic. Edgar Guenther wrote later:

> My wife and I spent many weary days in the saddle from morning till dark trying to find our people so that we might minister to their children. We were led to many a temporary abode by smoke rising from camp fires; others we came upon merely by chance. Having no medicines of any kind I

trapped skunks, rendered the fat, and mixed it with turpentine and coal-oil. To give the concoction a pleasant odor my wife added some of her precious perfume. For containers we begged extract and other bottles from the officers' wives at Fort Apache. For chest pads we cut up every spare piece of warm cloth on hand and when that was used up our long winter underwear was dedicated to the cause. Humanly speaking we saved the lives of many youngsters; everyone of our school children survived, but several hundred others died throughout the reservation for lack of proper care. For weeks we were awakened almost every morning by a rifle shot announcing that another family had lost one of its little ones.

If there were any doubts about the commitment of the Guenthers to the Apaches, the events of that fateful winter erased them.

The first year on the reservation the Guenthers met B-3, a Chiricahua Apache woman of Geronimo's band. She was alone and her small daughter was dying. The Guenthers visited often, sharing the message of Jesus with the little girl. B-3, of course, was there, too, silently listening. Later that year the girl died.

In February 1912 Minnie Guenther gave birth to her first child, a daughter named Wenonah. It was difficult for Minnie to give up her school duties, so she often strapped Wenonah into an Apache cradleboard and set her in a corner of the school room. One day B-3 walked into the classroom, picked up Wenonah and went out the door. She walked over to the Guenther's house, fussing over the baby, and began to do the dishes, sweep the floor, make up the beds— no doubt grumbling in Apache what a shame it was to leave things in such a mess. This routine was repeated almost daily. B-3 had found a new daughter. In fact, she called Wenonah "my daughter." The Guenthers reciprocated and with deep feeling called her "my mother" ("shi ma" in Apache). This became her name. Shima's Apache heart swelled with pride when her friends began to call her "the tall missionary's sister." She practically raised Wenonah and taught her to speak Apache, though Shima never learned much English.

Eventually the Guenthers had eight more children and Shima loved them all. Even when the Guenthers moved to Whiteriver, Shima often made the seven-mile walk just to visit and catch up with the growing family. Near the end of her life in

1945, she wanted to "receive Jesus' brand," was baptized, and died a Christian.

The winter of 1918-1919 was also one to remember. For one thing it was the coldest winter ever recorded. But it is remembered most of all for the flu epidemic that took so many lives. The Apaches again fled to the hills but could not escape. The Guenthers closed the school. Not wanting to infect his family, Edgar kissed Minnie and their four children good-by and left for Whiteriver. There he stayed with Dr. Fred Loe, the agency doctor. Minnie saw her husband only once during the next three and one-half months.

Guenther and Loe went out every day on horseback, looking for Apaches. The usual routine was to roll out several layers of building-paper to ward off the dampness of the ground. Next Dr. Loe would give the Apaches the medicine he had brought. Guenther would then speak words of comfort and cheer, offer a prayer, and off they went in search of another camp.

E. Edgar Guenther brings hope in Christ to an aged Apache.

When he was a young man Chief Alchesay became a U. S. Army scout. General Crook was so impressed with his service that he once told Alchesay, "I am not above you; we are both of the same rank." By the time the Guenthers came on the scene, Alchesay had settled down to civilian life on the North Fork of the White River. Guenther had heard conflicting reports about the chief and his temper, so he concluded it would be best if their paths didn't cross.

It happened one day that Dr. Loe decided to give his horse a rest and stayed home. Guenther took the building-paper and some medicine, and set out alone. After following a small trail he noticed the smoke of a campfire ahead. He had come to Chief Alchesay's camp, and the chief had the flu. Guenther proceeded as usual: insulated his bedding with paper, administered some of the medicine he had brought along, made some suggestions about food and drink, and after a short visit continued his rounds.

The next day it was Guenther's turn to stay in Whiteriver and give his horse a rest while Dr. Loe visited Chief Alchesay. The chief immediately asked, "Why did you not bring that tall missionary with you?" You can be sure the "tall missionary" (*Inashood N'daesn*) visited the chief the next day. Over the years Pastor Guenther and Chief Alchesay became like brothers. The name *Inashood N'daesn* was aptly chosen because of Guenthers's long stride and tall stature. The Apache is typically short with broad, flat features.

Rumors began to fly that the Roman Catholic Church might try to establish a foothold in Whiteriver. The Guenthers were promptly transferred there. It proved to be a wise move because eventually Whiteriver became the headquarters for the Public Health Services and Tribal Government. Again it meant starting "from scratch." The first church service was held on Christmas Day 1919 in an agency carpentry shop with space for 60. Two hundred Apaches showed up and tried to squeeze in.

The Synod then wisely appropriated $10,000 for a new church—an immense sum in those days. They got their money's worth. Under the watchful eye of Art Knoop, a skilled builder and Minnie's brother, the new church with a seating capacity of 400 was rapidly completed.

The dedication day on April 30, 1922, was, Pastor Guenther recalled many years later, the happiest moment of his long, exciting life as a missionary. In that service Chief Alchesay was baptized into the Christian faith and was followed by 100 members of his tribe, both young and old! Alchesay spoke to the assembly: "This is the only church I've put my mark on. You listen to the tall missionary when he speaks from the Book. Listen to the box (organ) when it makes music." Someone poetically described Whiteriver as "a village nestled in an amphitheater of mesas." On that day in 1922 it had a very special kind of beauty, an inner beauty because a "Pentecost" had happened in Whiteriver.

You will recall that when Harders died in 1917 Edgar Guenther was appointed superintendent. While he really enjoyed holding services and making camp calls, he didn't appreciate being a church administrator. This entailed writing lengthy reports on each mission station, training and supervising the new missionaries, and trying to solicit funds for the various Apache projects. He "loathed" (his own word) being forced to spend so much of his time doing paper work and finally, in 1936, resigned his position as superintendent of the Apache mission field. He was encouraged later that year when the church feted him for twenty-five years in the ministry. Someone pointed out that in those twenty-five years he had baptized over 1,000 Apaches!

Pastor Guenther kept going. He conducted services at Whiteriver, Fort Apache, and Canyon Day. But wherever Apaches lived and worked, he vowed to serve them. Therefore, when he heard the lumbering town of McNary was growing and Apaches were working there, he began holding services there. After struggling, he gathered enough funds in 1945 to build a church. While putting up the rafters, however, he suffered a serious heart attack and had to rest for six months. Only two years later, when he was sixty-two years old, he began holding outside services in a newer lumbering town called Maverick, some fifty-two miles east of Whiteriver, altitude 9,000 feet.

Something that gave him much satisfaction occurred on May 18, 1950. On that day, the White Mountain Apache Indians officially adopted him into their tribe. He was the first white man to be so honored. His life had come full circle. As a boy he had always wanted to be an Indian. Now he had actually become one.

It was now time to slow down. In November 1950, Edgar's son, Pastor Arthur Alchesay Guenther, was installed as assistant pastor in Whiteriver. Did you notice Pastor Arthur's middle name? There's a little story that goes with it. On the day Arthur was to be baptized, Chief Alchesay took him in his arms, marched into church with him and announced: "I am an old man. I now have one more son. His name is Alchesay!" Well, Minnie and Edgar had decided to name their son "Arthur" after Minnie's brother who had designed and built the church. But one doesn't argue with the Chief! He was baptized Alchesay

Arthur Guenther, but because of a clerical error he wa[s]
ly listed as Arthur Alchesay. You can be sure, howeve[r,]
Arthur isn't ashamed of his middle name.

On his deathbed Chief Alchesay asked for a shawl that ha[d] the key to the Whiteriver church wrapped inside. He reportedly took the key and said, "This is the key that opened the door to God's house. This is the key that opened the door to heaven." He died and was buried with the key in his hand.

Like many another Christian warrior, Pastor Ed Guenther never really retired. When he wasn't serving the McNary congregation, he was counseling his Apache friends. During the winter of 1960 he became seriously ill. In April 1961, although he was dying, he was permitted to leave the Tucson hospital for one final visit to his beloved reservation. A golden anniversary was held in honor of the Guenthers. Over 1,500 people gathered at the Whiteriver fairgrounds for the festivities. There was a pit barbecue, and simple, honest words of praise for the *Inashood N'daesn*. He thanked them from his heart for their love. Then the Apaches knew how tall the tall missionary really had been, and that they would see him again at the Savior's side.

The Guenthers had been on the Fort Apache Reservation 50 years. Edgar had been in the ministry 50 years. Edgar and Minnie had been married 50 years. Edgar Guenther died on May 31, 1961, a few hours before his seventy-sixth birthday.

It just would not be right to continue without a few special words about Minnie Guenther. After all, how many WELS mothers have been named "The American Mother of the Year!" In 1967 the church Ladies' Aid Society, unknown to Minnie, submitted her name into competition for "Arizona Mother of the Year." After she was declared the state winner, she went to New York City to compete against the other forty-nine state winners. Much

Minnie Guenther, missionary wife and "American Mother of the Year," 1967

45

as you already know, she was named "The ... of the Year for 1967." On the flight home the ...ounced over the intercom that they had the ...er of the Year" aboard and in honor would fly ...tion so that she could see her home from the ...rt Mrs. Guenther was met by state officials and ...d the entire high school marching band from Whiteriver.

That was only the icing on the cake, however. It would be just plain impossible to catalog all the incredible contributions this wife and mother had made to her husband, her immediate family, her extended Apache family, and her church. She was always just herself, Minnie Guenther, without any frills, no matter where she might be. One time the late movie actor, Charles Bickford, stayed overnight at the parsonage. (There was no hotel in Whiteriver at the time, so the big old parsonage often served as one.) Mr. Bickford was given the best room upstairs. He let it be known that his dog always slept in the same room with him. Minnie said no dog was going to sleep upstairs in one of her bedrooms. The dog slept downstairs.

After suffering a series of strokes, Minnie died in Whiteriver on January 8, 1982, at the age of ninety-one. As a rule the Apache is reticent and avoids showing emotion. But at the cemetery, in spite of a blizzard, several Apaches felt they had to make long speeches— which was their way of honoring her. We think *Inashood N'daesn* would have liked that.

The East Fork Orphanage

Sparta, in ancient Greece, was renowned for producing superb soldiers. Babies that didn't measure up were simply "abandoned" to die. The Apaches also "disposed of" unwanted children, especially in the earlier days of our Lutheran mission. When our missionaries became aware of it, they tried their best to rescue the little ones. A baby born with a defect was definitely "bad medicine."

Once Edgar Guenther was alerted to come to a campsite. A baby had been born with six fingers on each hand. The grandmother insisted it be killed immediately. "Bad medicine." Guenther calmly held his knife a few moments over the campfire, wiped it clean with his handkerchief, and quickly cut off the infant's tiny extra fingers. The child was then immediately accepted as normal!

The lives of twins born to an Apache woman were in even more danger. According to Apache logic, a woman who bore twins must be an adulteress. She was expected to smother or "abandon" the weaker of the two. So in rescuing the babe the missionary saved not only a life but also a mother from embarrassment.

At first the missionary families took the babies into their own homes. Of course the parsonage wasn't equal to becoming an orphanage, but they did the best they could. Pastor Art Guenther tells how his mother Minnie wrote to the Carnation Company and persuaded them to contribute dented cans of milk to the cause. A manufacturer of baby sleepers "with drop seats" was persuaded to donate "seconds." For years apple boxes and cartons served as baby cribs and bassinets. And so the East Fork Nursery was born.

Arnold Knoop, Minnie Guenther's brother-in-law, soon got busy building cribs, beds, "potty" chairs, and other furniture. In 1919 Arnold and Frieda Knoop had moved to Carrizo, some 30 miles west of Whiteriver, where they opened a trading post. Most of the Apaches were destitute, however, so the trading post became an economic disaster. The generous-hearted Knoops couldn't abide having a store full of goods while so many were hungry. At first they exchanged food and supplies for whatever the Apaches could give them in trade. Finally, they began just giving away their inventory

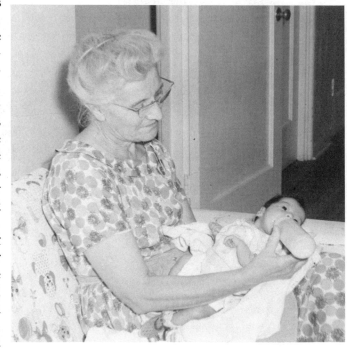

Louise Kutz dedicated her life to the happiness and eternal welfare of unfortunate Apache children.

until the shelves were bare. The Knoops later sold to the Guenthers the artifacts the Apaches had traded. These artifacts comprise the bulk of the Guenther Indian Collection now in the Arizona State Museum in Tucson.

It wasn't until 1957 that the East Fork Nursery and Child Placing Agency was created to find Apache Christian homes for abandoned children. Supporting this work has been a special project for individuals and ladies' organizations of our synod. Today the orphanage is a model facility. Among those who have cared for these little ones whom Jesus called "the greatest in the kingdom of heaven," we must mention Miss Louise Kutz. Born in Iowa, raised in Wisconsin, she worked at first at the Lutheran Children's Home in Wauwatosa, Wisconsin. From 1942 on, this Christian lady served as matron at the East Fork Nursery, dedicating her life to the happiness and eternal welfare of unfortunate Apache children. A dormitory for nurses and attendants has been named in her honor.

Apache Schools

The reader will remember that Missionaries Plocher, Harders, and E. E. Guenther began their mission work by teaching

Much early work was done in the mission schools.
Dorothea Uplegger with first graders in Peridot school.

Apache children. The mission strategy was simple: win the children for eternity through the gospel, and through them the older folks. This is certainly not the only way to proceed, but our Lutheran elementary schools in Apacheland have truly been a blessing. Our Apache congregations today largely consist of those who have enjoyed a Christian education in our four Apache Lutheran elementary schools.

The proof of the pudding. . . . Listen to this Apache girl writing (in 1934) on the subject, "Why I Go to a Mission School":

> I go to school at Bylas Mission. I like to go to school to learn God's Word of course. God's Word gives me more pleasure than any other thing. I like to stay with my Savior Jesus so that I do not go on the wrong road. I sin every day and He washes it away. He died for me, too, and arose again on the third day and went up into heaven, as you learned too. I like to hear the story of how he died for me. That's why I like to go to the Mission School.
>
> Sadie Starr, Seventh Grade

We were intrigued by this blurb in the January 1931 *Scout:* "*Ceterum censeo* (lest we forget), Arizona must have that Lutheran Academy!" Those Latin words were the favorite trademark of a famous old Roman patriot, Cato. He made a habit of closing every speech with a sentence beginning with the words, "*Ceterum censeo,*" and then he would continue, "Carthage must be destroyed." It must have worked because the city of Carthage was finally destroyed by the Roman legions, even though she was no longer a military threat. When Ed Guenther printed that blurb, he was stating his oft-repeated plea to start a Lutheran academy or high school. And it worked! The October 1933 issue of *The Apache Scout* announced proudly that such an academy "has been established at Whiteriver!"

Pastor Walther Grothe, a former teacher from East Fork, constituted the faculty. There were five charter students, including one Winifred Guenther. After the announcement there followed this paragraph: "No, there need be no arching of synodical eyebrows. Synod is not involved. The school is thus far purely a private undertaking." There was nothing wrong with Pastor Guenther's intentions. But alas, Apacheland wasn't quite ready as yet for its high school. It soon closed its doors. Nevertheless, the good seed had been sown.

In 1948 an Apache Lutheran high school came to stay. Its name was East Fork Academy, now the East Fork Lutheran

Arthur J. Meier, teacher in Apacheland for over 30 years

High School. It is a boarding school where teens are given an opportunity for a high school education with Christian teachers. One of them was Teacher Arthur J. Meier, who gave over 30 years of service teaching Apache youth. The Apaches must have admired him, too, because he showed us an official certificate (dated January 16, 1969) making him, like Ed Guenther, "an honorary member of the White Mountain Apache Tribe including, but without stint, free tribal hunting and fishing privileges." Arthur's son, William, who grew up on the reservation, is at the time of this writing the chairman of the WELS Board for World Missions.

East Fork High School was operating thirty years before an area Lutheran high school, Arizona Lutheran Academy in Phoenix, finally got started in 1978. But the East Fork school did not always enjoy smooth sailing. In November 1986 a devastating fire all but demolished the school. Could the school, like the mythical Phoenix, rise from its own ashes? It could and it did. This time the Apaches themselves had a direct hand in the construction of the new building and formed a school board that controls the affairs of the East Fork school.

The inspiring story, "Out of Ashes," appeared in the July 1988 *Northwestern Lutheran,* written by the gifted penman and missionary who lives just about a stone's throw from the new facility and grounds, Eric Hartzell. Eric is presently the superintendent of our Apache mission field, superintendent of the Nursery, and pastor of two sizeable churches. His father, Eugene Hartzell, preceded him at East Fork. After long, faithful service on the mission field, Eugene accepted a call to serve a parish just north of the reservation, where he served until he retired from the active ministry.

Some large congregations do not have elementary schools of their own, such as Whiteriver and San Carlos. These congregations, however, send children to neighboring schools. They also have active and efficient Sunday schools and Vacation Bible schools for Indian children, and Bible classes for Indian parents.

You know the old adage about not seeing the forest for the trees. Have you ever seriously thought of the impact our Lutheran youngsters have had over the years on these two large reservations? When we say "large," we're talking about over 10,000 Apaches on each reservation. Sanctified by the Holy Spirit, our young people have witnessed and testified and worn their faith on their sleeves for all to see. Of course sometimes their sanctification has been compromised by their sinful flesh, as is our common lot as Adam's children. Nevertheless, they have been a rewarding leaven in the corporate life of Apacheland. Many of the good things that happen in the land of the Apaches are undeniably traceable to a century of Bible instruction by Lutheran missionaries and teachers and by pious Apache fathers and mothers. *The Lutheran Journal* states flatly: "The Wisconsin Synod is the only large well-organized church mission in Apacheland!"

The Apaches all know about our schools. They've seen what kind of students they produce. For example, it surely didn't hurt our schools' collective image in the 1980s when three years in a row a student from our little East Fork Lutheran High School was named Miss White Mountain Apache. One of them, Miss DeAlva Rainbow Henry of Cibecue, had this to say to her people:

> I encourage the White Mountain Apache Nation to put God first in everything. There is nothing more important to me than to share with you as Miss White Mountain that the one to know is Jesus. No matter whom we know, we remain spiritual outcasts unless we know the only true God!

How many young people you know could have made a better, clearer confession of their Christian faith? We thank God for blessings he has given through Christian schools—also in Apacheland.

The Scout

You may have noticed by now that we have leaned heavily on information gleaned from that precious little periodical, *The Apache Scout*. It now appears under the more prosaic name,

The Apache Lutheran. The Scout was Missionary Edgar Guenther's brainchild. In the first issue—and subsequent issues—he personifies *The Scout,* speaking of it as if it were a person: "You will find the Scout to possess all the noble attributes of his race: he will look you squarely in the eye, tell you exactly why he has come. . . . So please let him be your guest for the whole-souled fellow that he is. . . ." Then in a neat apology for *The Scout*'s humble appearance, he continues, "and remember that even such couriers as *The Northwestern Lutheran* or *The Junior Northwestern* were once dressed in homespun."

The function of the scout in real life was still fresh in Apache minds. Many of their bravest warriors, such as Chief Alchesay, had been scouts in the U. S. Army, and so Guenther plays on the duties of the scout:

> When a fort was surrounded by enemies it was the duty of the old-time scout to sneak through the circle of the attacking party. . . . If someone lost his way . . . no one was better fitted for the task of trailing the unfortunates than the Apache Scouts. . . . If it should happen that one of our Christians loses his way in the desolate regions of self-interest, we shall not hesitate to put the Scout on his trail, feeling sure of his ability to find him, revive his lagging spirits, and bring him back to a life of Christian activity. Apache Scout, Godspeed!

After this modest introduction, one would hardly expect such an excellent little periodical. The cumulative variety crammed into each eight-page issue is amazing. Are you looking for something poignant, something with real feeling? The August 1923 *Scout* reports: ". . . with difficulty Tom said to his missionary, 'I think I am going to heaven today.' And he did."

About two years later, one of Tom's friends, Lon Bullis, one of the best Lutheran interpreters, lay dying of T.B. in a sanatorium in Phoenix. He wrote to his pastor, Francis Uplegger, at San Carlos: "Come! I want to have you with me once more below and by the sacrament be strengthened for the going to the home above." After the Lord's Supper and final blessing, Lon was the one who first said a parting word. Smiling, with a cheerfulness from the bottom of his heart, he said, "Farewell, then, till we meet again at the Savior's throne, who has called us into his kingdom and soon shall call me hence." The call came soon after that.

Are you looking for articles that would appeal to youngsters? How about these titles: "Feeding the Snake," "The Ants Are a People," "A Wonder Carpet," "Pig or Deer," "The Contented Knife-Sharpener," "The Gum-Chewing Girl." There were also many nature stories about cacti, juicy mescal buds, mountains, flowers, animals.

Are you interested in religious articles with real substance? We were amazed at the depth of the subject matter in the early years when many of the readers probably were rather uneducated people. For example, "Did My Baby Go to Heaven?" is a two-page article that says all we can say to a young couple who somehow postponed having their baby baptized, but who prayed faithfully and did not despise baptism. What a powerful reminder of the blessings of that sacrament! This article by E. E. Guenther from the September 1934 *Scout* could be reprinted as is in any of our church papers today.

The November 1933 issue of *The Scout* was written to commemorate the 450th anniversary of Luther's birth. Two articles deserve mention: "What Have the Apache Indians To Do with Luther?" by F. Uplegger and "Did Luther Start a New Religion?" by E. E. Guenther. These articles are not simplistic little Luther biographies cast in a primer setting; they're real meat, generously sprinkled with solid Luther quotes. Our respect and admiration for the writing abilities of these early missionaries has soared tremendously. We would have to say that Ed Guenther in particular must be considered one of the most imaginative and gifted of our early WELS writers who dared to write in the English medium.

"G'ad N'schahi" — Old Cedar, East Fork

If you were looking for columns with continuity, *The Scout* had plenty to offer. Dr. F. Up-

53

legger authored a fine series of articles, "As the Apache Says It," which gave the Apache a deeper insight into the grammar and usage of his own native tongue. "The Old Cedar Speaks" found the old tree talking English in the first person singular: "A year or two later a missionary came and pitched his tent right under my spreading branches." From his vantage point the Old Cedar could pass judgment on Apache life: "I see too much idleness . . . vices like drunkenness, gambling, adultery." The old tree also saw positive signs: "I see the steady growth of Bible mission work. . . . I hope that hundreds more may find lasting peace and rest under the larger and more beautiful Tree of Life. **G'ad N'schahi** has spoken." We assume that must be the Old Cedar's Apache name. The voice again was Ed Guenther.

Lengthy installments also featured the exploits of the Moravian David Zeisberger, the first great missionary to the American Indians. The episodes always had applications for the Apache reader: "These words of Zeisberger about medicine men are true to this very day, also in Apacheland." Or, "What a blessing if our Apache Christians would grow so strong in faith!"

The Scout became quite cosmopolitan, for it featured quotations from such periodicals as: *The Christian Indian, The Missionary Lutheran, The Tri-Parish Monthly Caller, The Moody Bible Institute Monthly,* and even thoughts from sermons by Rev. C. H. Spurgeon. Sometimes there were unusually creative articles, such as a detailed travelogue describing all the mission stations from an airplane flying over the reservations. *The Scout* was always bringing interesting little tidbits of information: "Lately the radio has designated Cibecue as being the most isolated community in the United States." Wouldn't you like to read an article about "Loco Jim," a converted medicine man who was always "talking with Jesus"?

There was always good advice for the Apache: "When you are sick, call the doctor, not the medicine man. Have you ever noticed that a medicine man hurries to the white man's doctor whenever he is sick?" And parents:

> Call the doctor at once and not after you have tried everything else. . . . Do not feed the baby meat, tortillas, or white flower gravy. . . . Give your children stewed and fresh fruits, milk, meat soup, boiled rice, and plenty of clean water. . . . Keep the child dressed with more than a smile when the

weather is cold. . . . Keep its eyes, face, head and hands clean *all the time*. . . . If your child seems hot, give it castor oil at once and follow with half a spoon of soda. The latter may ward off pneumonia. . . . You mothers, stay home and care for your children at all times instead of letting them roll in the dirt while you are off gambling and drinking. God will hold you responsible for any neglect.

The Scout was also the forum for announcements of all sorts: anniversaries, births, deaths, baptisms, "doings" at the various mission stations. It was a sort of glue that tried to keep our missions in Apacheland in touch with one another— and it did right well!

Tidbits and Treasures

Tufa is a valuable building material found near the Nantan Mountains. When quarried, it is easily sawed, but hardens under exposure to air and sunshine. Many of our mission buildings, such as the church and parsonage at (New) San Carlos, are of tufa. The mission at Old San Carlos was also of tufa. When the mission had to be abandoned in 1929, Henry Rosin, the reservation's unofficial "handy man," organized a team of Apache volunteers to dismantle it and haul it nine miles to Peridot. There they put it back together again as a school, which still stands.

* * *

The reason they had to abandon Old San Carlos was that it was about to be flooded by the waters behind Coolidge Dam. Remember the Pima Indians and Dr. Cook? For centuries they had made a living irrigating the land, using the waters of the Gila River. When the white man came, he settled upstream from the Pimas and monopolized almost all the water. Most of the Indian farms dried up. Then one heard of a great dam that was to be built. The dam would hold back the flood waters of the Gila for the "poor Pimas." Ed Guenther writes: "If the Pima Indians were the only ones to benefit from this dam then you and I would never live to see it built. . . . The white man wanted the dam to irrigate the many additional acres of land waiting for water."

But the story of the "poor Pimas" was a good lever for prying a concession out of Congress, and the dam was built. Gertrude Uplegger (who was there) tells us that most of the Apaches were opposed to the dam because it would flood their burial grounds. Her brother, Alfred, was instrumental in convincing them that the project should have their support even though the Pimas would be the chief beneficiaries.

Now you know what we meant when we said the Apaches would some day be able to thank their Pima brothers and Dr. Cook for sending the first Inashoods to Apacheland with the living water of the gospel. We thought of a parallel in Romans 15:26,27 where Paul's converts in Macedonia and Greece were able to raise a generous offering for the needy in Jerusalem whence the gospel had come to them.

* * *

At the dedication of the new Coolidge dam on March 4, 1930, ex-President Calvin Coolidge and many notables were present. Will Rogers, popular humorist and homespun philosopher, was also there. He did not eat at the table with the guests of honor, but grabbed his lunch from the hot dog stand with the crowd. Later Rogers mused in his inimitable way:

> A peculiar thing about the dam that you may not read in your dispatches— the dam is built on the lower side of the Apache Indian reservation, and the water is all to be used by the Pima tribe and the whites. In fact, they moved the Apaches out of the very valley where the water is backed up in, and moved them 10 miles up above. The only way the Apaches can ever get any good out of the dam, is for somebody to invent a way for the water to run uphill. And then they wonder why Apaches are wild!

* * *

Finally, we just cannot resist sharing with you a few of the tales told about our early missionaries. The following are about Missionary Edgar Guenther, and were told to us by his son, Arthur. You'll have to admit they're a bit wild, but they're true!

> During World War I, in the general hysteria about anything German, there was a certain shavetail lieutenant at Fort Apache who was obsessed with the idea that father was a spy for the German Kaiser. After all, his name was so German you could spell it with an umlaut, and he spoke German as fluently as English. Anyhow, he just didn't like father and began spying on him. Father had borrowed a transit, level and tripod to do some surveying on the San Carlos Reservation. He also had a stethoscope-like device called a sonascope, bought from Montgomery Ward. By listening, a mechanic could tell which rod of your Model T was going out. The lieutenant observed father as he drove by with this

equipment sticking out of the old Model T, and said to himself, "Aha, he's sending wireless messages to the Kaiser."

Then one night while the family was eating supper, the parsonage was surrounded by soldiers, and a squad of black troopers burst in, bayonets at the ready, to arrest father. Although father was a good friend to most of these soldiers, they had their orders. They began searching for evidence, prying open drawers, etc. In those days during summer the stove was disconnected and a colorful painted plate covered the hole in the chimney. It was pried off and they pulled out an old lard bucket and some newspapers— including an *Allgemeine Zeitung*, a German newspaper printed in Milwaukee—with a picture of the Kaiser on it! That was it! They marched father off to the guard house and locked him in a filthy cell. That night mother gave birth to Winifred— alone! (We called Winifred the other day and, incredibly, she somehow inherited the huge iron padlock and key that imprisoned her father while she was being born!) Of course, the lieutenant had acted on his own, without the commanding officer's knowledge. The next day the C. O. was furious. The telegraph wire to Fort Sam Houston, Texas, headquarters of the 10th Cavalry was really humming, and also to Washington. The letters of apology from the government are there to be read— and also the letters from father to Fort Sam Houston.

* * *

Arthur Guenther with an aged Apache woman and her daughter

For some time, there had been some in the military who were going to get father on something— perhaps disrespect for the flag. He used to ride or walk over to the fort in the evening to pick up the mail. Invariably it was time to lower the flag. So they made father stand at attention in front of the troop during the complete ceremony. But father had a sense of humor. When they asked what the military could do to compensate for this grave injustice, father thought a moment and said, "You know, I've just seeded in a big lawn over at East Fork. I'd like a load of horse manure for every time I had to stand at attention. Delivered personally by that lieutenant."

I interrupted and asked Art, "Did he really do it?"

Art's answer was a model of military preciseness, "So it was ordered, and so it was done!"

The Future

Before looking ahead we must at least mention the names of a few more people who gave so much of themselves in the Apache mission field. We think of Pastor E. Arnold Sitz who had come to Arizona for health reasons, organized the Cibecue-Carrizo district, became the first president of the Arizona-California District, and died at age 95. . . . There was Henry C. Nitz who labored so efficiently as principal of the East Fork boarding school before moving to Minnesota in 1929. . . . Paul Behn, who later served on the Apache Mission executive committee, was also at East Fork, 1934-1940. . . . Missionary Ernest Sprengeler served Bylas from 1930-1947 before his lengthy and fruitful ministry in East Fork. . . . O. P. Schoenberg served East Fork and then in 1911 opened the mission in Cibecue. It is said he was an adept teacher. . . . Probably no one had a more profound effect on the organization and administration of our Apache Mission in recent times than Pastor Raymond Zimmermann. Before his retirement, his position was that of Field Secretary. . . . Pastor Fred Nitz's heart was always in Apacheland. He proved this not only by his work on the field, but also by serving on the Board for the Apache Mission for thirty years. . . . For length of service we also mention Teacher Willis Hadler of Bylas, whose teaching career there spans over 30 years.

This list would not be complete without acknowledging the dedicated service of an Apache, Rankin Rogers. Although he had to walk with crutches and had only a seventh grade education, he was a natural-born teacher and taught the lower classes at Peridot from 1920-1935.

There is no denying that WELS' first venture into foreign mission work produced its share of mistakes. Prof. Koehler mentions some: for example— sending young unmarried missionaries like Mayerhoff into the wilds alone, not using Mayerhoff's linguistic gifts to tutor other missionaries, or not giving missionaries special pedagogical training to help them teach Indian children effectively. It didn't help matters that our work in Apacheland was at first placed under the direction of the Southeastern Wisconsin District, and was administrated by a board which at times showed little understanding or empathy for the workers. Sometimes it seems that the Apache mission was perhaps a sort of catch-all, where men were sent who couldn't seem to fit in anywhere else. But again, hindsight is easy. Thank God that our mission policy, forged in the crucible of trial and error, under God, has come a long way!

Churches at Canyon Day, Cibecue, Peridot, and San Carlos

There is little profit in rehearsing the obstacles that impeded growth in our Apache mission. Yes, we've come a long way since the government used policemen to "induce twenty half-wild little children of nature" to enter Missionary Plocher's classroom, as *Continuing In His Word* records. But the historic observation of the Apache disposition still remains true: they are "individualists" who are reluctant to take part in joint activity such as a congregation. In spite of outward changes in Apacheland, we are told that the Apache remains true Apache.

We've already mentioned the population boom in Apacheland. In 1972 the publication *You And Your Synod* listed the total Apache population at "a little less than 9,000." Today's figure is more like 21,000 and growing. It is disturbing to read that the majority of our Apache congregations do not have an accurate membership list. Still, the number of Apache Lutherans seems to hover about the 3,000 mark. In other words, the percentage of Apaches that are Lutheran Christians today is smaller than it was 30 years ago. Why?

Here are some possible answers. Before World War II, it is estimated that about 90% of Apaches claiming to be Christians were Lutherans. What has happened since? For one thing, after World War II, Congress opened up the reservations to all sects. Then there were sweeping changes made in tribal organization and government. The Assembly of God and Miracle Church grew by leaps and bounds. They came in with their "whoop and holler" religion (as Art Guenther calls it), with signs and wonders, miraculous healings combined with an emotionalism that has swept many of our nominal Lutherans away. Then there has also been a revival of the native Apache religion—complete with more sophisticated medicine men and women plus the popular Sun Rise dance, a ritual tied to the old religion that seems to affect all Apaches one way or another.

Nevertheless, there is reason for optimism. Our most experienced missionary, Art Guenther, says, "We're coming back with quality!" We have an excellent group of young missionaries and teachers. The tried and proven approach of Christian education through Christian schools has always had the Lord's blessing. To most Apaches, our work of missions and our Lutheran schools are synonymous. The sects can't match them and our commitment to excellence in education.

Unfortunately, the population boom does not mean that there is a general corresponding economic boom. Apacheland remains essentially a welfare state with many of its people living below the poverty line. The unemployment rate is listed at 70%. Many factors are involved here. Among them are a paternalistic attitude on the part of the federal government, the lack of a work ethic, and an almost complete lack of money-management skills among many of the people.

How much does this bleak picture affect our Lutheran Apache Mission? Considerably, of course. Nevertheless, statistics show a modestly growing commitment by our Apache members to support the Lord's work on both the local and synodical levels. In fact, our congregations in San Carlos and Whiteriver are within "striking distance" of total self-support. However, we must be realistic and acknowledge that total self-support for our churches in Apacheland is not achievable in the near future. Hindrances are: the rather expensive educational system we have in place, the low economic level of the Apache, and the welfare mentality that seems to go along with life on a reservation. But just remember: Apache missionaries 50 years ago would never have dreamed of the financial support coming out of Apache churches today!

We are happy to see the recent excellent and comprehensive Board for World Missions report focusing on the Apache Mission. It is an in-depth study of past performance and a courageous strategy proposal for the future. Through many years of experience we seem to be learning how to meet the unique challenge of the Apache mission field. It has been a long 100 years in Apacheland, but much has and can yet be accomplished under a gracious God's blessing, WITH PATIENCE AND PERSISTENCE!

Surrounded and all but submerged by the cross-currents of paternalism and welfarism, tugged this way and that by false prophets, superstition, and shamanism, may our brothers and sisters in Apacheland stand up on their own and take the right kind of pride in being an Apache, an American, a Christian, a Lutheran!

They say that when Minnie Guenther wanted to send greetings on special occasions, she did so by writing her own poetry. We came across one of her little gems recently and decided: why not close this chapter with some simple words written by someone who loved the Apaches almost as much as she loved her Savior.

In this world of sin and sorrow
   Jesus hold my hand.
Make me strong to meet the morrow;
   Jesus hold my hand.

When temptation doth surround me
   Be Thou ever near,
With Thy hand upon my shoulder
   I need have no fear.

O Jesus, take this heart of mine,
   Make it pure and ever Thine.
Thou hast bled and died for me;
   Let me ever live for Thee.

Lord Jesus, let me ever be
   Thy own dear child and follow Thee;
My hand in Thine will lead me right
   And guard my footsteps day and night. Amen.

Minnie Guenther

MISSION CURRENTS ONE STRENGTHENING THE STAKES

As we have seen, the Wisconsin Synod's first venture into heathen mission work came soon after the initial step toward the union of the Wisconsin, Minnesota, and Michigan Synods in 1892. The result of this union, however, was a rather loose federation of church bodies, at best an initial step toward limited cooperation in worker training, publications, and missions. Much strengthening of the stakes still needed to be done before the leaders of the respective synods felt that the time had come to form a single church body.

In the ensuing years, the federation progressed toward a much closer union especially by developing various worker-training programs.

It centered the headquarters for pastoral training in Wisconsin. In 1893 a new seminary was built at Sixtieth and Lloyd in Wauwatosa. Under the able teaching and leadership of professors John P. Koehler, August Pieper, and John Schaller, this institution emphasized a historical-grammatical approach to Scripture, known as the "Wauwatosa Theology." Under Dr. A. F. Ernst, Northwestern College in Watertown developed a more rigid educational system patterned after the German gymnasia

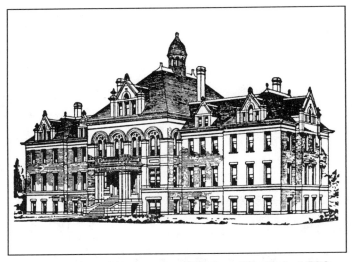

The home of "Wauwatosa Theology," built in 1893

or pre-university schools, better serving the purpose of preparing men for the ministry. This program continued in 1913 under the direction of Prof. E. E. Kowalke, who succeeded Dr. Ernst as president.

Dr. Martin Luther College in New Ulm, which originated as an all-purpose training school for the Minnesota Synod, was assigned to serve as the federation's teacher training institute in 1892. Its preparatory department also served as a feeder school for Northwestern College.

The Michigan Synod's seminary at Saginaw, which had closed in 1907, reopened as a preparatory high school for Northwestern College in 1910. Prof. O. J. Hoenecke, the first director of the institution, continued to serve in that capacity for nearly 40 years.

Professors August Pieper, John Schaller, and John P. Koehler provided able leadership for Wisconsin Lutheran Seminary in the early part of this century.

This educational development took much of the federation's energy during this period of internal growth.

In 1917, the loosely structured federation took a further step toward internal development by becoming a unified corporate body. The "Joint Synod of Wisconsin, Minnesota, Michigan, and Other States" became one in fact as well as in name, operating under one constitution. The Pacific Northwest District was added in 1918 and the Dakota-Montana District in 1920. This reorganization and expansion took place under the leadership of Pastor G. E. Bergemann, who served as the synod's president from 1908 to 1933. Historian Edward C. Fredrich, professor emeritus of Wisconsin Lutheran Seminary, has summarized the talents of synodical leadership in this succinct way: "Muehlhaeuser founded the synod, Bading shaped its confessional stance, and Bergemann gave it its organizational form." By the year 1919, the newly merged body numbered 698 preaching stations, 438 pastors serving 127,083 communicants, with 325 Christian elementary schools, and 272 teachers serving nearly 14,000 pupils.

With all this internal growth and development, it seemed to many that the synod had enough work on its hands without looking to the rest of the world for things to do. The outbreak of World War I in 1914, which the United States entered in 1917, also concerned the synod. Among the 325,000 American casualties, many came from Wisconsin Synod congregations, and even following the November 11th Armistice in 1918, many homes in the synod were affected by the war's devastating upheavals. Therefore, the Apache Indian mission and the Synodical Conference work among African Americans had to serve several generations as the synod's only "world mission" outlets.

At the synod convention in New Ulm that followed in 1919, Prof. August Pieper in his convention essay took up the theme of *reconstruction* and applied it to "The True Reconstruction of the Church." Of special interest in Prof. Pieper's paper are his words referring to the synod's response to Christ's commission to preach the gospel in all the world. After calling attention to a number of activities in which the church body had demonstrated some signs of spiritual malaise, Pieper said the following:

> The same indifference and half-heartedness shows itself also in the conduct of our missions. Our Indian mission up to the present appears as the plaything of a few interested people, something which a large part of the synod regards

as an unnecessary waste of money and strength, which "brings nothing in (namely, to the synod treasury)," which a person unwillingly and necessarily supports because he cannot rid himself of it in a decent way and doesn't want to hurt the feelings of its supporters. Upon a work carried on in such fashion the goodwill and blessing of God can certainly not rest.

Summing up the synod's attitude toward its entire mission responsibility, Prof. Pieper used even stronger language:

> Do we want to do it or not? One-half a heart, one-half a job, one-half the result! We have worked as in a trance. Mary as she sits at the Lord's feet has become a dreary dreamer. She has accustomed herself to a matter of hearing alone, her ear is dead, her heart is indifferent, her hands and feet have become heavy, lazy. Up, up, Mary! Rub the sleep out of your eyes, shake the drowsiness out of your body, it is time to get to work!

The synod showed its appreciation to Prof. Pieper for his timely words by thanking him for his "powerful witness," requesting him to make further presentations of the same nature at future gatherings, and resolving that his essay be distributed as a pamphlet in both German and English languages. Was it by plan or coincidence that the synod celebrated the 25th anniversary of the Apache mission at that same convention?

In a direct way, World War I also served to create interest in the synod's first overseas venture. Postwar Europe, in desperate need of reconstruction, looked to America for help both physically and spiritually. The tables of a century before were turned. In 1920 German-speaking Lutherans in Poland asked to be served by pastors from the United States. In 1922 Pastor Otto Engel was sent to Poland to investigate these possibilities. Prof. John P. Koehler of Wisconsin Lutheran Seminary was also asked to study this field while spending a year in Germany.

All this led to the Wisconsin Synod's return to the continent from which its founding fathers had come.

A BATTLE FOR CONFESSIONALISM MISSIONS IN EUROPE

POLAND

The story of the Wisconsin Synod's first overseas mission begins in Lodz, about 100 miles east of Germany's frontier with Poland. Our purpose in Poland was not the conversion of non-Christian people. We did not aim at winning people from Catholicism or the sects. From the beginning, the synod's purpose was to support true Lutheran confessionalism, and it was undertaken in response to urgent appeals.

Church Conditions in Poland after World War I

During the nineteenth century, many Germans left their homeland because of crowded conditions and the lack of economic opportunity. Some emigrated because of the forced union of Lutheran and Reformed churches in Prussia. At the invitation of large landholders and industrialists, many moved to Poland. They were guaranteed there would be no interference in religious matters.

After World War I, however, the new Republic of Poland revoked the religious guarantees. The Republic tried to unite

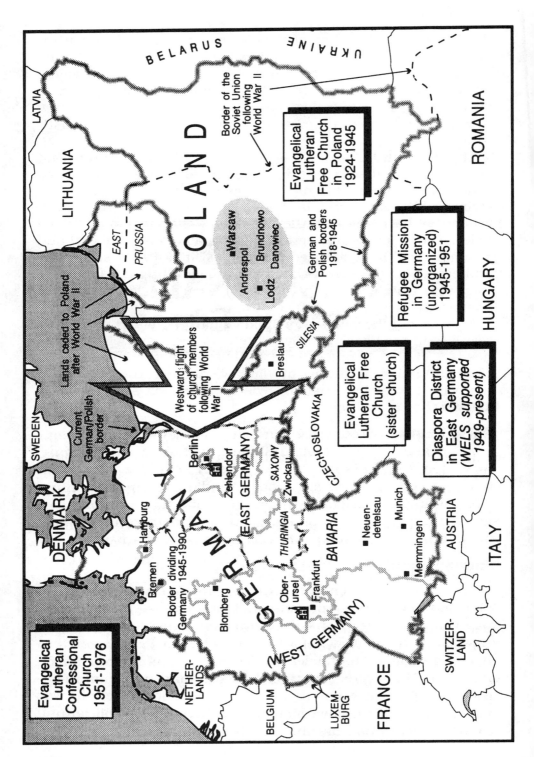

the Protestant churches of Poland into one church organization. This planned reorganization led to tensions within the Evangelical Augsburg Church of Poland, which had a vague Lutheran consciousness but did not uphold a strong Lutheran confession. Antagonism between native Poles and ethnic Germans frustrated attempts to draft a united church constitution.

The Augsburg Church was the only Lutheran church that could enjoy legal status in the republic. Its Lutheranism, however, was suspect. One of its ministers, Pastor W. P. Angerstein, published a tract in which he showed that the church was out of harmony with the *Augsburg Confession* in all 28 articles. The church's university-trained pastors were liberal and rationalistic. They practiced fellowship with various sectarians and even with the Polish National Catholic Church. Many pastors were uninterested in the care of souls. A fee system for pastoral services favored the well-to-do.

Even before the war, various individuals in Poland pleaded to relatives in the Wisconsin Synod to help them in their spiritual need. A circle of confessional Lutherans in the city of Lodz, about 50 miles southwest of Warsaw, renewed the pleas after the war. It was then that the Wisconsin Synod seriously considered the call for help.

Surveying the Field, 1922

In 1921 the synod authorized Pastor Otto Engel of Randolph, Wisconsin, a native of Lodz, to study the church situation in Poland and present a report. While in Poland during 1922, Pastor Engel preached and made presentations wherever he had an invitation to do so. He reported to the 1923 convention of the Wisconsin Synod that many preachers in Poland were apostate, that thousands of souls lacked a shepherd, and that many people hungered greatly for God's Word.

Gustav Maliszewski, an evangelist and teacher in the Augsburg Church in Lodz, led one of the confessional groups that had been meeting in private homes. Mr. Maliszewski had read some of Dr. C. F. W. Walther's writings and also had access to the periodicals of the Evangelical Lutheran Free Church (Saxon Free Church) in Germany. Pastor Angerstein urged him to enroll in the Saxons' seminary at Berlin-Zehlendorf. There he was introduced to a theology rooted in the Scriptures and faithful to the Lutheran Confessions.

Maliszewski returned to Lodz in 1923 and gathered a considerable number of people in that city and in nearby Andrespol. He hoped to organize a Lutheran free church. Since the government would not permit him to hold public services, he met with people in their homes, instructing them in the Bible and catechism. He appealed to the Saxon Free Church, the Missouri Synod, and the Wisconsin Synod. All three gave the appeal serious consideration, but it was the Wisconsin Synod that, by virtue of Pastor Engel's visit, was ready to take action.

Decision to Enter the Field, 1923

After hearing Engel's report, the 1923 Synod Convention resolved "that the Joint Commission on Missions should take on the mission in Poland with all energy." Ten thousand dollars was granted for this mission.

The resolution passed only after considerable debate. The field's remoteness, the synod's limited funds, and the lack of men for the work were cited as reasons not to undertake the mission in Poland.

In 1924 Engel accepted the call to superintend the work in Poland. Meanwhile, Maliszewski worked on a constitution for an Evangelical Lutheran Free Church. He translated it into Polish and submitted it to the Ministry of Public Worship and Instruction in Warsaw. The agency promised to approve the constitution and thus opened the way for public worship services.

Beginnings in Lodz and Beyond, 1924-1926

St. Paul's Evangelical Lutheran Free Church of Lodz was organized on May 11, 1924. Thirty-five men subscribed to Maliszewski's constitution and resolved to take up the struggle on behalf of the truth. They elected him as their pastor.

Since Professor J. P. Koehler of the Wauwatosa Seminary was intending to travel to Germany, the Commission on Missions asked him to visit Poland, study the situation, and determine what the synod ought to do there. He reported: "Poland presents a large and ripe mission field which ought to be worked by a Lutheran body."

After the beginning at Lodz, inquiries came from all over western Poland and beyond, mostly from disillusioned and disaffected members of the Augsburg Church. Maliszewski regarded every inquiry as a Macedonian call and followed up as best he could. He appealed to the Wisconsin Synod for more manpower. It was on the way, but not from the United States, as we shall see.

Providing Pastors

During his two years in the field, Engel helped organize and extend the work. He especially recruited young men for seminary training. The ethnic Germans in Poland would provide the manpower themselves, and the first man entered the seminary at Berlin-Zehlendorf in 1924.

Almost without exception the men who joined Maliszewski as pastors got their theological training at Zehlendorf. In order of their seniority they were Heinrich Mueller, Leopold Zielke, Karl Patzer, Armin Schlender, Eduard Lelke, Helmuth Schlender, Alfons Wagner, Alfred Reit, and Arthur Napp.

August Lerle, one worker who did not study at Zehlendorf, was, nevertheless, interviewed there for possible service in the ministry. Lerle was born near Lodz, studied theology at Neuendettelsau in Germany, and returned to serve as a pastor in the Augsburg Church. His last assignment in that body was as director of a school for evangelists in Zgierz. There, his strong Lutheran confessionalism was an important factor in making it impossible for him to continue. He found his way to Maliszewski's group and began to serve St. Peter's in Lodz in 1927.

Dasler's Directorship, 1926-1929

Engel returned to his family in 1925. Adolf Dasler, another native of Lodz, was called to take his place. Dasler had come from Poland to study at Northwestern College and the Wauwatosa Seminary. He had been serving the Wisconsin Synod congregation at Kingston, Wisconsin, when he accepted the call to Poland.

Dasler presented an optimistic report to the Wisconsin Synod convention in 1927. He reported 200 communicants at Lodz and 69 at Andrespol. These congregations were contributing to their pastors' salaries, helping the poor, and assisting the students at Zehlendorf. In Dasler's view, contributions were good, considering the tragic economic conditions in Poland. The Lodz congregation was asking for help in building a church because of the standing-room-only situation in their place of worship.

That same convention heard the synod's mission board recommend to discontinue or at best to minimize our involvement in the work in Poland. The board anticipated that costs would increase as the number of workers increased and requests for chapels and parsonages came in. In this respect, time and subsequent events would prove their forecast correct.

The synod, however, did not accept the board's recommendation, but in the providence and grace of God resolved to continue supporting the cause of a confessional Lutheran church in Poland. Though it might have been good business to do otherwise and though the synod would not always exercise perfect judgment in implementing this resolution, the decision to continue work in Poland was a good one.

The Bodamer Years, 1929-1939

Dasler concentrated his efforts on the inner development and strengthening of the mission. He initiated regular pastoral conferences. He worked in Poland until May 1, 1929. Then the mission board asked: "Where is a man to be found who has the synod's confidence, whose circumstances permit settling in Poland, who can muster the cheerful zeal to serve his Lord in this work?"

The Lord knew the answer, and he provided Pastor William C. Bodamer of Scio, Michigan. Bodamer began his work in Poland that same year. Until world events separated him from the field in 1939, he labored to lead the fledgling free church into soundly Lutheran doctrine and practice.

Pastor William Bodamer led the young church in Poland into soundly Lutheran doctrine and practice. Shown here about to leave for a 1949 visit to the Refugee Mission Church in Germany.

Bodamer's policy in extending the church was sober: Go only where there is a clear call. . . . Investigate the reason for the call (some people thought: "Free church means you don't have to pay anything"). . . . Inform inquirers clearly concerning the doctrinal position of the free church. . . . State clearly what will be expected of the members. . . . Explain our form of church government. . . . Instruct them in the nature and meaning of discipline.

The center of the work remained Lodz. Bodamer described the city in *The Northwestern Lutheran* in 1934. Lodz was only about 100 years old, a textile center with other industries as well, having a population of approximately 650,000. It was a dirty place, where factory workers earned about $3.75 a week and sometimes less. About 100,000 Germans, nearly all "Evangelical," lived there. Tens of thousands were only nominal members of the Augsburg Church.

Maliszewski served St. Paul's congregation in the center of the city. They worshiped in a brick chapel, built with the help of the Wisconsin Synod. St. Peter's was on the south side, meeting in a rented hall and served by Heinrich Mueller. On the north side was a preaching station, served by Eduard Lelke. Antipathy and apathy toward the church were highest on the north side, and Bodamer reported: "Here is heathen land."

The work spread to country towns and small cities. At Brudnowo, the seeds of Lutheran confessionalism had been sown by a German soldier from the Saxon Free Church during World War I. The congregation was visited every two months by Maliszewski, and served between times by Evangelist K. Biegalke, who had left the Augsburg Church in 1930. On a tour of the field in 1935, Bodamer preached almost every day, often more than once, for a solid month. Not long before his death in 1952, he reminisced in a letter to his successor Alfred Maas: "Those were good years because there was hunger and thirst for the gospel."

During Bodamer's first two years in Poland, the church grew from 521 to 1254 souls. In 1930 he began to edit the monthly paper, *The Evangelical Lutheran Free Church in Poland*. Signs of a healthy church were apparent: Sunday Schools and instruction classes, Youth Weeks and women's organizations, choirs and brass ensembles, increased giving for home and mission purposes.

Bodamer's work in Poland ended in 1939, when the onset of World War II kept him from returning after a furlough in the United States. When he left, there were twelve congregations, fourteen preaching stations, almost 5,000 souls, nearly 2,000 communicants, and ten church buildings. He had supervised the work of eleven pastors. The Lord had abundantly blessed his work in the name of a synod that had begun tentatively and had seriously considered discontinuing its first mission on foreign soil. At the time of Bodamer's death, Dr. Henry Koch of Morrison, Wisconsin, wrote to Executive Director Maas: "He steered the ship of church between the rocks of church and state." Rocks there had been!

Opposition of the Augsburg Church

From the beginning, the Evangelical Augsburg Church of Poland, which had the weight of the government behind it, fiercely opposed our mission in Poland. The 1925 WELS Convention Proceedings report: "As a result of misrepresentation and slanders concerning the purpose and aims of our work, Missionary Engel received . . . a peremptory deportation order from the government. . . . It turned out that enemies of the free church were behind the affair and moved the government to act." Engel was finally permitted to remain and continue his work unhindered.

Although the authorities permitted Maliszewski to begin conducting public services in 1924, the Evangelical Lutheran Free Church did not enjoy official recognition. For the most part the government tacitly tolerated it.

The congregation had to notify the authorities of all meetings, so that they could send observers if they wanted to. Reports of all business transactions had to be submitted to the government. Only Polish citizens could perform official pastoral acts. Where would births, marriages, and deaths be recorded? Civil records were kept by the clergy of recognized churches. If one belonged to an unofficial church, he had to go to the government office where the vital statistics of dissenters were recorded and where the wait for service was long.

Not until 1937 was the Evangelical Lutheran Free Church of Poland organized. Gustav Maliszewski was elected president. While they could still not gain official recognition as a church body, Polish law allowed them to incorporate as The Union of Adherents of the Evangelical Lutheran Free Church in Poland. The government worked out an arrangement under which magistrates and civil officials were instructed to furnish registry services wherever organized congregations of the free church existed.

In 1931 Bodamer's visa was about to be canceled. The WELS in convention humbly petitioned the Polish government to allow him to prolong his stay. The United States ambassador also interceded, and the visa was extended.

When Evangelist Biegalke led his Brudnowo group out of the Augsburg Church in 1930, Augsburg church officials sent the sheriff to collect dues from people who had not set foot in the state church for years. The state church people also barred free church people from using the only available cemeteries. The law of the land compelled the Augsburgers to admit them, but the law was frequently circumvented. Gates were locked and the keys "lost." Free church members were consigned to the plot reserved for suicides. At Skrypkowo a dozen policemen used rifle butts to disperse vigorously protesting mourners who were waiting at the cemetery gates to bury the body of their loved-one.

A chapel was built in Danowiec in 1930. The government padlocked the building before it could be dedicated. Not until April of 1934, after protracted legal proceedings, was the building finally released and dedicated. Other churches and chapels were locked and sealed before or just after completion.

Needless to say, this kind of harassment kept some people from joining a free church and scared away a few who had joined. Still, the Lord gathered and preserved his flock.

The Terror of September, 1939

On September 1, 1939, Germany declared war on Poland and invaded. The following day Warsaw newspapers and a radio broadcast urged: "Smite all Germans dead. They are spies!" The ancestors of most ethnic Germans had lived in Poland for generations, some for centuries. They were citizens. But it was not a time for fine distinctions, and more than 60,000 were murdered. In Armin Schlender's two congregations, 14 members were killed and a number of others disappeared. About 200 Germans in the area were butchered like cattle, recognizable in death only by their clothes. After the neighborhood mobs had done their worst, they were followed by Poles fleeing ahead of the German army, who together with numbers of released convicts terrorized, vandalized, and brutalized.

Under Nazi Occupation, 1939-1945

The Blitzkrieg was successful, and the takeover of Poland ended in a few weeks. Poland was partitioned between Germany and Russia, and the German portion was renamed

Warthegau. The military government conferred German citizenship on all ethnic Germans and changed Maliszewski's name to Malschner. Our mission lost its resident director. Pastor Bodamer had come home for the 1939 synod convention, and the German government would not let him return.

The policies of the military government were anti-church. Special permission was required to conduct services. No offerings could be taken during the services, and even the poor boxes were removed. The church's monthly newspaper could not be published because no paper was available for such purposes. Contact among the congregations and pastors was sustained through round-robin letters. They could have no contact with churches or congregations outside Warthegau.

The last restriction probably had the most far-reaching effect on our free church. In 1940 the pastoral conference and congregations of the Evangelical Lutheran Free Church of Poland decided to join the Evangelical Lutheran Free Church of Germany. The National-Socialist government forbade the merger. The history of our mission might have ended then, or taken a quite different course, but the Lord of the Church had other plans and used the power of the pagan state to bring them to pass.

Two young pastors were drafted, Reit and Napp. Neither ever returned from action on the Eastern Front. Some members of the church fled to Germany in 1939 and resettled there, no longer trusting their Polish neighbors. A few members defected during the war, but overall the church experienced a net growth of about 450 souls. Six pastors and one evangelist served 15 congregations and 30 preaching stations, about 5,000 souls. They received no salaries, only support in kind. In retrospect, however, Armin Schlender was able to write, "We could preach the gospel, administer the sacraments, carry on our religious instruction, make home visits, and care for souls unhindered." There was an influx of ethnic Germans from the Baltic countries, parts of Russia, Bessarabia, and Czechoslovakia. They did not, for the most part, join our congregations, but they swelled the responsibility list of our mission to about 8,000 by 1945.

Collapse and Flight, 1945

In early 1945 the front lines were getting closer as the Russians advanced. Schlender wrote, "Millions of German people left their homeland and headed west, either on their own initiative or because they were compelled to. Among those millions of westward fleeing people most of our Christians were also to be found. Thereby our church in the East (in Poland) ceased to exist."

The church would continue in the West under much the same leadership. The pastors and people who fled, however, would often remember the years of beginning and growth in Poland as the best years.

GERMANY

Conditions after World War II

Legal documents, mortgage papers, and savings passbooks had been left behind in Poland. A pastor wrote: "The synod (WELS) must tell us what we shall do in the future."

Even before the war's end, Germany was devastated. It could barely sustain its own population, let alone care for millions of displaced persons pouring in from the East. The situation did not improve with the war's end. People who had been hated as Germans by the Poles among whom they had lived for so long were as welcome as a plague of locusts in the land of their ancestors.

Regrouping for Action

Members of our Poland Mission were scattered all over Germany, many of them separated from family members. The pastors who had struggled to serve them in Poland now began a truly heroic effort to serve them in Germany. Whatever personal shortcomings and lack of practical wisdom they might display in later years, it must be said of each: "He had a pastor's heart for his people."

While still in Poland, the pastors had agreed to meet at Zwickau in East Germany at the publishing house of the Saxon Free Church. Pastors Malschner, Lerle, Mueller, Zielke, and Armin Schlender met there in 1945 to regroup. To begin with they ministered to the various congregations of the Saxon Free Church whose pastors were in military service. They were soon joined by Pastors Helmuth Schlender and Alfons Wagner. By late 1945 these seven men were dispersed around Germany. They wrote to Bodamer, asking that the synod replace their lost ordination certificates and provide them with credentials as pastors of the Wisconsin Synod.

In February 1946 Malschner invited the others to a meeting at Memmingen in southern Bavaria, where he had been working since June 1945. Knowing that they and their people could not return to the land of their birth, the pastors from Poland decided it was their God-given duty to search out their people and resume their ministry to them in Germany. In June they met again to organize as The Evangelical Lutheran Refugee Mission Church. The name these pastors chose defined their reason for being. There would be later name changes, but in some part of their minds this original group would always be refugees, serving refugees, dependent on the Wisconsin Synod to help them do it.

Reestablishing Contact

The pastors of the Refugee Mission had resolved to see to the spiritual needs of their scattered people. Meanwhile, they and their people continued to be in dire physical need. The synod authorized a Committee on Relief for War Sufferers, with Pastor Karl Krauss of Lansing, Michigan, as chairman. The committee appealed to congregations of the synod to hold door collections and special offerings. By April 30, 1947, a remarkable total of $160,125.99 had been raised.

A two-man committee, Pastor Bodamer and Pastor Alfred Maas, who later became the mission's Executive Director, was authorized to go to Germany and reestablish contact with the remnant of the Polish Mission. In the immediate post-war years, military commanders determined who could visit Germany. Permission for men from our synod was denied a number of times while representatives of other bodies were making regular visits. Maas called on his congressman for help, appealing to the constitutional principle of equal treatment for all religious groups. Permission was finally granted in May 1947.

In November of that same year, Maas began to purchase CARE packages on a regular basis. Cash payments could not be sent to Germany at this time because no rate of exchange had been established.

Itinerant Ministry

This is how the six pastors were deployed in 1947: Malschner was stationed at Memmingen in the extreme south of Germany, in the American Zone of Occupation; Armin Schlender, Leopold Zielke, and Alfons Wagner were responsible for the

Pastors W. Bodamer and A. Maas were finally able to meet with Refugee Mission pastors in Germany in 1947. (From L to R: Lerle, Bodamer, Schlender, Maas, Zielke, Malschner, Osbahr, Wagner)

British Zone in northwestern Germany; Helmuth Schlender and August Lerle labored in the Russian Zone. Access to the French Zone was not yet possible. All the pastors were circuit riders, traveling widely and laboring mightily. They traveled by train, bicycle, and on foot, Armin Schlender in a disreputable sheepskin mackinaw and second-hand shoes. When Helmuth Schlender was too tired to pedal his bike, he walked it and kept on going.

Armin Schlender and August Lerle would be gone from home for three months at a time. In 1947 Schlender had 100 places and three islands on his circuit. In the spring of 1950, he confirmed 67 children between Palm Sunday and Pentecost at 14 stations, some of them separated by hundreds of miles. Lerle had lost 90% of his vision, but did much of his traveling by bicycle. "When they see me com-

O'pa August Lerle fathered the courageous Refugee Pastors in Eastern Germany.

79

ing, they should have enough sense to get out of the way," he said. Once when crossing the border from one occupation zone into another, Lerle was challenged by a border guard for including a Bible among his papers. Lerle simply said, "Here is the Bible. Read it. I'm willing to sit here all day until you have finished." The guard let Lerle pass without further delay.

A New Free Church in Germany

From 1947 on, a new free church gradually developed out of the Refugee Mission. The nuclei of the congregations were the remnants of the congregations in Poland. Some in the Wisconsin Synod argued, after the fact, that the synod should not have brought a new free church into existence in Germany. It should rather have urged Lutheran refugees to join the conservative Lutheran free church bodies already existing. Not doing so, however, did help an existing, uprooted church survive in new surroundings. In any case, the importance of maintaining confessional alliances that had been forged in Poland prevailed as a deciding factor in forming a new free church.

In a few places, the state churches tried to make the Refugee Mission's work impossible. Some representatives of the other free churches, however, seem to have harbored more resentment and offered more resistance. There were personality clashes, and our men were at least partly at fault. The refugees felt that the German free churches did not welcome them. Maas and others on this side of the Atlantic felt that our refugee pastors were not at all ready to move in the direction of amalgamation with the other free churches. To force the issue would have been extremely difficult, if not impossible.

Additions to the Ministerium

The 1951 Synod Proceedings recorded that, in the Russian Zone, 5 pastors and 24 lay teachers were serving 3,000 souls in 14 congregations and 110 preaching places. In the 3 western zones, 11 pastors were serving 18,000 souls in 11 congregations and 100 preaching stations. The ministerium had grown from the original 6 men to 16. The additional 10 had come from various sources, and it would be a challenge to blend them into a cohesive group. As we shall see, the challenge was never fully met.

The Seminary at Oberursel

With the encouragement and help of the Wisconsin Synod, the mission tried to recruit and train young men from its own midst to serve as pastors. The Evangelical Lutheran Free Church (Saxon) and the Evangelical Lutheran (Old-Lutheran) Church—the Breslau Synod—had established a seminary at Oberursel/Taunus, near Frankfurt. In the late 1940s, young men from the Refugee Mission began to attend this school. The Wisconsin Synod contributed to the seminary at Oberursel by giving direct subsidy and by helping with a building program. Our synod also provided indirect subsidy by paying tuition for members of our mission who were studying there. In 1951 we also sent 25 sets each of Hoenecke's *Dogmatik* and Pieper's *Jesaias II* for the students' use.

In 1950 our mission had five students at Oberursel. By 1955 enrollment was in decline. Reasons assigned were the partition of Germany, the general atmosphere of unbelief, and the service of materialism.

Amazing Growth and Rapid Decline

Concerning the development of a new free church, in February 1948 Alfons Wagner wrote to Dr. Henry Koch, who for a short time had been his professor at Zehlendorf: "The charity of our American brethren of the Wisconsin Synod . . . is becoming rather well known, and the refugees, about whom no one cares and who have no way at all out of their difficulties, come to us. . . ." (Dr. Koch himself, in an unofficial capacity, lectured on the Refugee Mission, raised money, gave his own money, and advised Maas.)

In that same year the German mark was devalued in a currency reform. This aggravated the unemployment situation, and the first victims were refugees trying to gain a foothold in the German economy. About five percent of the people in our churches were employed in the summer of 1949. Yet, the soul count of our mission kept growing until it reached the amazing total of 21,000 in 1951.

Were the numbers exaggerated? More likely there was a connection between the rapid growth of the field and the charitable work that Wagner mentioned in his letter to Koch.

By 1952 some slippage was noted. Membership was being reduced by relocation, especially as younger families went to the industrial centers. Others were joining the mass of émi-

Refugee congregations made use of band instruments to accompany congregational singing.

Pastors of the reorganized Evangelical Lutheran Confessional Church meet in West Germany with Director A. Maas and Executive Secretary E. Hoenecke.

grés to the U.S.A., Argentina, Brazil, Canada, and Australia. "CARE Package Lutherans" defected. Some people left when they discovered that membership in a free church calls for more financial commitment than does paying small taxes for the support of a state church.

Reorganization

The Refugee Mission, which had named itself Refugee Mission Church and thereby defined its task at Memmingen in 1945, was really only an association of pastors. It was not officially constituted as a church body and had no lay delegates at its conferences. Malschner explained in the mission's church paper, *Durch Kreuz zur Krone,* June 1951, that the pastors had wanted to involve the laity for some years but had not been able to follow through. That was regrettable, for it made later efforts to invest the laity with more responsibility that much more difficult.

In the same issue, Malschner announced a name change:

> At our pastoral conference in Blomberg, at the suggestion of our synod's representatives (Maas and Koch) we changed the name of our refugee church to "Evangelical Lutheran Confessional Church in the Dispersion." This change proved to be necessary because the name "Refugee Mission Church" was a stumbling block and that designation no longer appeared to be timely.

In late September 1952 at Blomberg, a constituting convention was held. Ten pastors and ten lay delegates elected the circuit-riding Armin Schlender as their president.

Durch Kreuz zur Krone

When Bodamer was unable to return in 1939, Gustav Malschner had taken over the editorship of *The Evangelical Lutheran Free Church in Poland*. He kept the round-robin letters going during the years when the Nazis refused to allot paper for religious periodicals. Resettled in Germany, he published *Mitteilungen* ("Sharings" or "Communications").

On January 1, 1950, he published the first issue of *Durch Kreuz zur Krone* ("Through the Cross to the Crown"). On the first day of 1953 Armin Schlender, Johannes Fiedler, and Johannes Forchheim became the paper's editorial committee, replacing Malschner. The paper's editorial focus was always on the cause of Lutheran confessionalism. Beginning in 1954, mimeographed sermons were included for the benefit of those who lived in remote places. For many years Schlender was the paper's chief contributor. In addition to its confessional and devotional articles, it contained news items from the church body's congregations and helped promote a unified spirit among them.

The last editor, Karl Wengenroth, summed up the purpose and the accomplishments of the paper in the final issue, December 1975: "We praise our God and Lord, that through the ministry of *Durch Kreuz zur Krone* he comforted many a Christian in suffering and cross bearing, strengthened weak faith, gave support and wisdom for life and churchmanship, and preserved the hope of the eternal crown of life."

Internal Development

Changing the church's name did not change its perspective, even when the "in Dispersion" was dropped a few years later.

Although a few native Germans were joining the mission by 1949, the refugee complex survived, partly because some of the pastors themselves were still housed under conditions not far removed from those of 1945. Many of the lay people were still unemployed.

Beginning in 1949, budgetary support from the Wisconsin Synod included funds for building. By 1956 there were seven churches and five parsonages. In the late 50s the policy was that two-thirds of a project's cost was granted by the WELS and one-third was a loan to be repaid by the congregation. Payment of salaries held in trust by WELS gave the pastors great help, enabling some of them to acquire their own houses. In 1947 six Volkswagens were provided. Four of the Poland veterans received them outright from a rehabilitation fund. The other two cars were to be paid for with small monthly payroll deductions.

Church and parsonage in the foreground were part of the seven churches and five parsonages built in West Germany with WELS support.

Automobiles ought to have made the pastors more efficient in riding their circuits. For some of them, however, improved mobility simply resulted in enlarging the geographical areas they tried to serve. Moreover, as a result of this constant travel to serve tiny groups, the pastors sometimes neglected the needs of the larger congregations and did not always nurture them to stability.

Administrative Problems

Both Malschner and Schlender were zealous missionaries but not particularly good administrators. The constituents of the church tended to suffer. A report to the districts of our synod in 1954 emphasized this problem.

> Our men have been overextending themselves, spreading their work too thin over an expanse of territory they simply

cannot cover adequately. Time and again we have brought this to the attention of our workers, telling them that they were dissipating their strength in a task they simply cannot accomplish, and in so doing endangering the very future of the mission through a lack of thorough and purposeful endeavor. . . .

In 1949 seven pastors formally petitioned President John Brenner, asking that a permanent representative of the synod be stationed in Germany. They felt the need for a leader who would function as Bodamer had in Poland. The position of resident director was authorized in 1949, and calls were extended during 1950. The calls were declined, however, and instead the mission board decided that Executive Director Maas should visit the field at least twice a year.

For two decades, when Maas was not in Germany, policies were interpreted, problems were addressed, and decisions were made by means of overseas airmail. Predictably, this method of supervision led to many misunderstandings. Among other things, the church was not able to fit itself into this pattern of administration, and its work and outreach failed to prosper as anticipated.

Executive Director Alfred F. Maas

Pastor Alfred F. Maas, the mission board's executive for the Poland-Germany field from 1938 to 1962, bore the brunt of such long-distance administration for those 24 years. He served as non-resident director of the mission from 1951 to 1961.

Beginning in 1947 he visited the field annually, sometimes twice a year, missing scheduled visits only because of stomach ulcer surgery and a heart attack. During the earlier years, he also had home mission responsibilities. His

Pastor A. Maas made frequent trips to Europe as the Mission Board's executive for the Poland-Germany field.

85

congregations loved him and the cause of missions enough to grant him regular leaves of absence.

Internal Dissension

The Maas correspondence files show an unhealthy tendency persisted in some of the workers to compare themselves with their co-workers as to what they did, spent, and needed. They had long memories for past grievances. At almost every conference, some pastors did not commune because they were at odds with their brothers. One pastor lamented in a heated conference debate: "We are suffocating ourselves in our own atmosphere!" Discouraged and disillusioned by the attitudes and actions of some of their seniors, a number of the Oberursel graduates left, some for the state churches.

Conditions in local congregations sometimes mirrored what was going on among the pastors. Pastor and lector squabbled over where the lector should stand when the pastor was not present. In one congregation strife arose between refugee Balts and refugee Poles. A congregation refused to accept a newly-assigned Oberursel graduate as arrogant and called one of the refugee Polish pastors instead. Another congregation raised the issue with their pastor that he had been born in Germany and not in Poland.

In 1955 Maas received several letters explaining why pastors could not ask their people to give more or do more. The business manager advised Maas that, if people were asked to contribute more generously, some of them would leave. Evidently some, or many, congregations had no idea what their pastors were paid or just how they were paid. In that year the per communicant average giving for all purposes was $2.58. Furthermore, each member communed on average only 1.46 times annually.

In 1953 the mission lost most of its largest congregation, Ebenezer at Blomberg, along with a church building that had been mostly financed by the Wisconsin Synod. The building was eventually returned, but most of the members became and remained adherents of the territorial church. This apostasy was a reaction to questionable politics on the part of one of the senior pastors from Poland.

New Policies and Emphases

Edgar Hoenecke, chairman of the Board for World Missions, wrote to Pastor Ernst H. Wendland in December 1960:

> It appears that our brothers over there are living and laboring under the delusion that our synod is both able and responsible for their perpetual support. I believe that we once upon a time created and encouraged that delusion because we were guilty of some very foggy thinking and planning regarding this "mission" in the "fatherland."

Wendland was appointed to the executive committee for the German mission in 1955. He and Maas, sometimes accompanied by other officials of the synod, made a series of trips to Germany between 1955 and 1960. Their objective was to teach the brothers self-sufficiency in church matters, and not only with regard to money. In July 1957 they recommended to the General Mission Board that no more building funds should be sent until the congregations in Germany began to repay their loans. They also recommended a 15% budget cut. If the pastors regarded stewardship and evangelism efforts as impolite, perhaps the laity would take hold. Some did.

At the synod convention of the Evangelical Lutheran Confessional Church at Varel in 1960, Wendland presented the essay: "The Indigenous Church: It Governs Itself, Reproduces Itself, and Supports Itself." He said, "This is your church, not ours. These are your buildings, not ours. . . . We would rather hear, 'How can we take hold of this work together?' than, 'What can you do for us?'"

The church eventually became self-governing, but never really self-propagating or entirely self-supporting. That year, detailed instructions were provided on how each parish's budget should be drawn up. Maas also wrote to Schlender that a mandated salary increase would offer a beautiful opportunity to let the congregations handle the increase themselves. At least one congregation refused to submit a budget. Another, after repeated reminders, sent a budget under the pastor's signature, with no lay signatories. Still another congregation built and, with borrowed money, totally financed a bell tower for its modest, synod-financed chapel, on which they were not repaying the loan. The pastor explained that this had given the people the "joy of giving and of self-help."

Hoenecke's Extended Visit in 1966

Maas retired in late 1961 and entered his eternal rest in early 1962. The office of non-resident director was discontinued in order to give the confessional church more control of its own affairs and have it assume more responsibility for its own support. Pastor Karl Krauss took Maas's place as chairman of the Executive Committee for Germany. He and Edgar Hoenecke continued during the 60s what Maas and Wendland had done during the 50s. They admonished and instructed to achieve more lay involvement, reduced subsidy, and tighter organization at the congregational and synodical levels. They also encouraged the church to consider merging with the other free churches in Germany if it could do that without compromising its clear confession. Edgar Hoenecke put forth a valiant effort on behalf of this church, which in his view and that of the Board for World Missions was not properly a mission. He spent several months in the field in 1966 as interim director.

Hoenecke reported to the synod in 1967 concerning the defeatism, loss of confidence, and lack of harmony that he had observed. He acknowledged that the synod's administrative policies had inadvertently contributed to the situation. He stated, "A factor which retarded the development of a strong independent German church was the administrative policy which required it to defer all its decisions and problems to the executive director or committee in the U.S." It was reported in 1969 that subsidy had been reduced by $30,000 in six years and that the congregations of our sister church were "raising substantial sums for world missions and charitable causes".

Karl Wengenroth (right) replaces Armin Schlender (left) as president of the Evangelical Lutheran Confessional Church in 1968.

The Final Decline

In 1971 the church in Germany was stabilized, with practically no change in membership. President Karl Wengenroth, who had succeeded Schlender in 1968, wrote that the older members of the church, who had joined it in the early years, were no longer understood by their own families. He wrote: "The young don't want to hear about deportees anymore and don't want to belong to a church. What do our youth know about the true goals of our church? What understanding do they have of the confession for the sake of which we exist and struggle as a separate Lutheran Church?" What to do? He went on to point out that families must try harder to inculcate these things.

The education of children and youth had been a problem from the beginning. As early as 1948 it was noted that, due to the unsettled conditions and the itinerant ministry, instruction classes could not be conducted in Germany as they had been in Poland. Summer classes were planned, where children from remote areas could gather at a central location. A youth pastor was regularly elected by the ministerium, usually a man fresh out of the seminary. Youth weeks and youth camps enjoyed mixed success. Meanwhile, the public schools were effective in alienating youth from the church and the truth of God's word.

Unfortunately, too, little attention was given to carrying out any kind of personal evangelism program. This was in line with the premise expressed by one of the leaders of the church: "The people know where the church is and are welcome to come. I'm not going to run after them." These conditions together with young families moving to where employment opportunities existed and where they lost touch with the church, contributed to the graying of the church and its ultimate decline.

In September 1975 the Evangelical Lutheran Confessional Church held its last convention. Three months later the ELCC disbanded. Its four active pastors and their congregations merged with the recently organized *Selbststaendige Evangelisch-Lutherische Kirche* (Independent Evangelical Lutheran Church), hereafter referred to as SELK. A fifth pastor, Reinhold Buchholz, had earlier announced his disagreement with the decision to merge and entered instead into the ministry of the territorial Lutheran Church of Hannover.

The Movement toward Merger

From the beginning it was the Wisconsin Synod's policy to encourage cooperation of the Refugee Mission with the Saxon Free Church. Personality clashes, the isolationism of the refugees, and the coldness of some of the free church laity toward the refugees all served to hinder such cooperation. The charge was raised in the mid-50s that the other free churches were happy to receive members from the Refugee Mission but loath to release them to our congregations. The other free churches continued to challenge the Refugee Mission's right to exist.

Three such free churches existed before the Refugee Mission came into being.

The first was the Saxon Free Church, which in a name change became the Evangelical Lutheran Free Church (ELFC). Our synod was in fellowship with it from the time of its founding in 1876. In East Germany the Diaspora Circuit of our mission became a district of ELFC. This East German Church is generally referred to as ELF (*Evangelische Lutherische Freikirche*).

The second, the Independent Evangelical Lutheran Church in Germany (IELC), was the product of a union of several smaller free churches. The Wisconsin Synod never entered into fellowship with this body because of differences in fellowship practice as well as problems in the matter of biblical inspiration and inerrancy. The IELC in Germany was most vehement and unrelenting in its opposition to our mission's right to be a church body.

The third body was the Evangelical Lutheran (Old Lutheran) Church, commonly referred to as the Breslau Synod. It was organized in 1845, in opposition to the Prussian Union, the forced merger of Lutherans and Reformed into one Evangelical Church. Breslau entered into fellowship with the Saxons in 1948 and with the Wisconsin Synod in 1949. Our sister Evangelical Lutheran Confessional Church (ELCC) was thus also drawn into fellowship with Breslau. Fellowship was established on the basis of the *Einigungssaetze,* Union Theses, of 1947. These were a clear doctrinal statement on the sensitive issues of Scripture, church and ministry, and fellowship issues. Unfortunately, it became increasingly clear in the late 1950s that many of the Breslau pastors did not regard the doctrinal statements of the *Union Theses* of 1947 as binding.

In spite of evident differences in doctrine and practices, the three free churches, excluding the ELCC, had entered into a "working fellowship" in 1957. The action was a first step toward ultimate merger.

For confessional reasons the ELCC refused to be a part of the working fellowship and continued to warn against the practice of fellowship without full doctrinal agreement. The other free churches, however, generally ignored the testimony of the ELCC men. That testimony was undercut by a series of ELCC moves at the congregational level. In the late 60s and in 1970, no fewer than seven mergers of various free congregations and pastorates were effected. ELCC congregations or pastors were involved in every one of them.

Through the 60s and into the early 70s, the situation in Germany became more and more the concern of the WELS Commission on Doctrinal Matters. Under the dedicated leadership of Professor Carl J. Lawrenz, there were visits and conferences and correspondence with representatives of the various free churches. As later developments bore out, and as our ELCC men warned, those leaders did not speak for their rank and file when they gave assurances of their orthodoxy. There was hope that a realignment could be effected along liberal and conservative lines. What finally occurred was the merger of liberal and conservative elements into a single new Independent Evangelical Lutheran Church, *Selbststaendige Evangelisch-Lutherische Kirche,* (SELK).

Formation of SELK

The Saxon Free Church and the Breslau Synod each held its last convention in 1971. Each voted overwhelmingly to adopt the proposed constitution of the new SELK. On June 25, 1972—on the anniversary of the Augsburg Confession of 1530—the new SELK came into existence. It numbered about 42,000 souls and 33,000 communicants.

The ELCC watched these developments with great interest and mixed emotions. At year's end Wengenroth said: "Our hearts would be lighter if we could declare to our congregations today that all reservations regarding this future church have been removed and that we could enter it confidently. . . . Love for the brethren is genuine only if it does not deny Christ and his truth."

The Mequon Meeting, 1973

On July 17 through 20, 1973, a meeting of theologians was held at the seminary in Mequon. President Wengenroth of the

ELCC was present, along with four pastors and professors of SELK. The men agreed on the doctrine of Scripture, including the creation days. They also agreed on the doctrine of church and ministry, including fellowship principles. The meeting closed with a joint service.

Unfortunately, the results of this meeting were repudiated by SELK's church leadership. Just as leaders of the free churches had not always spoken for their rank and file in earlier meetings, so now the representatives of SELK had not really spoken for their leaders. SELK's leadership was unwilling to recognize the basic premise of the so-called Mequon agreement, namely, that full doctrinal agreement is an indispensable prerequisite for confessional fellowship. The Commission on Doctrinal Matters could not recommend fellowship with the new SELK, and the 1977 synod convention agreed.

The End of a Cherished Fellowship

Wengenroth and the ELCC took the outcome of the Mequon meeting at face value. They hoped for some further clarifications from SELK but did not hesitate to declare fellowship at their Jubilee Synod at Oldenburg, May 23-26, 1974. They also resolved to seek organic union with SELK and scheduled a special convention for that purpose. Fifty years and fifteen days after the organization of Maliszewski's congregation at Lodz, our "Poland Mission" arranged to go out of existence. The actual resolution came in June of the following year, with 19 ayes, no nays, and no abstentions. Discussion was brief. The merger with SELK became effective on January 1, 1976.

The special convention also thanked the Wisconsin Synod for 51 years of fellowship and financial support. A mission begun on the basis of confessional concern ended with a break in fellowship between that mission and the synod that had nurtured it from beginning to end.

EAST GERMANY

Developments in East Germany

Recall that we also had a mission in the East, in what became the German Democratic Republic (GDR). There, August Lerle asked the Saxons to accept people who had fled from Poland. When the people lived close enough to a Saxon congregation, this was done. Then Lerle went into the northern sec-

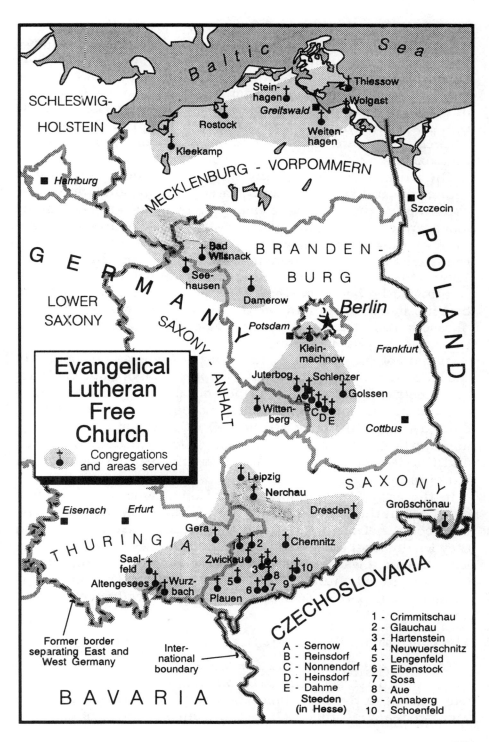

tion of the Russian Zone of Occupation, where there were no congregations of the Saxon Free Church. There, from September 1946 to October 1947, he made eight "missionary journeys." In 1948 and 1949 he and Helmuth Schlender, with the help of a pastor named Rachner, gathered about 4,000 souls into 5 parishes comprised of 14 congregations. They became the Diaspora District and affiliated with the Saxon Free Church. They were supported by the Wisconsin Synod through the Saxons.

The work in East Germany was done under very difficult economic and political conditions. Yet, in some ways the churches in the East were healthier than in West Germany. Maas wrote to Lerle: "Would God that the reports from the West were as thoroughly enjoyable." In 1955 the Diaspora District remitted $250 for Wisconsin Synod missions. In the early 1960s, the pastors declined an increase in salary subsidy, not wanting to be better off than their people and not wanting to become more dependent on the Wisconsin Synod. To paraphrase a 1957 letter of Lerle to Maas: We tell our people it's a sin not to do what they can, to look for outside help.

In spite of the difficulties, the word of God was not bound in the GDR. On the one hand, some baptized children of the Diaspora District were never confirmed because they chose to participate in the communist youth movement, lest they be excluded from university studies. On the other hand, young adults who had been steeped in atheistic philosophy hungered and thirsted for God's righteousness and became members of our church.

In the early 1970s, efforts toward amalgamation of the free churches in the East paralleled the efforts in the West. Legally, they could not act jointly with the West Germans, nor could they legally form a new joint organization. They were, nevertheless, moving toward an arrangement whereby they would function as a united church without state sanction. They anticipated merging in 1978. Meanwhile, they had already declared fellowship with SELK.

The Confessionalism of the Saxons in East Germany

Some of the Saxons and Diaspora men were not ready to move toward merger with SELK without concern for true doctrinal unity. At the same time, they saw more clearly that SELK was not really a unified church. Through a series of contacts with the WELS, they had grown to understand and accept the WELS doctrinal position. Their long and patient efforts to bring SELK to a clearer doctrinal position did not meet with success.

As a result this group of Saxons and Diaspora men in the East who were joined in the Evangelical Lutheran Free Church (ELF) suspended fellowship with SELK in October 1989. They numbered about 3,000 members, served by 18 pastors. Their president was Pastor Gerhard Wilde, who had attended Wisconsin Lutheran Seminary for the 1952-53 school year. Dr. Gottfried Wachler presided over the Leipzig seminary, where seven students met in two rented rooms.

Professor Wilbert Gawrisch, chairman of the Commission on Inter-church Relations, and commission member Pastor Martin Janke attended the ELF convention at Crimmitschau in May 1988. On their return, they reported they were impressed by the strong desire of the Free Church to remain faithful to Scripture and the Lutheran Confessions. The Free Church was now protesting its fellowship with SELK because SELK tolerated false teaching with regard to Scripture and fellowship.

Gawrisch and Janke returned to East Germany for the convention of the Evangelical Lutheran Free Church in October 1989. On October 15 they brought back the news that ELF had courageously held fast to its confessional positions even though this meant suspending fellowship with SELK.

On November 9, 1989, the German Democratic Republic began to ease exit and entry restrictions for its own citizens and for visitors from the West. Thus the hated Berlin Wall was opened. In the days and weeks that followed, the Iron Curtain, which had divided communist Europe from the free West for forty years, was lifted. One by one the countries of eastern Europe rid themselves of socialist regimes that had been put and kept in place by the USSR. That vast empire could no longer maintain an artificial and ineffective economic system or sustain its tyrannical political control.

In the same month, a fact-finding team of the WELS Board for World Missions visited Germany especially to consult with President Wilde and other leaders of our sister church, ELF. Upon their return they recommended and gained approval for calling two men to work for two years with this five-fold objective:

1) Encourage ELF in gospel outreach.
2) Assist ELF to follow its members westward and organize congregations.

3) Offer support to ELF in its confessional struggle.
4) Evaluate the potential for expanding mission outreach to other countries.
5) Explore the possibilities for expanded radio work throughout Europe and Asia.

As we shall see, the fifth objective was later expanded in scope. Meanwhile, the Lord provided two men who would not need much brushing up in the German language to work with ELF: John Sullivan had been serving German immigrants among the members of his congregation in Canada; Harris Kaesmeyer taught German during part of his long tenure at Michigan Lutheran Seminary in Saginaw. He had also spent a year of study at the Oberursel seminary in the late 1940s. The synod allotted non-budgetary funds for both positions.

Even before the reunification of Germany, ELF had managed to organize a congregation in the Federal Republic of Germany at Steeden, an hour's drive northwest of Frankfurt. When the German Democratic Republic folded on October 3, 1990, however, Karl Marx Stadt, where ELF held its decisive 1989 convention, regained the ancient and honorable name Chemnitz, indicative of what the event means for the church.

The people of East Germany, including the pastors and people of ELF, have suffered some with the change. Prices rose, factories were closed, unemployment increased. But they have gained much, too: freedom of movement, freedom to evangelize, the removal of restrictions on the Christian education of children and youth.

A second fact-finding team of the WELS Board for World Missions visited Leningrad and Moscow in January 1991. On the basis of the information they gathered, the board resolved to expand and actively pursue the fifth objective mentioned above. Pastor Kirby Spevacek, long-time missionary in Central Africa and then on the Apache field, accepted the call to explore possibilities for mission work and radio and television outreach in the countries of the former USSR and in other parts of Europe and Asia. A second man, Gary Miller, has joined him. As in the case of the men working with ELF, non-budgetary funds were tapped for this undertaking.

A confessional church survives, small in numbers, but not as small as our mission was in its beginnings. Is the cause worthy of our further support? Were the efforts in Poland and

Germany justified? For those who love the Lutheran confession the answer is an obvious "Yes."

SWEDEN

Biblicum

Stiftelsen Biblicum, Institute for Biblical Research, was founded in Uppsala, Sweden, in 1968. It was established to train and support scholars who would produce up-to-date materials in the interest of a biblically-based Christianity.

Among the seven founders was Dr. David Hedegard, who in the 1930s had raised his voice against the liberalism and apostasy rampant in the Church of Sweden. His recognized scholarship and ability as a readable author made him a voice which his liberal adversaries could not stifle.

Another widely respected member of the founding group was Gustav Adolf Danell, dean of the cathedral in Uppsala. He had been crying out against the apostasy of the state church, Lutheran in name only, since the late 1940s.

Biblicum, the Bible Research Center in Uppsala. The building was enlarged in 1980.

A third co-founder was Lars Engquist, pastor of a large congregation at Råneå in northern Sweden. He had resisted the false theology of the state church to the point of forbidding his bishop to speak or function in the church at Råneå.

Stiftelsen Biblicum was supported by gifts from individual pastors and lay persons of the Church of Sweden. At first the work enjoyed wide popular support, but its teaching of biblical inerrancy alienated various individuals and groups who were

conservative in other respects. Support dwindled more rapidly when Biblicum began to speak out on the subject of church fellowship principles. Biblicum had come to recognize the WELS positions on inerrancy and fellowship as biblical, and it was applying them to people in the church of Sweden, which was forsaking the truth of God's Word. Nevertheless, its bimonthly magazine *Tidskrift Biblicum,* Magazine for Bible Research, enjoyed a circulation of more than 1,500.

Another member of the board was Pastor Per Jonsson of Landskrona, on the west coast of Sweden. When Jonsson left the Church of Sweden as a testimony against unionism, Dean Danell resigned his position as member and president of the Biblicum board. Two other members resigned with him, regarding Jonsson and conservative theologian Dr. Seth Erlandsson as guilty of "separatistic actions." That left control of the institute to men who were coming to understand that one cannot remain a protesting member of a false church indefinitely. The time comes when in faithfulness to our Lord and his word one must separate from such a false-teaching church body.

The doctorate in theology was conferred on Seth Erlandsson by the University of Uppsala in May 1970. In June, at the age of 28, he began his work as the director of Biblicum. That October he and his mentor, David Hedegard, began conducting independent Lutheran services in Uppsala. This was a step in the process that ended with Erlandsson giving up his ministry and membership in the Church of Sweden. Erlandsson resigned from the Church of Sweden in 1973 while Dr. Siegbert Becker and Board for World Missions Executive Secretary Edgar Hoenecke were in Uppsala. So seriously did Dr. Erlandsson take this step that he had these two men accompany him and witness that he actually dropped his letter of resignation into the postbox.

When Hedegard died in the autumn of 1971, Erlandsson had been chosen to take his place on the board of Biblicum. The son of a state church pastor, Erlandsson was a brilliant young man, well able to lead the confessional movement that would lead to the formation of a confessional Lutheran free church in Sweden.

Swedish Confusion in Fellowship Matters

Early critics of the Swedish state church, though respected by pious Lutherans who were not happy with their pastors and bishops, had to contend with a law that prohibited leaving the Church of Sweden. That law remained in effect until January 1, 1952. Both confessional and pietistic leaders advised the faithful that they could look to the church for its sacraments while staying away from false preaching and teaching. Still others believed that their place was in the state church until God gave them a clear sign to leave.

Danell, who practiced selective fellowship with individuals in the state church who agreed with him, always said, "Not yet." His idea of a confessional church seems to have been to set up a chapel in Biblicum after his retirement, preach orthodox sermons, serve like-minded people, and remain in affiliation with the Church of Sweden. One of the founders of Biblicum and one of the two board members who resigned when Danell did was Pastor Ingvar Hector. He was concerned about the validity of an ordination that was not conferred at the hands of a bishop in the "unbroken apostolic line." To that Lars Engquist gave a truly Lutheran answer: "That the laying on of hands by erring and sometimes downright ungodly bishops should mean more than the teaching of the apostles is beyond my understanding."

First Contact with WELS

Kjerstin Jonsson, wife of Per, seems to have made the first contact with the Wisconsin Synod. She had read a number of essays of Dr. Siegbert W. Becker and become acquainted with *This We Believe,* Wisconsin's pamphlet summary of its doctrinal position. She translated those writings and her husband disseminated them in confessional circles at their own expense. Some years later she also translated the WELS catechism.

The Biblicum leaders invited Dr. Becker to come to Sweden and confer. The Board for World Missions used non-budgetary funds to finance Swedish language training and a month's visit so that Becker could offer guidance to the confessional group. Hundreds attended his lectures, and the Swedish secular press reported his Bible-centered theology as refreshing news. The Lord had opened a door in Sweden!

Organization of St. Matthew's and St. John's

Back in Uppsala a recent theological graduate, acquainted with Biblicum and in agreement with its position, was awaiting ordination. Sten Johansson did not believe he should be ordained by any Swedish bishop, for all were heretical in their teaching. In 1972 he and two of his friends took formal leave of the state church and founded the Evangelical Lutheran Mission in Uppsala. Johansson was called as their pastor. The mission attracted a growing number of adherents, and in September 1973 St. Matthew's Evangelical Lutheran congregation was organized.

St. Matthew's congregation in Uppsala, Sweden, was one of the first groups to organize and become a member of the LCCS.

Seth Erlandsson played a leading role in the organization of this first free Lutheran congregation in the history of Sweden. The constitution included a strong renunciation of all religious unionism, partly as a testimony against a church in which Baptists, Pentecostals, and atheists could hold membership. Just as Matthew left behind his tax collector's bench and the whole life connected with it, so this small group left behind the religious establishment that had been such an important part of their lives. Like Matthew, they did so in order to follow Jesus.

At Yxenhult, a little village in southern Sweden, lived a former lay preacher, Ruben Christianson and his wife Hanna. In 1932 she had built a small chapel on her own land, where she invited friends to hear the kind of preaching that was not to be heard in the state church. After contacts with Erlandsson, the Christiansons and a few others organized St. John's congregation of Yxenhult.

Meeting in Uppsala, 1973

In late April 1973, Dr. Becker and Edgar Hoenecke met at Uppsala with the leaders of the free church movement. In their report on this meeting they stated, "It was quite apparent that no hindrance had been found to a declaration of church fellowship."

At this meeting the Swedes decided to publish a monthly *Lutersk Sandebrev*. This four-page *Lutheran Dispatch* was to present the cause of the confessional free church movement to people all over Sweden. Also during this meeting, a strong confessional statement was drafted. This *Upprop,* or proclamation, was sent to orthodox Lutheran leaders for their signatures. Then it was mailed as a challenge to thousands of pastors and people to take action that meant leaving the Church of Sweden.

Organization of the Lutheran Confessional Church in Sweden

In a meeting at Uppsala, September 6 to 8, 1974, three congregations and scattered believers met in a rented building near the Uppsala cathedral. They organized the *Lutersk Bekaennelse Kyrkan i Sverige,* the Lutheran Confessional Church in Sweden (LCCS). Forty-six men, including an eighty-year-old, signed the constitution. Six were pastors: Sten Johansson, Seth Erlandsson, Per Jonsson, Erland Pettersson, Alvar Svensson, and Arne Svensson. The congregations were St. Matthew's of Uppsala, St. John's of Yxenhult, and Our Savior's of Landskrona.

In a country with a population of over eight million, 90% of whom are nominally Lutheran, the three congregations and a few scattered believers totaled 68 souls. Per Jonsson was elected president.

Early Development of LCCS

Erlandsson and Johansson wrote and lectured on scriptural doctrine and practice. Jonsson published the *Lutheran Dispatch,* paying for it out of his own small salary. Cassette tapes of services and sermons were sent out on a weekly schedule to scattered groups all over Sweden. The pastors visited these groups at regular intervals to instruct and encourage.

Growth in numbers was slow. Jonsson's congregation at Landskrona included his family and ten other persons. Members of his Church of Sweden congregations were reluctant to follow him out of that body. Former friends, people who knew that the state church was corrupt but who were scandalized by the idea of leaving it for a free confessional church, now openly opposed and attacked the young church.

Up at Råneå, a few miles short of the Arctic Circle, Lars Engquist was patiently instructing his large congregation of 5,000 members and urging them to take the necessary step with him. He did not want to leave his flock to the wolves of heresy until he was sure they understood why it was necessary for him to leave the parent church and join the LCCS. The members of the congregation would then be able to decide for themselves whether to follow their pastor out of the state church or not.

Establishment of Fellowship with WELS

On October 3 and 4, 1973, the WELS Commission on Doctrinal Matters met with Seth Erlandsson, Per Jonsson, and Lars Engquist. The resolution of the Commission on Doctrinal Matters at the end of those two days was threefold:

1) to declare agreement with St. Matthew's of Uppsala, with no hindrance to the practice of fellowship;
2) to inform the synod of these findings;
3) to declare doctrinal agreement with Jonsson and Engquist but to refrain from entering into fellowship with them until Engquist had withdrawn from the state church and Jonsson had left his association with the *Bibeltrogna Vaenner*, "Bible-believing Friends." The latter was an association whose membership consisted mostly of people who were still in the Church of Sweden.

In 1975 WELS formally established fellowship with the LCCS and encouraged its sister churches to do the same.

Expansion and Growth

The 6 pastors and 68 souls in 3 congregations of 1974 grew to 15 pastors and evangelists serving 423 souls in 11 congregations and 9 preaching places by 1985. And they were not all in Sweden. There were three congregations in Norway and a number of preaching places in Finland. The Lutheran Confessional Church in Sweden became the Lutheran Confessional Church in Scandinavia in 1986. More recently, because of distance and the difference in language, the preaching places in Finland have formed a separate organization, the Evangelical Lutheran Confessional Congregation. This congregation continues in fellowship with the LCCS and with the WELS.

In 1976 Lars Engquist finally left the Church of Sweden, following legal proceedings that gained national attention. He organized St. Peter's of Råneå. On Reformation Day that same

Members of the LCCS worship in chapels which are small compared with the state churches they have left.

year, Bror Roslund, a former lay preacher, was ordained and became the assistant of St. Mark's in Ljungby. Its head pastor was another former lay preacher, Gideon Gisselsson. Dr. Ingemar Furberg, who had been pastor of a large state church congregation in Göteborg was now serving a small LCCS congregation there and commuting to Uppsala to assist Erlandsson at Biblicum.

Ole Brandal was the head of the Lutheran Laymen's Mission, a pietistic group in Stavanger, Norway. He wanted to be truly Lutheran. After correspondence and personal contact with Becker and the Swedish leaders, he resigned his position at tremendous personal sacrifice and left the Church of Norway. In 1978 he organized a congregation of 41 souls at Avaldsnes near Stavanger. He served these people until his death in 1983. A second Norwegian congregation, St. Luke's of Stavanger, was organized in 1980. Four laymen were publishing a Norwegian-language paper *Bibel og Bekjennelse,* Scripture and Confession.

By 1981 individual Finns held membership in a number of Swedish congregations. In 1984 the first of several preaching stations was established in Finland.

The tape cassette ministry and mission continued. More than 400 recorded lectures were available, including a series by Erlandsson, "What is Christianity?" Paul Waljö, a retired layman, donated his time and the use of his tape machine to produce 2,000 cassettes in a single year.

Reaction of Swedish Authorities

For the most part the Lutheran free church movement and the LCCS were not harassed by the authorities in Sweden as our pastors in Poland had been between 1924 and 1939.

Lars Engquist, however, did run into legal problems. He was still a member of the Church of Sweden when he ran afoul of the government. Chief pastor at Råneå since 1966, he was fined $500 by a civil court for dereliction of duty. There were two counts, both dating to 1972. In that year he refused to take up a collection for combating racism because he knew the monies would be used to support guerrilla fighters. He also refused to take a special collection for the Swedish mission in China because he knew the mission accepted Marxism as a practical application of the gospel.

Engquist appealed his conviction, but the appeals court denied his appeal. "It is clear," he said, "that we must now leave the Church of Sweden. . . . I will continue to fight for the souls of men. but this verdict shows that it is not permitted to fight according to God's Word and the Lutheran Confessions within the Church of Sweden."

Pastor Lars Engquist left the Swedish state church and with members of his flock organized St. Peters of Råneå.

For several Sundays after Pastor Engquist left the state church, those who followed him used a cemetery chapel for worship services. On October 31 they found the doors locked. The rules had been changed the previous Friday evening, and the chapel, which had always been open to all faiths and those of no faith, was no longer open to this faithful flock. In snow and raw cold, Engquist conducted a half-hour service for about 50 people. On the following Sunday the congregation gathered for worship in the basement of his house, which soon proved too small.

LCCS's Mission Mindedness

At the time of organization in 1974, the LCCS resolved to support the Lusaka, Zambia, seminary of the Lutheran Church of Central Africa as its foreign mission. The following year they added the WELS mission in Japan as a recipient of their gifts of love. Through the years this tiny church has been generous in its support of missions in other lands, and recently has sent funds to help support the work of its German sister church, the Evangelical Lutheran Free Church (ELF).

Their first mission field was, of course, their own land. In the fall of 1974, Sten Johansson came to the United States to receive evangelism training and to become acquainted with congregational life in the WELS. Regrettably, this promising young man was lost to the LCCS a few years later, when he began to espouse an erroneous view of the Lord's Supper.

The Work of Siegbert W. Becker

Dr. Becker's visit in 1973 began a series of visits that continued until his death in 1984. He attended the LCCS conventions and counseled them as they faced the problems of developing a young church. He advised them on how to establish a training program for pastors. Above all, he lectured! All over Sweden and then in Norway he made Bible-based presentations to hungry souls. His patient instruction bore fruit particularly among pietists, whose focus until this time tended to be on subjective response rather than on God's declaration of acquittal for all people on the basis of Christ's work.

Dr. Siegbert Becker of the Wisconsin Lutheran Seminary made Bible-based presentations to hungry souls all over Sweden and Norway.

In 1983 he announced his retirement from Wisconsin Lutheran Seminary, effective in May 1984. The LCCS called him to spend a year working at Biblicum. He was to help train pastors and serve as a consultant to the Biblicum staff as they prepared a new Swedish translation of the Bible.

The church celebrated its tenth anniversary in September 1984, four days after Dr. Becker's funeral. He had learned in

May that he was suffering from a malignancy that the physicians correctly regarded as incurable.

In addition to all he did in Sweden, Dr. Becker worked energetically to promote the cause of the LCCS in this country. With articles in *The Northwestern Lutheran* and with countless lectures before Lutheran Women's Missionary Society rallies and other groups, he told the story of the LCCS and gained support for it. The Scandinavian church sorely misses him to this day.

WELS Support for the LCCS

Experience with our mission in Poland and Germany had taught the WELS a hard but useful lesson. When Hoenecke reported on his and Becker's 1973 visit to Uppsala, he included this information: "We warned with brotherly candor against too much dependence on help from the outside, and the advice was taken in the same friendly spirit in which it was given."

Nevertheless, both parties recognized that LCCS would need some assistance, and a plan was developed that would not require the use of WELS budgetary mission funds. Generous gifts from various groups and individuals were used to establish a "Sweden Conference and Aid Fund." This fund, now known as the "Scandinavian Fund" has modestly subsidized the Scandinavian church to this day. In 1977 WELS made a one-time grant of $50,000 to establish a Church Extension Fund. The amount of annual subsidy has gradually declined. In 1987 it was $8,400, none of it from regular budgetary synodical offerings.

Pastors of the LCCS often work with their hands to help with their support.

The Sacrifices of Pastors and People

How do the pastors support their work when congregations are obviously too small to pay full salaries? One pastor works in the office of a local police department, another has a morning paper route, a third does public relations work for the post office. Others are an electrician, a security guard, a tree farmer, a proofreader, a chain-saw salesman, a teacher. Their wives help support their husbands' work by teaching, nursing, baby-sitting.

One-third of the entire baptized membership attended the LCCS's convention in July 1986, a tribute to the wholehearted commitment of these people to God's truth and the Lutheran confession. That commitment led them also by 1979 to average more than $350 in annual offerings per communicant member.

At Yxenhult, Ruben and Hanna Christianson turned their tree farm over to their pastor so that he could support himself by harvesting and selling the trees. At Råneå a couple donated space in an apartment building, to be remodeled for use as a church. The cost to the congregation was only $4,400 because pastor and people did all the work. When Biblicum needed an

When an addition of Biblicum was needed, donated labor and private gifts from members of WELS and the LCCS paid for the project before this happy day of dedication.

addition to its building at Uppsala, the project was paid for before the day of dedication, partly because of private gifts from WELS members, but largely because of the Scandinavian people's gifts and their donated labor. One group came to Uppsala from Norway to help with the construction.

108

The Seminary Program

Dr. Seth Erlandsson and Dr. Ingemar Furberg were called to provide seminary training at Biblicum. Gunnar Edwardsson, the first graduate of the seminary program, was ordained in 1979.

Edwardsson was raised by pietistic parents who used devotional literature that, in his own words, was "so legalistic that when I moved away from home in 1971 to go to school in Lund I did not know the gospel." At Lund he was exposed to liberal theology but that did not assure him of his salvation. He met Ingemar Furberg, at the time still a member of the Church of Sweden. Furberg encouraged him to read Franz Pieper's *Christian Dogmatics*. As Edwardsson later recalled, "In two months I had read Pieper and *The Book of Concord*, and I was a new man. What I had never dared to believe, I had found, the forgiveness of sins and the righteousness that avails before God."

Two Great Tragedies

God spared Dr. Becker the experience of two great tragedies in the church for which he labored. The 1987 WELS convention was given the saddening news: "With heavy hearts we report that Dr. Seth Erlandsson has, for personal reasons, resigned his various positions in the church." The LCCS's premier theologian, writer, and only full-time seminary professor was gone from its public ministry. He remains a member of the church but his great abilities and energies are no longer being used, sorely needed as they are. His co-worker at Biblicum, Ingemar Furberg, lives in retirement at considerable distance from Uppsala.

Furthermore, it was reported in May 1987 that Professor David Valleskey and Pastor Martin Janke of the Interim Committee were trying to arrange a meeting with LCCS's church board to discuss matters that were disturbing our fellowship. President Per Jonsson would not permit such a meeting, just as he would not let board members who disagreed with him attend board meetings.

Per Jonsson and a few others were accusing WELS of false teaching in the Lord's Supper and the doctrine of the public ministry. He insisted that the true Lutheran teaching is that the Lord's Body and Blood are present from the moment when the words of institution are spoken. His view cannot be established from Scripture. In the matter of the public ministry he insisted, contrary to Scripture, that only the pastoral office is divinely instituted, to the exclusion of teachers, professors, and other called workers.

Only members who agreed with Jonsson, the president of LCCS, were permitted to be qualified as voters at the church convention of July 1987. Nevertheless, only about 75 souls sided with Jonsson and left our fellowship. About 277 remained. The majority reorganized, elected a new board, and set out to plan the future of the LCCS.

By 1991 there were seven pastors serving about 700 souls in seven congregations and several preaching stations. In recent years, pastors and lay persons have attended the annual Evangelism School of Outreach at Wisconsin Lutheran Seminary. The 1990 LCCS convention resolved to establish a fund to provide some support for a pastor to concentrate on gospel outreach. A number of women have undertaken the translation of WELS Sunday School materials. The chairman of the church board is a layman, Thomas Lindgren, an accountant who lives near Uppsala.

Bloodied but not bowed, this little church has been aptly described as "optimistic as it seeks to hold high the banner of confessional Lutheranism in a land which is home to the largest Lutheran church in the world, but where confessional Lutheranism is seen as an anachronism."

God bless the efforts of these courageous Christians and crown their optimism with success.

MISSION CURRENTS TWO
POSTWAR INTERNAL PROBLEMS

One would think that the years following World War I might have been more placid as far as synodical development was concerned. A confessional stance had been taken. A well organized synodical structure was in place. World peace had been declared. All systems were set to move forward. Sadly, the last half of the "Bergemann Years" didn't work out that way.

First there was the language problem. Following the war, it became clear that the German idiom of the forefathers would have to give way to the official English of the country. Understandably, this was a gradual process. Church members during those years had to be bilingual to fit into the scheme of things—in school, in church, in worker training, in development. Sometimes it was difficult to know whether to be confirmed in English or in German, which of the two language services to attend with the family, which grammar to use for studying Greek or Hebrew, which medium to use to teach or to proclaim the good news. Nowadays much thought is being given to the problems of adapting to other cultures. The people of our synod went through this process the hard way, and it required more adjustments than is often realized.

Unfortunately a number of doctrinal as well as jurisdictional problems muddied the synodical waters during the decade following the war. One matter involved a divisive dispute between board and faculty at Northwestern College in matters of disciplining students. The other was occasioned by a controversy concerning a conference paper on justification, which eventually brought the seminary faculty into the picture and ended in the withdrawal of a group of pastors who called themselves the "Protes'tants." This rift sent its shock waves throughout the entire synod.

Perhaps the most unsettling problem affecting the synod's expansion into other parts of the world had to do with finances. The somber aftermath of World War I was followed by the decade known as "The Roaring Twenties." Economically the United States seemed to be flying high. But did all the noise and bluster really reflect productive activity? Were these years reflecting the symptoms of a hysterical reaction to the war? The whole world had suffered a severe blow to its ego. Somehow, in spite of expectations to the contrary, the war didn't seem to have improved things much. Perhaps that realization led to blowing off some steam while the opportunity was there. Here today, gone tomorrow! Enjoy life while you can!

Then came the inevitable day of reckoning. An economy that was soaring toward seemingly limitless heights ended up in a terrible crash. "The Early Thirties" that followed hard upon "the Roaring Twenties" brought an economic depression such as the world had perhaps never known before.

The church doesn't exist in a vacuum. The Wisconsin Synod during the so-called "good times" was swept into building activities that failed to take sufficiently into account the inevitable day of reckoning. In most cases the building itself was needed. But it was done often without full certainty of how to pay for it once it was completed.

Dr. Martin Luther College, for example, underwent a rebuilding program during the twenties involving dormitory, classroom, and administration buildings. The Cost? Close to $400,000. Northwestern Lutheran Academy was established at Mobridge, South Dakota, involving a number of building projects. Michigan Lutheran Seminary added a refectory to its

The new seminary at Thiensville was built at a cost of nearly $440,000.

complex of buildings. The cost of these projects was modest, but added to the deficit already in the treasury. On the Indian Mission a boarding school for the Apaches was begun that included a girls' dormitory. Bit by bit the debt continued to grow. The cap to all of this was the move of Wisconsin Lutheran Seminary from Wauwatosa to Thiensville in 1929, costing nearly $440,000. Northwestern College came in for its share and had plans approved for a new classroom-library-science building, but before the building began, the crash of 1929 put an end to any and all further building activities.

By the end of 1930, the Wisconsin Synod had accumulated a debt of $752,649. In normal times this may not have seemed so insurmountable. In the country's depressed situation, the effect was disastrous. Banks were failing. Jobs were scarce. Contributions fell dramatically. All salaries paid by the synod were cut to the bone. Candidates for the ministry graduating from Wisconsin Lutheran Seminary were left without calls. Professors and missionaries receiving salary or subsidy from the synod experienced months when no salary was forthcoming at all.

An apt comment at this time by Professor John Meyer of our Wisconsin Lutheran Seminary deserves repeating:

> Until very recently there was always a shortage of men for our work. Why? Many people withheld their sons because there was more material success luring them to other professions. What did God do? When we withheld our sons from His service, He sent the World War and we had to let

our sons go to the shambles of a foreign battle field (Reference to World War I)! God showed us that He can—very painfully too—take our sons if we refuse to give them to Him willingly. After the war we gradually got more men. Yet, although our country, and our Christians along with the rest, was practically wallowing in money, contributions toward missions were far from keeping step with the general prosperity. We withheld our money from God. He sent us the Great Depression and many lost practically all they had. God can get at our money, if we withhold it from Him, get at it so that it hurts, while we might have enjoyed the pleasure of giving for His saving cause.

Under these conditions, President Bergemann, who had worked so energetically toward organizing a viable church body, ended his leadership of 16 years in 1933 with the report:

> Under existing circumstances there has been no thought of expanding into new mission fields. . . . The harvest is great, but it must go to waste because the workers whom the Lord has given us cannot be put to work.

It's a pity that Bergemann, who had a real heart for mission expansion, had to end his tenure on this sad note. Regretfully many delegates remembered the strong exhortation that he had made at a previous convention:

> The preaching of the Gospel was and ever will be the one great and peculiar mission of the Church. Not until the Church has gone into all the world and has preached the Gospel to all creatures, has it performed its mission!

Pastor John Brenner succeeded Pastor G. E. Bergemann as president of the synod in 1933.

In 1933 John Brenner was elected president and had this burden of debt placed on his shoulders. Two years later he faced his first convention in which every proposed increase met with a negative response. On the last morning of the convention, an event of far-reaching significance took place. As the time of adjournment was approaching, a young delegate by the name of Edgar Hoenecke, deeply troubled that the debt was thwarting our mission endeavors, proposed that the synod "retire [its] debt without delay." A lay delegate, Mr. Frank Retzlaff, with hat in hand, about to leave the convention floor, declared, "I like what that young man has proposed, and I want to second the motion." Although it seemed rather late to do anything about this motion, it had to be called. Much to the surprise of President Brenner it passed with a large majority.

With renewed vigor the debt retirement resolution was implemented under the leadership of Professor E. E. Kowalke. Pastor Hoenecke was put in charge of publicity. Through a plan devised by the Michigan District to use striking informational bulletins, the synod made a strong appeal to all congregations. The effort began to take hold. The country's prosperity, which had for so long been "just around the corner," was gradually returning. The ground was being prepared during the 1930s for what was to follow in the decade just ahead. Unfortunately, a terrible second world war intervened, and the promise offered by the 1935 convention to retire the debt "without delay" could not be carried out until 1945.

In the meantime a cooperative venture in world mission work was undertaken by the synod through its membership in the Synodical Conference. The Synodical Conference was a federation of the Missouri, Wisconsin, Norwegian, and Slovak Synods, a fellowship of church bodies engaged in mission work among the blacks in the United States. Beginning in Little Rock, Arkansas, as far back as 1877, this work had spread to most southern states as well as to metropolitan centers in the North. In connection with the Conference's fiftieth anniversary in 1927, the desire was expressed to extend its work to the continent of Africa. Over $7,000 was collected among the black congregations for this purpose. It was at a conference of black congregations, incidentally, that the idea to carry the gospel to Africa arose.

A few years later, in 1934, an appeal from the African continent came directly to the Synodical Conference itself, an appeal which was just too "Macedonian" in nature and substance to refuse (See Acts 16:9-10). As a member of the Synodical Conference our synod found an outlet for involvement in world mission work in spite of postwar financial difficulties. Thus the Lord had his own way of leading us to a "Dark Continent" that was indeed "ripe for harvest."

Marvelously, this move into Africa took place and captured the mission spirit of many in our synod through the events that followed.

ANSWERING WEST AFRICAN APPEALS
NIGERIA AND CAMEROON

NIGERIA

The African continent is easy to illustrate because it consists of two ovals that form a right angle. At the western hinge of this right angle are two independent countries that form the focus for this chapter of WELS World Mission History. The countries are Nigeria, with a currently estimated population of 115 million, and Cameroon, with an estimated population of 10 million.

Our synod's mission work in Africa began in Nigeria. As previously mentioned, this African mission was a cooperative effort with the synods that formed the Synodical Conference. After 25 years of cooperative work in this venture, this joint work ceased as a result of the breakup of the Conference in the early 60s. The Lutheran Church-Missouri Synod, which had, by virtue of its size, financed 88 percent of this field's needs, thereupon assumed total support and supervision of the field.

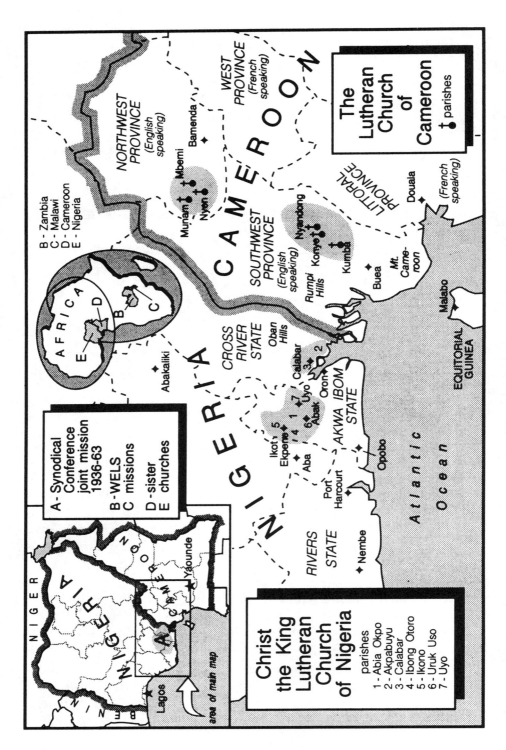

This left WELS without a mission in western Africa. But not for long! As an aftermath of our participation in this joint work in Nigeria, our synod undertook independent mission work with two smaller church bodies that had their roots in the Synodical Conference work in Nigeria. These two smaller bodies were Christ the King Lutheran Synod in Nigeria and the Evangelical Lutheran Church in Cameroon, a country adjacent to Nigeria's eastern border. WELS made official contact with these two church bodies in the late 1960s.

The Evangelical Lutheran Church of Nigeria

We turn our attention first to the joint work of the Synodical Conference in Nigeria. The miracle of God's grace that led to this undertaking can only be explained by the words, "Go" and "Lo," words contained in the King James Version of Christ's Great Commission. To our Lord's command, "Go and make disciples of all nations," Jesus attached the promise, "Lo, I am with you alway." Our black congregations in southern United States had raised their voices in response to Christ's "Go." They also provided offerings to support the effort. Whites, too, from the South and the North promoted the mission. In spite of adverse economic conditions, Synodical Conference leaders made sure African mission work appeared on the agenda of their conventions. Articles urging mission outreach began appearing in official periodicals of Synodical Conference church bodies.

"We Have Waited for You to Come"

With a growing desire to fulfill the Savior's command to "Go," how did the church finally spring into action? Here the church was to experience the sureness of the Lord's promise in a marvelous way, as the Lord began "opening doors that no man can shut" (Revelation 3:8). An appeal came from 16 churches in the densely populated coastal region of Nigeria. Members of the Ibesikpo clan of the Ibibio tribe wrote to the Missionary Board of the Synodical Conference on January 22, 1934, stating:

> We have informed the government officials in Nigeria about your coming into Ibesikpo as missionaries of the Gospel of Christ. They have given their approval, and no objection is offered by them. We hope that when the Lutheran Synodical Conference will hold its convention in 1934, they will give earnest consideration to the Ibesikpo appeal and be

ready to bring the Good News into our land. We have waited and waited patiently to see you coming to us. Do not despise our tears. We have waited so many years for you to come.

Truly amazing, isn't it, for such an appeal to come at such an opportune time? An equally amazing series of events preceded this appeal. Christianity since earliest times had been no stranger to northern Africa. Due to internal strife and a lack of missionary vision, however, it was all but obliterated by Islamic conquest. During the succeeding centuries, forays were made by European colonial powers along the coastline of Africa, west and south of the Sahara, seeking not only gold and ivory but also introducing the Christian faith to colonies they controlled and supervised. Unfortunately, slave trading also prevailed, until this was vigorously opposed and halted in the 19th century. This century also saw a mission activity so intense that it became known as the "Great Century of Missions."

Jonathan Udo Ekong

Nigeria came under the English sphere of colonial influence. Several "faith missions" from the British Isles entered Nigeria's densely populated southern coastal zone. One of these faith missions was the Qua Iboe Mission, which concentrated its efforts among the Ibesikpo clan. In 1930, from this Qua Iboe Mission, 16 churches with schools seceded to form the Ibesikpo United Church. This secession began with dissatisfaction among the people, stemming from the mission's refusal to baptize infants. It led to the closing of the mission's central school at Obot Idim. Since the money collected from the churches was used to support the schools, the Ibesikpos felt they should have a greater say as to how the schools were run. Meanwhile, an Ibesikpo who had been sent to America to receive an education and to find a church body that would help bring his people the true word of God was giving glowing reports of the mission to the Synodical Conference.

Jonathan Udo Ekong

This student was none other than Jonathan Udo Ekong, who later became a leading figure in the establishment and work of the Lutheran Church of Nigeria. More than 40 years old at the time, he spent a number of years gaining a college education before becoming aware of Synodical Conference plans for African mission work. He enrolled in Immanuel Lutheran College, which was supported by the Synodical Conference, and became well acquainted with its president, Dr. Henry Nau. Following his ordination into the Lutheran ministry in 1938, Ekong returned to Nigeria and began a ministry there that extended over a period of 46 years. He was 101 years old when he died in 1982, having participated in all phases of the development of the Evangelical Lutheran Church of Nigeria.

A Visit to the Ibesikpos

Through Ekong's contacts with Synodical Conference officials, a survey commission was authorized to visit the Ibesikpos. Pastors Immanuel Albrecht of the Wisconsin Synod, Otto Boecler of the Missouri Synod, and Dr. Nau were selected to serve on this survey trip. They arrived in Nigeria on February 4, 1935, after a month-long sea voyage. After visiting the 16 churches two of the team returned, and Dr. Nau remained for another six months.

Convinced that the Ibesikpo congregations that had seceded from the Qua Iboe Mission had reached a point of no return, the survey committee recommended that these congregations be assured of the support of the Synodical Conference and of the sending of resident missionaries as soon as possible. Upon receiving affirmative replies from the constituent synods that same year, Synodical Conference President Ludwig Fuerbringer instructed the Missionary Board to proceed at once with the opening of the work in Nigeria and the calling of missionaries. Dr. Nau received a leave of absence from Immanuel Lutheran College and returned to lay the groundwork for establishing a mission among the Ibesikpos. At its 35th convention, which met in Indianapolis in 1936, the Synodical Conference officially ratified Dr. Fuerbringer's decision.

Dr. Henry Nau

A better advance man than Dr. Nau could not have been found. The best description of his work is contained in his 414-page book entitled, *We Move into Africa*. The book, unfortunately no longer being published, makes for absorbing reading. It pictures Nigerian life and culture, presents the church situation with its problems and promises, and contains a vision for the future. Above all the book reflects Dr. Nau's firm convictions concerning the building of a sound confessional church as well as the establishing of indigenous principles based upon the thorough training of competent national workers.

Dr. Nau's policies were followed by the team of expatriates that came after Dr. Nau's advance work. The team included Pastor and Mrs. William Schweppe of the Wisconsin Synod,

Dr. Henry Nau remained in Nigeria for six months to work with Missionaries William Schweppe and Vernon Koeper after their arrival in 1937.

Pastor and Mrs. Vernon Koeper of the Missouri Synod, and nurse Helen Kluck. The latter member of the team was included to show the mission's concern also for the physical needs of the Africans.

The First Missionary Team

The mission work of Pastor Schweppe deserves special attention by the people of our synod, since he was the first missionary of the synod to work overseas in a heathen mission field. His life-story and letters have been compiled by Missionary E. H. Wendland in a paperback entitled *IBIBIO*. Rev. Schweppe served as superintendent of the Nigerian field for its first 22 years. In grateful recognition for his longtime leadership during this pioneer stage, Rev. Schweppe was awarded the Doctor of

Divinity degree at the Concordia Theological Lutheran Seminary in St. Louis on June 5, 1958. Dr. Schweppe also did advance work in the establishment of a mission in Ghana and completed 33 years of foreign service in Zambia, Africa, before meeting an untimely death by a road accident in 1968. His faithful wife Leola worked tirelessly at his side during these years of distinguished service to the cause of missions. "Bill," as his friends knew him, truly exemplified his own watchword: "The greatest work in the world is mission work."

The team of missionaries that disembarked from the ship Wilberforce at Port Harcourt on April 24, 1937, to greet Dr. Nau was under no illusion about the type of work it was to encounter. They had accepted calls that many had refused. They were well aware that living conditions would be a far cry from what they were accustomed to in America. They knew they would be working in a totally different cultural atmosphere. While on shipboard from London for several weeks, they were together with other experienced missionaries headed in the same direction. Dr. Nau immediately began a six-month briefing before he returned to America. In Leola Schweppe's words, he was a "real driver."

The Schweppe House at Obot Idim, Nigeria

Dr. William Schweppe soon became the superintendent of the field. We in America can hardly even begin to understand the problems that these early missionaries faced. Nevertheless, there were many plus factors too. People in large numbers were everywhere— 800 per square mile. British colonial influence had eliminated some of the language barriers. Quinine had been discovered to cope to some extent as a preventive against malaria, the "white man's killer." The Bible was already trans-

123

lated into the leading African dialects. Although the climate was extremely hot and humid during the rainy season, the people were able to raise enough yams, cassava, and fruits for their livelihood. Native huts could be built out of bamboo poles and thatch. Even churches, schools, and mission dwellings could be constructed largely out of materials at hand.

Tribal Beliefs

But let's not forget the minuses. One of these was the problem of dealing with African tribal beliefs. Traditional religions in Africa placed great emphasis on the importance of ancestral spirits and magical practices. A "high god," the people believed, carried on his rule through a system of spirits who could be manipulated by native practitioners, or "witch doctors." In the final analysis, the tribes were steeped in a superstitious belief in the powers of witchcraft. Such things as sickness and death were the result of evil spirits. Charms and various "medicines" were needed for "protection." Unusual events such as the birth of twins were believed to be caused by evil spirits, and the twins were abandoned. In addition to problems with tribal beliefs, some tribal customs went contrary to the teachings of Scripture. The practice of polygamy, taking more than one wife, was just one of them. These beliefs and customs, although countered to some extent by the coming of Christianity, are still very much a part of African life today.

Working with Great Zeal

Schweppe and his growing team of workers carried out their mission primarily by organizing courses of thorough indoctrination for pastors, teachers, and headmen. Although congregations and schools had been organized previously, knowledge of basic Christian doctrine had been superficial. Requests for outreach to new village areas kept coming in. In his daily log, Schweppe lists the following items as having taken place during the course of one week: six adult early morning instruction classes, three afternoon instruction classes with children at the central school, three conferences with school teachers, one headman's class, one church council meeting, one funeral, two examinations of confirmands followed by church services with holy communion, and five emergency calls resulting from cases of sudden illness, abandonment of twins, and altercations between members. On one day Dr. Schweppe records how he taught several classes, served as mediator in a family dispute, took care of a social obligation, and acted as a paramedic and assistant undertaker. With such zeal on the part of the Nigerian mission staff, the seed of the gospel under God's blessing germinated and grew rapidly and abundantly.

Even furloughs during those early years had their problems. On the Schweppe family's first furlough in 1939, their trip home took three months and included many harrowing experiences at sea. These were the years of World War II, with German U-boats lurking in the waters. Not until 1944 was Dr. Schweppe able to return to Nigeria. In the meantime the Vernon Koepers, the Justus Kretzmanns, and nurse Christine Rapier held the fort.

Following Dr. Schweppe's return to Nigeria, the staff of expatriate missionaries grew steadily in order to care for the expanding needs of the field. The post-war history of the Nigerian field can best be described by the word *growth*. When the mission observed its 10th anniversary in 1946, it already numbered over 10,000 baptized members and nearly 4,000 communicants in 72 congregations. From 1944 to 1948, 11 expatriates were added to the missionary staff. Included among these were the following members of the Wisconsin Synod: Rev. and Mrs. Norbert Reim, Rev. and Mrs. George Baer, Rev. and Mrs. Edgar Greve, Rev. and Mrs. William Winter, Rev. and Mrs. Alvin Werre, and teachers E. J. Baer and R. A. Spangenberg. During these years the mission field became an organized church body known as the Evangelical Lutheran Church of Nigeria (ELCN).

Training Nigerian Pastors

A key factor in the remarkable growth of the Nigerian Lutheran Church was the establishment of a seminary program for the training of national pastors. Begun in a home during the war years, the school had to be closed because of lack of manpower. The seminary was reopened in 1949, and in 1953 eight students graduated and were ordained. Rev. M. N. Uko writes in the Golden Jubilee Edition of the *History of the Lutheran Church of Nigeria:* "It was a happy day for the Evangelical Lutheran Church of Nigeria because eight of its sons were entering the ministry."

A seminary classroom building was dedicated in January 1951, the first of several mission buildings on the Obot Idim compound. Dr. Schweppe served not only as superintendent of the mission but also from 1949 to 1958 as president of the seminary. Working closely with him as instructor and dean of students was Missionary Norbert Reim (1951-1959). Missionary Edgar Greve held the post of Manager of Lutheran Schools from 1954 to 1958, and was helpful in developing courses of study and processing teacher certification requirements. Reim, now semi-retired and living in Arizona, writes: "We always considered the work in Nigeria to be the most satisfying part of our ministry."

The Growing Years

The years between 1945 and 1960 were years of numerical and spiritual growth. This included the establishment of a secondary school, a normal school for the training of teachers, a foundling home to care for abandoned twins and orphaned babies, a Bible institute for pre-seminary students, a print shop, several schools for girls, and a hospital. The mission's outreach was extended to the Ogoja Province and to many larger cities of Nigeria. A rest home for missionary families was acquired in the highlands of Nigeria at Jos. Incidentally, the hospital was built largely through the generous donation of a consecrated Christian couple, members of the WELS, who donated the original funds in memory of their daughter Kathy.

On December 31, 1960, as the Evangelical Lutheran Church of Nigeria neared the end of its twenty-fifth year, it numbered 194 congregations, 33 preaching stations, 33,433 baptized members, 13,645 communicants, served by 18 African pastors and 18 missionaries. The mission staff also included nine medical workers, seven teachers, and two lay workers. This was truly a remarkable growth, especially when one recognizes the thorough indoctrination and high training standards that went along with it.

In many other ways, the church in Nigeria has been a model and an inspiration for mission efforts within our own synod. One feature

Dr. William Schweppe preaching at the 25th anniversary service of the Evangelical Lutheran Church of Nigeria, April 25, 1961 that immediately impresses a visitor from America is the singing. Hymns are not only translated into the Efik language, but an Efik hymnal complete with Lutheran order of service has been developed, with notes indicated according to the "do-re-me" system. Most of the members have been trained in this system, and both hymns and liturgy are sung with gusto.

Nigerians love to express their faith in other ways. When the offering is taken, the entire congregation moves in procession to a table in the front of the church, keeping time rhythmically with anthems sung by the choir. When a special need arises in the congregation, additional offerings are collected to take care of the need. Lay participation is outstanding, with important boards and committees chaired by competent laymen. The people have erected impressive church edifices, seating hundreds of people, and the national church body has taken over entirely the support of national workers.

Breaking of the Ties

In 1962, following the ending of fellowship ties in the Synodical Conference, the Wisconsin Synod participation in the Nigerian Lutheran Church ceased. The Lutheran Church-Missouri Synod, which had been subsidizing the giant share of the church body's annual budget, took over the support and direction of the work, which now involved over 55,000 baptized members and 35,000 communicants in 250 congregations. When a former Wisconsin Synod worker in Nigeria was asked, "Did the intersynodical tensions of those days have any effect on the national staff and the churches there?" he replied, "There was some tension between what one might call 'conservatives' and 'liberals,' but this did not always follow synodical lines."

Our synod offered to assume financial responsibility for the work in Nigeria, should the Evangelical Lutheran Church in Nigeria join in the WELS scriptural stand. A visit was arranged in which representatives from the WELS were given opportunity to discuss matters with the Nigerians. The meeting was held at Obot Idim on August 25, 1964, with the WELS represented by President O. J. Naumann and Professors C. J. Lawrenz and O. Siegler. The September 1964 issue of the *Lutheran Herald,* a periodical of the Nigerian Lutheran Church, reports as follows:

> The Wisconsin representatives made their points quite clear. . . . The delegates appeared very friendly, frank and

bold and tactful in pressing their points. They came and went. The idea that the Wisconsin visit was to take over the ELCN was purely out of misconception by many people. Instead of bringing gold they brought the living Word of God, and instead of breaking the framework of the ELCN they advised and prayed for the growth of the church.

The ELCN stayed with Missouri.

Thus came to an end a close relationship that bore rich fruit for many years and exposed the people of our synod to the work of introducing the gospel to a foreign mission field.

Christ the King Lutheran Church of Nigeria

With the ending of one phase of church work in western Africa, another phase soon began. Our synod's work on the western hinge of Africa had not ended. Two appeals for help from that area came in 1969. One came from Nigeria, involving people who had really been our "spiritual children" as a result of our previous work in the Synodical Conference. The other appeal came from Cameroon, also to some extent an outgrowth of previous work in Nigeria. In response to these appeals, the WELS is now working cooperatively with Christ the King Lutheran Church of Nigeria and with the Lutheran Church of Cameroon, just southeast of Nigeria.

We look first to Christ the King Lutheran Church of Nigeria. This church body began with nine congregations and about 2,000 souls, located in the Akwa Ibom State region of southern Nigeria. Most of these congregations are around the town of Abak, although work has spread out to other areas, such as the coastal city of Calabar. The church originated with pastors and congregations who once were a part of our synod's joint work in the Synodical Conference and who still subscribe firmly to the confession and practice of the Wisconsin Evangelical Lutheran Synod.

A history of Christ the King Lutheran Church (CKLCN) cannot ignore the "silent" years from 1962 to 1969, during which our synod had very little contact with Lutheranism in Nigeria. During the latter part of these years, the country was torn by a civil war. A group of army officers sought to set up an independent republic in the southeastern region called Biafra. This war ravaged the Cross River State, where Lutheran work was centered, and for a time seriously disrupted church activities. Although two million Nigerians died in this conflict, the church survived and the country remained united.

CKLCN actually formed in 1969 when its nine congregations and three pastors were among those seceding from the Evangelical Lutheran Church of Nigeria (ELCN). Although it might seem that tribal differences played a part in this step, there is little doubt that there was a loosening of doctrine and practice within the ELCN during the 1960s, particularly in the area of church fellowship. The ELCN had joined the Lutheran World Federation and the National Christian Council of Nigeria, both unionistic organizations. The CKLCN was taking a confessional stand.

A New Appeal for Assistance

The three pastors who served the seceding churches were Edet U. Eshiett, their leader, and two men he had helped train, Edet A. Akpakpan and Jonah U. Ekpo. Another member of the CKLCN, Ikpe B. Udofia, was studying in Yonkers, New York. Udofia addressed a moving appeal to WELS President Oscar Naumann and the World Mission Board's executive secretary, Edgar Hoenecke, in behalf of his church body. His personal appeal coincided with appeals from the pastors in Nigeria. The whole scenario is somewhat reminiscent of student Jonathan Ekong's appeal to the Synodical Conference in the 1930s. The requests centered in a desire to "receive the Bread of Life in its truth and purity."

E. U. Eshiett, E. A. Akpakpan, and J. U. Ekpo were the first pastors to serve Christ the King Lutheran Church in Nigeria.

As our synod officials inquired further, ELCN sources stated that the appeals were not for confessional reasons, but to obtain material, educational, and medical benefits. Faced with these opposing opinions, our mission board representatives had to be cautious in their judgments. While further investigation was going on, modest financial grants were sent to CKLCN from the "Aid to Sister Synods Fund" administered by President Naumann.

By late 1973 Pastor Eshiett felt that appeals to the WELS for aid were getting a negative response. He accepted an invitation from the Lutheran Churches of the Reformation to attend their seminary at Shepherd, Michigan. After experiencing some doctrinal differences with this church body, however, Eshiett again turned to our synod for help and was enrolled as a special student in 1974 at our synod's Wisconsin Lutheran Seminary in Mequon. Later that year, Eshiett returned to Nigeria to serve there once again as leader of CKLCN. Appeals for aid continued to come from this church body to our synod's Board for World Missions. Meanwhile, limited support was sent by a few individuals and from WELS restricted funds.

WELS Resolves to Help

In 1975 our Synod Convention resolved to ask the Board for World Missions to arrange for a visitation to the Nigerian field. In a joint meeting with the synod's Commission on Inter-Church Relations, the board, with some hesitation, agreed "that our synod has a special obligation over against former members of our mission in Nigeria."

Following this meeting on April 20, 1977, a team of three pastors experienced in world mission affairs— Arnold Mennicke, Richard Lauersdorf, and Theodore Sauer— were sent to Nigeria to investigate the situation further. The team returned with a positive report, and the 1977 Synod Convention resolved "to ask the Board for World Missions to explore the best possible way of standing at the side of Christ the King Lutheran Church in keeping with our confessional principles."

To implement this resolution, the Board for World Missions placed the Committee on Interim Missions, a sub-committee of the board, in charge of this request from Nigeria as well as any other fields not having an expatriate missionary. Plans were set in motion to conduct a worker training program involving periodic visits by qualified men from our synod to Christ the King

Lutheran Church (CKLCN) to assist this body in the development of a national ministry.

In this way our Board for World Missions developed a pattern for work in areas where it is extremely difficult or even impossible to send expatriate missionaries. In such cases a national church organization has already been established and agrees with us in doctrine and practice. WELS, in turn, desires not to disturb the independent status of this church body. Still, assistance is desired and needed, especially in the training of church workers.

In order to meet this need, Rev. T. A. Sauer, executive secretary of the synod's Board for World Missions, and Prof. E. H. Wendland, former missionary to Central Africa and instructor at the Wisconsin Lutheran Seminary, undertook two trips to Nigeria in 1980 and 1981. They thoroughly studied the situation and inaugurated a plan for assistance in the training of workers.

CKLCN congregations are administered by a Board of Directors consisting largely of consecrated laymen such as elders M. E. Hanson and I. A. Okon.

The visitors were both amazed as well as thrilled by what they found on their visits. The congregations were well organized and administered by a Board of Directors, consisting largely of consecrated laymen. Worship services and Sunday school sessions were well attended. At a synod convention service lasting two hours and 45 minutes, over 400 communicants received the Lord's Supper. The singing of both congregation and choir was outstanding. Churches were well maintained, and a joint ladies' organization functioned with the same precision as our stateside LWMS. Clearly, the good seed planted by the workers in the former Synodical Conference mission was still bearing abundant fruit.

A joint ladies' organization functions with the same precision as our stateside LWMS.

The people often spoke appreciatively of the work of Wisconsin Synod missionaries, some of whom had lived and worked in that very area. A booklet prepared by Wendland and Sauer entitled *A Nigerian Safari* gives descriptive and photographic details of their 1981 visit, in which the first two-week seminar for the training of workers was inaugurated. Earlier in that same year formal fellowship relations had been declared between the WELS and the CKLCN.

These visits have, to a great extent, set the course for the work that has followed under the direction of Rev. John Kurth, World Mission Counselor for the Board for World Missions. Two-week training seminars have been conducted twice a year according to a pre-arranged curriculum, which includes the

The training of national workers began with seminars conducted twice a year by visiting instructors from America.

chief areas of theological study. A pool of men with mission experience has been gathered from which to draw for instructors. Those serving in this capacity, in addition to those previously mentioned, have been Pastors Don Fastenau, Kirby Spevacek, Michael Hintz, and David Sternhagen from the United States, and Pastor Salimo Hachibamba and Dr. E. R. Wendland from Central Africa. On these visits John Kurth usually participates and serves as liaison between the WELS and CKLCN.

Gratitude

On one of these trips, both Kurth and Sauer in a special service of gratitude were formally presented with tribal tunics and other gifts. Elder Frank U. Etim, a 90-year-old Nigerian chief and a founding father of the Nigerian Lutheran Church, spoke special words of gratitude and, placing a chief's cap on Pastor Sauer's head, made him an honorary chief. This was a special way of saying thanks to WELS for all it has done to help this young church. Pastor Sauer remembers this as one of the most moving experiences of his life.

Uruk Uso to Calabar

In 1986 a $35,000 grant from our synod's "Reaching Out" offering enabled CKLCN to complete a "Theological Study Centre," located near its largest congregation in Uruk Uso village. The Centre provides living space for visiting WELS instructors as well as classroom facilities for training church workers. Arrangements were at one time made for Pastor Eshiett to carry on much of the program during the year as outlined by seminar leaders. Following Eshiett's disappointing resignation, however, Pastor Akpakpan was appointed by the CKLCN Board of Directors to guide this part of the work. In the meantime Pastor Ebong Ukpong, who received much of his training in America, has replaced Eshiett on the CKLCN roster of pastors.

Elder Frank U. Etim, a 90-year-old chief and a founding father of the Nigerian Lutheran Church

Meanwhile, CKLCN is growing and has a critical need for more pastors. At this writing, the Board for World Missions is implementing steps to temporarily provide a larger measure of assistance in the development of the CKLCN worker training program to help fill that need. According to this plan, experienced theological teachers from the United States, preferably men with mission experience, are being called for a two-year period to provide the needed help. It has often been said in our circles that the confessional stability of a church rests with the training of its pastors. We hope, then, that the critical need for more pastors for CKLCN can be best met in this way.

Latest reports from this sister synod show an ever greater desire on its part to expand its work to new places. Most of its congregations are in rural areas, but it is also reaching out to urban areas such as Calabar, to which many of its members are moving. Nigeria with its teeming millions has been one of the world's most productive mission fields. For us it is a real privilege to be able to assist these more than two thousand brothers and sisters in Christ in this undertaking. Oh the joy of sharing Christ with others! Our hearts can then truly sing to the Lord:

"Lift up thine eyes in wonder.
See nations gather yonder.
They all come unto Thee!"

"See nations gather yonder.
They all come unto Thee!"

CAMEROON

The Lutheran Church of Cameroon

In a time frame that almost parallels the appeals from Nigeria, similar requests came to our synod from the Republic of Cameroon, which borders Nigeria to the southeast. Here a Lutheran Church came into being as a result of the Biafra civil-war crisis in Nigeria, referred to in our previous section. During this war, which lasted three years (1967-1970) and which ravaged the Cross River area in which the Lutheran Church was headquartered, many people from Nigeria fled across the border into neighboring Cameroon. They found refuge in the adjacent English-speaking section of Cameroon. Among these refugees were products of our Synodical Conference mission work.

Two Lutheran pastors, E. E. Udofia and Isaac Eduok, both from Nigeria, were instrumental in organizing the Lutheran Church of Cameroon (LCC). They formed the church with four families and held worship services in their own homes in 1965.

Lutheran pastors E. Udofia and I. Eduok, pictured to the left, with Bruno Njume, present head of the Lutheran Church of Cameroon.

Other Nigerians, no doubt Biafran war-refugees, were attracted to these services. A Cameroonian by the name of Paul Chonason joined the church. There is no concrete evidence that he had any special Lutheran training or even much Lutheran background, yet he was an opportunist who evidently saw possibilities of using this fledgling body to his own advantage. He succeeded in becoming the leader of this group and was chosen as its chairman. In the meantime another pastor coming out of a sectarian background, Bruno Njume, joined this young body of Lutherans.

A Church in Need of Help

A series of interesting events led to LCC's appeal to our synod for help. As a result of the Biafra crisis, the border between

Nigeria and Cameroon was closed. Assistance could no longer come to these people from the Lutheran Church in Nigeria. Missionary Kirby Spevacek, who was serving in our Zambian mission in 1969, saw an article in the *Worldwide Evangelist* magazine in which Chonason was requesting that tracts be sent by a "conservative" church body. Correspondence between the two men followed, eventually leading to Chonason's request to our synod's office for spiritual guidance and financial assistance. This appeal, which reached America on January 29, 1970, was received with some understandable hesitancy on the part of our synod's Board for World Missions. But the board authorized Prof. E. H. Wendland, then serving as missionary in Zambia, to visit Cameroon on a fact-finding mission. He went there in late December 1971.

The trip got off to a bad start, making him wonder if it wouldn't be best to return to Zambia immediately. Professor Wendland explains:

> My suitcase was lost enroute when I changed flights in Kinshasa. I was met at Douala, Cameroon, by Chonason together with a Chief Wilson with a black Mercedes. He offered to take us to Kumba where the church was headquartered. On the way the chief pleaded for American teachers to staff his private secondary school, promising that his whole tribe would 'become Lutheran' if we could make a deal. In Kumba I was quartered at the town's only hotel with running water, the Hotel Authentique. Unfortunately the hotel's running water was confined to its one and only lavatory, and the only food available for 'Europeans' was stewed chicken and fried eggs. The only place to replenish a missing wardrobe was an open-air marketplace. Quite a prospect for a planned stay of six weeks!

In spite of all this the field itself seemed promising enough for Prof. Wendland to submit the following report: "Quite obviously help for this church is very much needed, particularly in sound worker training and in materials to help do the job. This field deserves a closer look." Acting on the report, the Board for World Missions decided on minimal interim funding with supervision from our Central African field.

WELS' Response

Two visits to Cameroon followed in 1972, one by Executive Secretary Hoenecke from the U.S. and Missionaries Sauer and Wendland from Zambia and the second by Sauer alone. On the basis of reports from these visits, the World Board resolved "to endorse the cautious program being carried on in Cameroon without committing the synod." Soon after this, things began to fall apart in Cameroon. A power struggle for leadership among the members of LCC led to internal dissension of such proportions that the district governor closed the church and impounded all church properties. This crisis, however, had a salutary, sobering effect on the church in Kumba. Paul Chonason was removed from the presidency and replaced by Bruno Njume. He, together with his pastoral colleagues Udofia and Eduok, worked hard to set their house in order. In April 1974 they succeeded in having the closure order revoked and the properties restored to the church body.

After renewed appeals from Cameroon another visit was made in 1975, again by Hoenecke, Sauer, and Wendland. New congregations and fields had been opened, especially in the nearly inaccessible Nyandong area from which Pastor Njume had come. This is possibly the remotest and most primitive area in which our synod is at work. The visitation team met

New fields are opened up in the nearly inaccessible Nyandong area of Cameroon.

with several chiefs from this area, who pleaded that we come to this field. The resultant report and recommendations to the Board for World Missions and to the Synod Convention brought about a major synodical decision. The synod in 1975 resolved:

1) To provide guidance and financial support to LCC.
2) To call two expatriates as resident missionaries.
3) To place this church body under the jurisdiction of the Lutheran Church of Central Africa and its executive committee.

A sum of $40,000 was added to the synod's annual budget for this work.

Pastor E. Hoenecke with Cameroonian chief

Repeated efforts were made to obtain permission to send expatriate missionaries to this field. The Cameroon government, at long last, granted this permission in late 1991. Other churches, organizations, and businesses have met with similar delays. Meanwhile, the work of the church has continued under its national leaders. We have had no difficulty in obtaining visas for field visits for the purpose of helping LCC and counseling its workers.

In 1979 we decided to introduce regular worker-training seminars, conducted by expatriate personnel twice a year. In this way, we could continue to strengthen the pastors and religious workers in Lutheran doctrine and practice and to offer advice and encouragement to this young church body.

Worker-Training Seminars

Missionary R. G. Cox from Central Africa and Prof. E. H. Wendland from Mequon introduced these seminars in 1979. Others serving in follow-up capacities have been Pastor Mark Krueger coming from Central Africa, and Pastors Paul Wendland, Michael Hintz, and Duane Tomhave from America. World Mission Counselor John Kurth has taken on the direction of this work and has been its chief participant. We hope these worker training seminars will ultimately provide the Cameroon church with the pastors it needs.

Both Kurth and Cox, perhaps the most frequent visitors to Cameroon, were honored for their service in a special recognition ceremony held in Kumba in 1986, in which they were presented with gifts and "crowned" with peace-hats. A great honor indeed from their Cameroonian brethren! Other field trips have been made both to visit the congregations and see the progress of the work and to discuss business matters with the church's Board of Directors.

Horse Or Helicopter?

On several visits the helicopter service of "Helimissions," an organization based in Switzerland, was used to gain speedy access to congregations located in areas inaccessible by conventional means of travel. In the Bamenda area toward the north, for example, a group of congregations can be reached only on foot or by horseback. An effort was made to purchase a horse for evangelist Elijah Koffi who works in this area. Appeals in *The Northwestern Lutheran* were made to buy "A Horse for Elijah." Enough donors were found to purchase a veritable stable of horses. Yes, a horse was purchased, but Elijah was unable to ride the animal and is footing it again in the rugged hills!

Via helicopter a visit was finally made to the home village of Bruno Njume, President of the Cameroon Lutheran Church. This village lies in a jungle area so remote, as one visitor expressed it, that "Tarzan could almost be heard calling in the distance." Of one of these visits Prof. Wendland writes: "Wherever we landed people looked at us as if we came from another planet. We prayed with them, listened to their pleas for help, to their words of thanks and greetings to their fellow Christians in America."

"Reaching Out" funds have helped provide a church in Kumba.

The Other Ten Million

As we in our synod are privileged to celebrate the centennial of WELS world mission work, we shall not want to forget this fledgling church body of 1,400 members. Nor will we want to forget Cameroon's other ten million people, living in a beautiful country close to the equator but having a life expectancy of only 47 years. For its many souls who are still living under the shadow of Islamic and animistic beliefs, there can, by God's grace, be an "eternal life expectancy" through faith in the world's only Savior. For this blessing we continue to pray and work.

MISSION CURRENTS THREE
THE HAPPY CONVENTION

After the delay mentioned earlier, the Wisconsin Synod's resolve of 1935 "to retire the debt without delay" began to take hold. One of the Michigan Plan bulletins used to help arouse interest by means of a clever cartoon illustrates the gradual progress of this effort. It shows a railroad train carrying missionaries toward fields of potential mission areas. Between the train and the mission fields, however, lies a deep washout labeled, "W.E.L.S. DEBT." Year by year the washout is being filled, filling the gap. The 1943 debt shows the remaining amount of $97,682, with words added, urging that by 1945 the entire debt be retired. The conclusion suggested by the cartoon is that once the debt is finally retired, the synod's missionaries will be able to share the gospel with the many fields ripe for the harvest.

At the 1945 convention, the synod's Board of Trustees could bring the good news that the debt was not only retired, but that a sizable surplus was to be found in the treasury. The report stated: "All accounts and requisitions could be paid as presented. The budget reserve fund amounts to $350,000. . . .

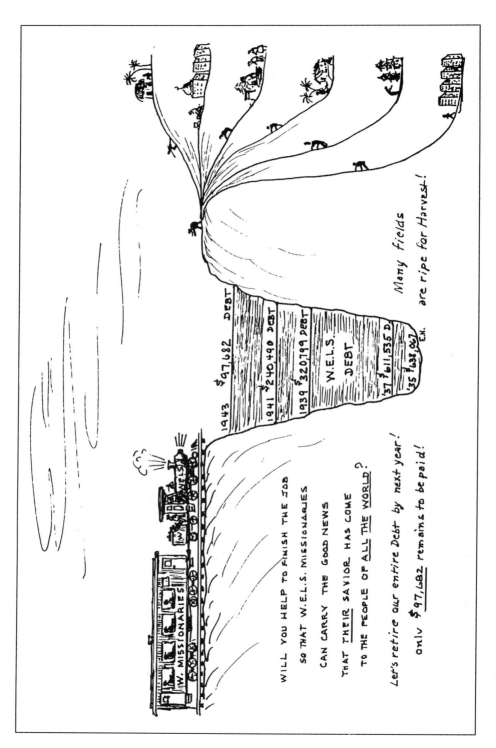

All professors and missionaries are now being paid a 25 percent increase above their basic salary. . . ." One can imagine the sense of relief enjoyed by a church body that had felt its every progressive step forward curtailed by a deficit in the treasury. One can also appreciate the happy feelings experienced in the hearts of those who at long last could think again in terms of expanded world mission outreach.

Another reason for a happy convention in 1945 was the hope that the war was about to end. In 1943 President Brenner had reported that 15,000 of the synod's members were absent from their homes because of World War II. "It is not necessary to go into details picturing the destruction and horrors of war, for there is no one on earth that is not affected and moved deeply by it," he had to report. In 1945, however, it was clear that the war's days were numbered. In fact, on the closing day of the 1945 convention the first atom bomb was dropped on Hiroshima, Japan. The end of the fighting was but days away.

Therefore, the delegates to the 1945 convention at New Ulm, Minnesota, assembled in a much more optimistic mood. President Brenner reflected this mood when he spoke of world missions as follows: "Until now we have not been planning to enter foreign fields, but the Lord may call us into such work at any time. May we then be ready to respond to his call, willing to work and to sacrifice." Yet he added the words of caution: "But let our expansion be a quiet steady progress in which the available manpower and the means to employ it keep pace with each other."

As the various divisions of the synod reported in May to the General Synodical Committee prior to the 1945 convention, the report on the Indian Mission called attention to the synod's many years of blessing and the "vastly increased opportunities resulting in so many ways from the present war." "We cannot shirk these issues much longer with impunity," the report declared. "As your committee in charge of the only heathen mission . . . which our Synod conducts independently, we earnestly urge this session of our Wisconsin Synod to take thought and action in the matter of mission work among those who have no opportunity to hear the sound of the saving Gospel (Isaiah 49:6)." The report was submitted by Pastor Edgar Hoenecke, the executive secretary of the Apache field, and Pastor Alfred Maas and Mr. Alvin Burkhardt, members of the Apache Mission Executive Committee.

This report as it had been read to the General Synodical Committee in May had met with no objection. It had been heartily endorsed by the General Mission Board, and its author had been encouraged to present it without change to the 1945 synod convention.

The report clearly challenged the synod on the strength of God's command and promise to give serious consideration to expanding its mission program into foreign fields. Lending credence to the challenge, the Board of Trustees had announced that there was a surplus in the synod's treasury. Consider also that the whole purpose of the debt retirement program had been to place the synod once more in a position to reach out with the gospel. One can imagine, therefore, how shocked Pastor Hoenecke felt when, after reading this report on the floor of the convention, he was declared "out of order" by the chair.

No doubt President Brenner was of the opinion that Hoenecke should have restricted his report to Indian affairs, rather than including in it a strong plea for mission expansion. Moreover, having worked for a decade under a cloud of debt, Brenner was extremely cautious lest such a situation happen again.

In any case, Pastor Hoenecke objected to this ruling by the chair. He based his objection on Jesus' Great Commission in Matthew 28:18-20 and on Isaiah's words in chapter 49:6. A lively discussion followed on the floor of the convention. Some, including synodical leaders who had faced the lean years when payroll demands could be met only with borrowed money, were defensive about what would happen to the newly established "reserve fund." Others stated that the synod must have a direct "Macedonian" call to undertake world mission work, rather than to seek it out. A few went so far as to say that this entire matter had been "staged."

In spite of these negative reactions the discussion ended with a resolution "that the President appoint a committee to gather information regarding foreign fields that might offer opportunity for mission work by our Synod." Although some may have thought that the resolution was just a convenient way to end discussion of this controversial issue, by referring it to a committee, progress was made. The door was opened for the report that was to follow at the next convention.

Reporting for the Committee on Foreign Missions at the Watertown convention in 1947, Pastors Arthur G. Wacker and

Henry C. Nitz began with the words of Isaiah 49:6: "I will also give thee for a light to the Gentiles, that thou mayest be my salvation unto the end of the earth." The report continued: "The Lord is speaking here also to us. Our Home Missions program has more than doubled in the last ten years, but we have a clear call to do both, Home and Heathen Mission work. . . . Foreign heathen fields where our Synod can begin work are at hand."

Again the discussion that followed on the floor was fast and furious. This writer remembers having attended the convention as a visitor and being enthralled by the lively use of Scripture passages on the part of those favoring world expansion. A large contingent from the Michigan District was especially noticeable, speaking for expansion. Again, many administration leaders expressed serious misgivings.

After a lengthy debate, the convention resolved "that the Synod authorize the expansion of our mission work in foreign heathen fields." The General Mission Board was instructed "to continue its investigation" and report its findings through the proper channels.

A beginning had been made. The Wisconsin Synod had declared itself to be "a light to the Gentiles," an instrument of the Lord's salvation "unto the end of the earth." In the months following the convention Pastors Wacker and Hoenecke were persuaded, after much urging by the Board, to explore possible mission fields in Africa. The result of their experience is a fascinating story in itself and merits a special section of "Mission Currents" in this historical presentation.

Eventually the synodical action following the exploration trip to Africa was combined with appeals to begin work in Japan as well. In 1951 the Wisconsin Synod Convention at New Ulm resolved not only to call and to send two missionaries to the Northern Rhodesian field in Africa but to ask the Lutheran Spiritual Welfare Commission of the synod to place a man in Tokyo, Japan. He was to care for the many men and women in the armed forces who were stationed in the Japan-Korea area. He was also to "investigate mission opportunities in Japan."

Thus the move to go with the gospel to foreign lands began, one might say, with a "Happy Convention" in 1945 and the appointment of a committee "to gather information regarding foreign fields." The gathering of information led to subsequent action in which the synod committed itself to foreign work. An important part of that action was the sending of Pastor Frederick G. Tiefel to Japan. Missionary Tiefel arrived in Tokyo in 1952. On the basis of his positive report, the 1953 Synod Convention resolved that two men be called to the Japan field as missionaries. They were also to continue the spiritual welfare work among the synod's members in the armed forces there. Serious mission work on the part of the Wisconsin Synod was about to begin in the Orient, a work that will occupy the next section of our historical presentation.

TO THE ISLANDS OF JAPAN
JAPAN MISSION

How has our ascended Savior used the WELS to help bring his saving gospel to the people of Japan? The Japanese are a people who for the most part have been living according to their own religions and serving their own gods for thousands of years. By contrast, we have been working in Japan for only a short period of time and within a limited geographical area. Nevertheless, the WELS mission experience in the Land of the Rising Sun serves to show how our ascended Savior works mightily by the power of His Holy Spirit through word and sacrament as he gathers his people to himself. In this brief resume of our Japan Mission, we will try to trace that work of our Savior God.

Learning to Know the Japanese

The recorded history of Japan goes back to only about the sixth century A.D. This makes Japan a relatively new country in the Orient. Nevertheless, its history seems ancient to us, when we compare it with that of the United States.

Japan's own religion is Shinto. It has to do with the origin of the Japanese people, their emperor, their destiny. Shinto also

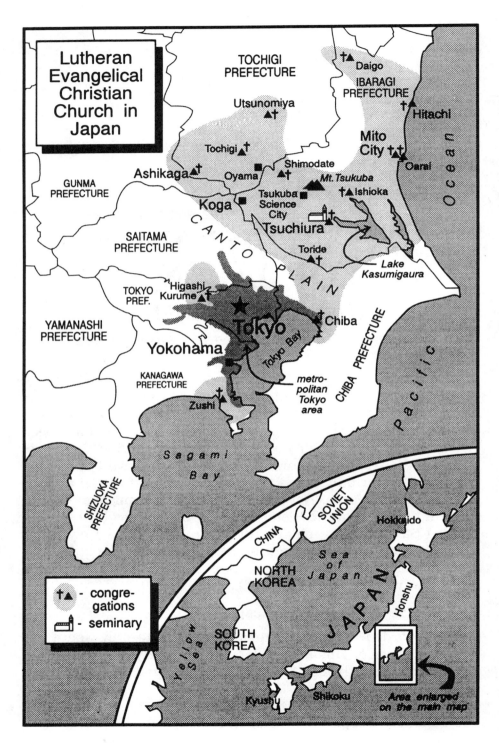

provides a way of seeking practical, day-to-day help such as good crops, safety on a construction site, or the ability to pass a college entrance examination. The Japanese seek these benefits from gods whom they call *kami*.

In the sixth century A.D. Buddhism, which had originated in India, was brought to Japan by way of China. This religion is more contemplative. It has much to do with a person's condition after death. In Japanese Buddhism much effort is exerted so as to achieve enlightenment, particularly through intensive meditation. Such enlightenment is a grasping of absolute truth or ultimate reality.

Many Japanese still worship their Shinto gods.

Confucianism, which also came to Japan from China, continues to have perhaps the strongest influence on the daily life of the Japanese. Among other things, Confucianism stresses moral responsibility to the group to which you belong, such as your family, your neighbors, your fellow students and teachers at school, or the people at your place of work.

Japan is a country where these three religions, Shinto, Buddhism, and Confucianism, determine to a great extent the religious thinking and the daily life of the people. It has been this way for over a thousand years. By comparison, Christianity has had very limited opportunity to affect the daily life or the culture of the people of Japan. We are still in the very early stages of having such an effect on their culture, if this change is ever to take place at all. As a result, Japan still is an unchristian society with a non-Christian culture. Only about one percent of the Japanese consider themselves to be Christian. In practical terms this means, for example, that Christmas is not a legal holiday. Of more importance for the missionary, it also means that most Japanese do not have any higher regard for the Bible than for any other book. The Lord has called us to proclaim his saving gospel in this unchristian setting.

Christianity in Japan

The Lord has his own ways of opening doors for his gospel. Up to the year 1500, the Christian people of Europe knew little or nothing of Japan. Then some Portuguese sailors were blown off course by a typhoon and landed on one of the Japanese islands. Some years later, in 1549, the Roman Catholic priest, Francis Xavier, began mission work in Japan. Xavier's strategy was to try first to convert the princes or rulers. It seems he hoped that a converted ruler might promote Christianity as the favored religion under his rule, much as European rulers of the time often determined the dominant religion in their territories.

These first efforts at mission work seem to have been quite successful. In fact, the number of Christians grew to such a degree that their percentage of the population was greater then than it is today.

Before long, however, the rulers began turning against Christianity. They had hoped that Christianity would bring unity to their land, but when Dutch Protestants appeared, who were bitter enemies of the Portuguese Catholics, the Japanese rulers saw that Christianity could breed controversy. They also soon realized that becoming a Christian meant dropping all their other religious practices. They weren't ready to do that, nor were they ready to run the risk of having these missionaries convert the entire nation. As a result, Christianity was outlawed and before long outright persecution began. In 1599 the first Japanese martyrs died for their faith. The Christians were forced to take their religion underground. As decades and even centuries passed, only a few tiny isolated groups, who were clinging to a distorted faith, remained.

Christianity virtually vanished from Japan. Not only did the persecution cause this but shortly after the persecution began, Japan closed its doors to all people from the outside, effectively blocking any new Christian influences. With just a few exceptions, Japan lived in total isolation from the rest of the world from 1614 to 1854.

Admiral Perry of the United States with his fleet finally led the way in forcing Japan to open its doors again to the outside world. In 1854 the Japanese entered an agreement allowing limited access to their country. This agreement gradually led to more treaties and a gradual renewal of mission efforts in Japan by both Roman Catholics and Protestants. The Lord had again opened the door to Japan for those who were to bring his word there.

Nevertheless, Christian missionaries were not always welcome. Until the end of the Second World War patriotism in Japan was centered in the emperor. According to their Shinto faith, the emperor was considered to be a divine person descended from the Sun Goddess. This meant that in Japan, patriotism and Christianity were in direct conflict with each other. Whenever patriotism was on the increase, Christianity was suppressed.

WELS Makes a Beginning

It is interesting to note that a proposal to begin mission work in Japan came before our Wisconsin Synod already at a very early date. In 1891 our synod's Mission Committee reported to the synod convention that, after investigating and comparing various fields, they were recommending we begin mission work in Japan.

Our convention decided to refer the matter to the Lutheran Synodical Conference, which was to meet in convention the following year. The conference then was made up of the Minnesota, Missouri, and Wisconsin Synods and the English Synod of Missouri and Other States. There is no record of any further action taken on the proposal, either by the Synodical Conference or by our synod. When our synod met again in 1893, we decided to begin work among the Apache Indians in Arizona. Our forefathers obviously were convinced that faithfulness to our Lord included seeking out opportunities to bring his word to people of distant lands and different cultures.

We did not again give serious thought to doing mission work in Japan until after the Second World War. Actually, we began to think of it during the Korean War. At that time rather large numbers of WELS members who were in the military were stationed in Japan and Korea. Our synod's Spiritual Welfare Commission, today's Special Ministries Board, was responsible for providing spiritual care for our people in the armed forces. As already noted previously, in its 1951 convention the synod authorized the Spiritual Welfare Commission to call a pastor to care for our men and women who were in military service in Japan and Korea. This pastor was to investigate mission op-

Pastor Frederick Tiefel was the synod's first missionary to Japan, serving from 1952 to 1957.

portunities in Japan as well. Pastor Frederick Tiefel received and accepted the call. He sailed for Japan in February 1952.

Pastor Tiefel soon reported that Japan offered great opportunities for mission work. Even before he learned the language well enough to work in it, he had Japanese people coming to him to study the Bible in English. He soon involved many of these people, most of whom were students, in translating materials such as the catechism into Japanese. Pastor Tiefel reported that he couldn't keep up with the demand for his services.

Pastor Tiefel's enthusiastic reports led our synod's 1953 convention to adopt a resolution formally committing itself to do mission work in Japan. The same convention also authorized calling a second missionary for this field.

These were the years in which the relationship between WELS and the Lutheran Church—Missouri Synod was deteriorating. Within our synod, there were sharp differences of opinion as to when WELS must make a complete break with the Missouri Synod. Missionary Tiefel was of the opinion that the time for WELS to break with Missouri had come. It appears that Missouri Synod missionaries in Japan were straying far from their synod's past teaching and practice. Observing this could only strengthen Missionary Tiefel's conviction that the time had come for the WELS to break fellowship with Missouri. Our synod in several conventions, however, was saying that the matter should be given more time. These were, no doubt, the chief factors that led to Pastor Tiefel's resignation from our synod early in 1957.

The group of Japanese Christians that Missionary Tiefel had gathered remained loyal to him. The work he had begun and was continuing in Japan was no longer a WELS mission.

We Begin Anew

In the meantime the call for a second missionary to Japan was finally filled. When Richard Seeger graduated from our seminary in the spring of 1956, he was assigned to Japan. Pastor Seeger arrived in Japan in the spring of 1957. By this time, however, Missionary Tiefel had already resigned from our synod.

Nevertheless, the Lord saw to it that our new missionary and his wife did not arrive in Japan without a welcome. When their ship docked in Yokohama on April 26, 1957, three WELS leaders were there to meet them. They were Pastor Oscar Naumann, the synod president; Pastor Harry Shiley, chairman of the Japan Mission Board; and Pastor Edgar Hoenecke, chairman of the Board for Foreign and Heathen Missions. While the Seegers were underway by ship, these three men had flown to Japan in an attempt to discuss matters with Pastor Tiefel. He, however, refused to meet with them, and although they were unable to carry out their plans to meet with Pastor Tiefel, they were there to welcome the Seegers when they arrived. One can only imagine how grateful this new missionary family must have been to have these men there to encourage them as they began their adventure in this new and strange country.

For the Seegers, getting started meant living temporarily in a hotel, saying good-by to the three men from the mother church

Missionary Seeger and his family were soon joined by R. Poetter, who already had experience as a missionary in Japan. Deacon Igarashi is looking on in the background.

153

in the U.S.A., finding a more permanent place to live in Tokyo, and then beginning an intensive study of the Japanese language. Japanese is an extremely difficult language for most Americans. Missionary Seeger put a great deal of effort into its study during his first two years in Japan.

During this time, Missionary Seeger also began conducting Bible classes in English. Probably many of the people who came to these classes did so at first for the purpose of learning English, but the Holy Spirit certainly used the word of God they were studying to testify to them regarding their Savior.

Early in 1958, our Japan Mission Board received word that Pastor Richard Poetter and his Japanese wife were back in the United States. Pastor Poetter, though coming from a WELS congregation in Wisconsin, had been a missionary in Japan for the Lutheran Church—Missouri Synod. He had left the Missouri Synod for conscience reasons and had once more become a member of the WELS. After gathering further information about him, our Japan Board extended a call to Pastor Poetter. He accepted, and he and his wife arrived in Japan in August 1958.

The disturbed relationship between WELS and the Lutheran Church—Missouri Synod had cost us one missionary. The Lord, however, used this same disturbed relationship to provide us with another missionary in the person of Pastor Poetter. Pastor Poetter was more than just a replacement. He already had about seven years of experience as a missionary in Japan, as well as being a man who had left another church body and joined the WELS out of conviction.

Ibaragi Prefecture the Main Target Area

As our two missionaries, Seeger and Poetter, settled in, they gave much thought and effort to the matter of choosing the area in Japan where we would carry on the main part of our work. Our missionaries seemed to be aware that the decisions they were making at this early stage would have a lasting effect upon our mission in Japan.

Japan is divided into state-like political areas called prefectures. Their size is similar to that of our smaller states in the U.S.A. Ibaragi Prefecture, which is located a short distance north of Tokyo, was chosen as the main target area of our mission thrust.

If you travel southwest from Tokyo, you find that the area continues to be industrialized and cosmopolitan for several hundred miles. If you go north from Tokyo and enter Ibaragi Prefecture, however, you find that quite abruptly the way of life becomes distinctively rural. The Japanese government is consciously infusing science and technology into this characteristically rural prefecture. The national government has been building and developing a research city called Tsukuba Science City in Ibaragi. Over thirty basic government research institutes are located there. Private research institutes continue to move in so as to be close to the government facilities. Many of Japan's top scientists, people who are working literally at the leading edge of human knowledge, are living in Tsukuba Science City in Ibaragi Prefecture.

Much of Ibaragi Prefecture is within the Canto Plain. This is the largest relatively level area in Japan although it does have scattered rolling hills. This makes it good land for farming. As you drive or ride the train through Ibaragi you see many rice paddies and orchards. The climate is mild. Temperatures don't get much lower than twenty degrees above zero Fahrenheit in winter. (Japan uses the Celsius scale as well as other metric measurements.) Summers are hot and humid with temperatures in the nineties for over a month at a time. Mt. Tsukuba, which has twin peaks and is covered with forests, rises out of the Canto Plain. Kasumigaura, the second largest lake in Japan, lies between Mt. Tsukuba and the sea.

Ibaragi Prefecture has several sizeable cities. At the time WELS missionaries began work in this prefecture it had a population of 2,064,000. Mito, the second largest city in Ibaragi and its capital, had a population of 120,000. Mito is a city rich in history. Its scholars played a major part in the fall of the last shogunate or military dictatorship in the 1860s. This led to the Meiji Restoration, which, after long years of isolation, was Japan's entrance into the modern world.

Several factors apparently led our pioneer missionaries, Poetter and Seeger, to choose Ibaragi as our first area of major mission work. Its proximity to Tokyo, where we had already begun, must have been a factor. Perhaps more important was that no other Lutheran church body was working in Ibaragi or in adjacent Tochigi Prefecture. The Lutheran Hour, which was being broadcast throughout Japan at that time, had received a number of responses from this region. The sponsors of the Lutheran Hour had no intention of sending missionaries into these two prefectures so they were very happy to refer any and all responses to their radio program to us. For these reasons and others, our missionaries concluded that Ibaragi Prefecture was the place where we should begin intensive work.

Mito City had received heavy shellfire from American warships during the war. At a place within the city just beyond the line where the devastation from the shelling ended, there was a somewhat "foreign" looking house. It had been built as a home and a clinic for a Japanese dentist who had moved back to Japan from Hawaii. This person had died, so his building was vacant. When this house came to the attention of the Poetters, they soon made arrangements to rent it and moved in. At this former dentist's clinic, our work in Mito, the capital of Ibaragi Prefecture, began. Missionary Poetter wrote that he preached from just about the spot where the dentist chair had stood.

Later we purchased land and built a parsonage, chapel, and small office in Mito. The headquarters for our mission in Japan has been located there since these early beginnings. Missionary Poetter continued to serve in Mito throughout his long ministry in Japan. He was appointed field administrator by the Japan executive committee. Later, when the national church, the Lutheran Evangelical Christian Church (LECC) came into being, he was elected its president or *Rijicho*. Pastor Poetter continued to serve in both of these offices until shortly before his retirement in 1991.

A Seminary at Tsuchiura

Tsuchiura is a somewhat smaller city than Mito. It is located on the main railroad line between Mito and Tokyo. In those early days of our mission when roads were poor and few Japanese owned cars, being near a main railroad line was very important.

Our missionaries had several contacts in Tsuchiura and the neighboring city of Ishioka. Before long a congregation was founded. Eventually Tsuchiura became and still remains an important center for our work in Japan. Perhaps the chief reason for Tsuchiura's importance is its location. It is about in the center of the region of Japan in which we are working. This, plus its location on a main railroad line, made Tsuchiura a city that was relatively easy for all our missionaries and Japanese pastors to reach.

When a building was needed to house the seminary program, it was erected in Tsuchiura. The church wisely put up a build-

The main building at Tsuchiura houses the seminary on the second floor while providing a worship area for the local congregation and larger gatherings on the first floor. The printshop is directly behind the main building.

ing that would serve as a meeting place for joint services, rallies, conventions, and other gatherings of our entire church body, as well as a home for our seminary. At the same time a printshop was built, and this operation, which had been carried on in Mito, was moved to Tsuchiura.

One thing led to another. Since the seminary program was to be conducted at Tsuchiura it followed that the fourth missionary, who was to be in charge of worker training, should live there. This meant the mission had to build another home in addition to the one already occupied by the pastor of the Tsuchiura congregation. Pastor Harold Johne was called to head the seminary program. He and his family moved into this new home as soon as it was completed.

Work at the seminary frequently involves three languages such as Japanese, Greek, and English.

This flurry of building all took place at the same time. The new buildings were dedicated on September 15, 1971. Doing so much building at just that time proved to be a special blessing from our ascended Lord. In 1971 each American dollar was still worth a fixed amount of Japanese currency, namely 360 yen. Shortly thereafter the yen was "floated" or allowed to freely reach its own level of value on the international currency market. As a result, the U.S. dollar immediately began to decline in value over against the Japanese yen. In other words one received fewer yen for each dollar that was exchanged. Had we built just a short time later the entire project would have cost us many thousands more in American dollars.

In 1978 Missionary David Haberkorn and his family joined the staff in Japan, and he was assigned to Nozomi (Hope) Congregation at Tsuchiura. Tsuchiura has since become a city of about 125,000 people. Missionary Haberkorn's field of labor also included nearby Tsukuba Science City and the surrounding area.

Spreading to Other Areas

Whether traveling by car or by train, one skirts Mt. Tsukuba in going from Tsuchiura to Shimodate City some thirty miles west. Shimodate was served by Pastor Yamada, a man who came to us from the Missouri synod in the early days. When Pastor Yamada resigned for reasons of health, he was followed by Pastor Menuhide Nakamoto. Nakamoto served Shimodate already as a student and vicar. When he graduated from the seminary in Tsuchiura he was given a permanent call to Shimodate. The special offering that our WELS congregations gathered for the twenty-fifth anniversary of the mission in Japan made it possible for the Shimodate congregation to build an attractive and functional chapel-parsonage combination.

The distinctively "Western" design of this church building serves to attract the attention of people living in Shimodate City.

Contacts in Utsunomiya City, the capital of Tochigi Prefecture, caused our missionaries to give early attention also to this area. One of our contacts in Utsunomiya wrote:

> A new bright life has opened for me through the gospel of Jesus Christ. Each day I find a time when I put everything else aside and read the Bible, study, and worship. Please send me names of others like myself who live nearby.

In February 1960 Missionary Seeger began classes and institutional work in Utsunomiya. Not until 1976 was a missionary, Roger Falk, assigned there. Land was purchased and a fine chapel-parsonage combination built. Through the continued work in Utsunomiya, the Lord has given us a small but firm foothold there. When Missionary Johne accepted a call to the United States in 1986, Pastor Falk became administrator of the seminary program. He continued his work in Utsunomiya while serving as the head of the seminary.

The records of our missionaries' activities are interspersed with accounts of personal, individual triumphs worked by the Holy Spirit. For example, on September 8, 1960, one of our recent converts, Mr. Keiichi Takahashi, lost both legs above the knees in a mining accident. It was on the third day after the accident that he said to our missionary, "Now I will have more time to witness to my Lord and Savior." These were not empty words. A short time later this man learned Braille and carried on our outreach to the blind and visually impaired until the Savior, whom he served so faithfully, called him home in 1989.

Work in Ashikaga City, which is also in Tochigi Prefecture, began in 1963 with English Bible classes. Our missionaries also conducted Bible classes in Japanese for the patients of a psychiatric hospital. The doctor who headed the hospital was not a confessing Christian himself but had high regard for Christianity and continued to favor our work in Ashikaga for many years.

One of our national pastors, Fukuichi Oshino, was called to Ashikaga after his graduation from our Japan seminary. Through Pastor Oshino's efforts the Lord provided us with a stable, growing congregation in that city. The architecture of the Ashikaga church building might seem a bit strange to Americans. The church itself has only a second floor. It is supported on pillars. This leaves the ground level open for parking. This unique architecture testifies to two developments in Japan: 1) The extremely high cost of land and 2) The increasing number of motor vehicles.

Our missionaries must have had their eyes on Hitachi City soon after our work in Ibaragi Prefecture began. Hitachi is some distance northeast of Mito. It is an industrial city with a harbor and is the largest city in Ibaragi Prefecture. In driving through Hitachi one gets the feeling that the city is being squeezed between the mountains and the sea. This squeezing has caused it to extend lengthwise up and down the coast.

Pastor Tadashi Yoshida was the first graduate from our Japan seminary.

The first graduate from our seminary, Pastor Tadashi Yoshida, was assigned to Hitachi. Some years later Pastor Yoshida was called to serve in Chiba, a major city across the bay from Tokyo. Pastor Elwood Fromm, who came to us from the Missouri Synod, was called to replace Pastor Yoshida at Hitachi. Pastor Fromm had passed a colloquy (a doctrinal oral examination) and had spent a year studying at the WELS seminary in Mequon, Wisconsin before he was called to Japan. Pastor Fromm was taken to his eternal home in the summer of 1988. Pastor Wakichi Akagami who had been serving a preaching station at Toride, a city between Tokyo and Tsuchiura, was called to continue the work at Hitachi.

The work in Tokyo has continued to progress since Pastor Seeger's time. After Pastor Seeger accepted a call to Hong Kong, Pastor Norbert Meier was called to Japan and placed in Tokyo. When Missionary Meier accepted a call to Alaska in 1974, Missionary Kermit Habben and his family moved from Tsuchiura to Tokyo to continue the work there.

Pastor Habben had been assigned to Japan when he gradu-

Missionary Kermit Habben, who was assigned as a seminary graduate in 1967, succeeded Richard Poetter as field administrator and chairman of the national church.

ated from Wisconsin Lutheran Seminary in 1967. He began his ministry in Tsuchiura as a replacement for Missionary Luther Weindorf, who had accepted a call to the United States. With Poetter's retirement in 1991, Habben became field administrator for the mission and chairman of the LECC. The Mito congregation, which Poetter had served for so many years, came under the care of Missionary John Hering.

The Tokyo congregation is located in Higashi Kurume, a western suburb of Tokyo itself. It is in a good location since it is on one of the major commuter lines leading out of central Tokyo. In addition to the main work of serving and extending the Japanese congregation, our missionaries in Tokyo frequently conduct English services for the benefit of Americans and other *gaijin* or foreigners living in the Tokyo area.

When one of the families in our Tokyo congregation moved to a city named Zushi in 1977, they asked Missionary Habben to conduct Bible classes and start a Sunday School there. Zushi is located somewhat south and a bit west of Yokohama. Beginning work there meant entering a new prefecture, Kanagawa. Because it is somewhat remote from the main area of our mission activities, the work at Zushi has progressed with difficulty. Nevertheless, the little group that is being served there has shown remarkable perseverance.

Reaching Far and Wide

Already in 1963, we began proclaiming the Savior to the Japanese by means of radio. These radio broadcasts serve to illustrate that the Church is one body made up of many parts with each part having its own function and purpose. Japanese pastors, American missionaries, and laymen all preach over the radio. The missionaries usually need to have their sermons checked by a Japanese for grammar. The Japanese laymen in turn need to have their sermons checked by a pastor or missionary for content before they go on the air. The result is a broadcast that proclaims the comforting truth of God's word in Japanese to anyone who will listen.

One has no way of knowing the total number of people who are listening to our gospel message on any given Sunday morning. Listeners are encouraged to contact us. Some do. Usually it is by mail. These contacts are followed up, not only with mailings but with a personal visit whenever possible. Our radio broadcasts cover roughly the two prefectures, Ibaragi and

Tochigi, where we are doing our most intensive work. One can't help wondering how many people have come to repentance and faith in the Savior through our broadcasts but as yet have not found the courage to contact us. Perhaps many, like Nicodemus in the time of our Lord, have faith but have not as yet confessed it openly.

Our church in Japan has also continued to reach a great number of people through literature. Printed materials range from evangelism pamphlets to Sunday school lessons to adult instruction courses to sermon books. A church periodical has been published regularly since 1961. The literature produced in our printshop in Japan has been an effective means of bringing the teachings of Scripture to many Japanese.

The Japanese Language
Is It Worth It?

From the start our missionaries and executive committee were determined that if we were to communicate with the Japanese people, our missionaries would have to learn the Japanese language rather than rely on interpreters. For this reason most of our missionaries spend their first two years on the field in intensive language study.

The Japanese language is extremely difficult for most Americans. The English-speaking person has many things working against him when he tries to learn Japanese. To begin with, Japanese has no words that are related to words in English, although the Japanese borrow some English words and use them as if they were a part of their language. One example is the word "hamburger". They, however, pronounce it "ham-ba-gaa." (The "a" is pronounced like the "a" in "account".) Japanese also has a separate character, or you might say a complicated letter, for each

The church sign at Tsuchiura uses the three Japanese writing systems and English.

word or concept. Each such character has one or more pronunciations. This means that for basic Japanese one has to learn how to recognize, write, and pronounce over 1,800 characters rather than only the twenty-six letters that we have in English. A Japanese typewriter has about 3,000 of these characters.

Furthermore, Japanese grammar is different from the grammar of European languages such as English. Japanese thought patterns also are different from those of English-speaking people. These differences make Japanese composition exceptionally difficult for Americans. All of these difficulties make it just about impossible for an adult American to master the Japanese language.

A Japanese typist has about 3,000 characters from which to choose.

Our missionaries, however, do learn to communicate in Japanese, and the Japanese people appreciate it. When a missionary once expressed his appreciation to a Japanese lady for coming to church Sunday after Sunday in spite of his poor Japanese, the lady answered, "I can tell that what you say comes from your heart." It was her polite way of telling him that his Japanese indeed was poor, but she did appreciate the message, the missionary's sincerity, and his effort to bring that message to her in her own language. There probably are times when the new missionary wonders whether learning the language is worth all the effort. Moments such as the one just mentioned assure him that it is.

Because they recognize not only the benefits but also the necessity of doing so, the missionaries' wives also make every effort to learn the language. Most missionary families have found that their children pick it up naturally and soon use it more fluently than their parents.

Learning the language is necessary for making friends and winning the confidence of people outside the church. Our mission families in Japan have always lived among the people.

This life style, which involves such things as living in a Japanese neighborhood rather than in a foreigners' "ghetto" and shopping in the same stores as the Japanese do, enables our families to become part of the community. This intermingling, in turn, provides contacts and opportunities to introduce Japanese people to the Savior.

A Church That Can Stand On Its Own Feet

As a synod we believe we can best serve our Lord in the cause of missions if we try to establish mission churches that can, so to speak, "stand on their own feet." This is called the "indigenous church policy." Under this policy, we encourage our mission churches toward independence in four areas: 1) winning new converts for the Savior, 2) administering their own affairs, 3) paying their own expenses, and 4) maintaining Biblical teaching and practice.

From the early days of our work in Japan our mission had an extremely capable, full-time lay worker, Mr. Ryuichi Igarashi, who was given the title "Deacon." He served as seminary instructor, literary editor, translator, writer, and in a number of other capacities as well. After working tirelessly for many years, failing health caused him to request a diminishing work load. The Lord

For many years Missionary Poetter and Deacon Igarashi consulted with each other almost daily.

called this dedicated, scholarly servant home to eternal rest in July 1990.

At this writing, a promising student, Takeshi Nidaira, is in his last year of studies in our six-year seminary program. The Lord has indeed blessed the Japanese church with gifted and capable national spiritual leaders.

The Lord's blessing reaches also into the area of maintaining and safeguarding biblical teaching and practice. The relationship between a sponsoring church body and its mission church develops somewhat like that of a parent and child. Since the missionaries who founded this mission and continued to serve it were from WELS, the infant church naturally believed and taught the same as WELS does. The time comes, however, when a child needs to confess his or her own faith. For our children, this confession usually takes place at confirmation. When that time came for our daughter church in Japan, the pastors and people of our mission made a study of the doctrinal statements that have been adopted by WELS. The Lutheran Evangelical Christian Church of Japan then by resolution declared itself in agreement with these confessional statements and requested a formal declaration of fellowship with WELS. In its 1981 convention our synod responded with a resolution declaring fellowship with the LECC. This formal bond of fellowship serves as a continuing reminder that there in Japan we have a maturing daughter church that shares our confessional position.

Where Are We Now?

After more than thirty years of labor, the LECC lists fewer than 200 communicants. Certainly statistics are at best only a rough indication of what the Lord has accomplished through us. He alone can see the faith in the hearts of his people. Nevertheless, when confronted by a statistic like this, faithfulness to our Lord and responsible use of people and funds require us to take a hard look at where we are in Japan.

Can we possibly expect that soon the Japanese people as a whole will be more open-minded toward Christianity? After all, Japan is being influenced by the West more and more. The Holy Spirit, however, tells us in the Scriptures that the mind of natural man is at war with God, and the gospel of Jesus Christ is so much foolishness to him (1 Corinthians 2:14). This natural opposition to the gospel remains true no matter what changes may take place in the culture of a people.

What does change through cultural openness is the opportunity to enter a country and proclaim the gospel to its people. While many countries are discouraging or even forbidding entry to foreign missionaries, Japan's doors remain wide open. Once he is within the country, the missionary is also free to preach the gospel without restriction by the government. Japan's constitution guarantees freedom of religion and the separation of church and state. The missionary works in this atmosphere of freedom all the while he is in Japan.

Through political developments, the Lord has caused Japan to be open to foreign missionaries since the close of the Second World War. Unlike the other defeated nations, Japan was not divided into occupational zones by the Allied Powers. No zone was placed under Communist rule. As a result, foreign missionaries were welcome and could work freely anywhere in the country. When the U.S. military occupation came to an end in 1952, the people of Japan were free to elect a government of their own choosing according to their new constitution. The Liberal Democratic Party won the majority of the seats in both houses of the national legislative body, which in Japan is called the Diet. This party remained in power for over thirty-five years and favored strong ties with the West, especially the United States. These ties made it easy for our missionaries to enter the country and work there for so many years.

In 1989 the Liberal Democratic Party lost control of the upper house of the national diet. This loss in itself didn't bring any major changes since the upper house has far less power than the lower house. Whether or not this change in control marks the beginning of a change of government attitude toward the West and toward missions remains to be seen. We don't know what the Lord has in mind for the future. We do know that for now the door to Christian missions in Japan remains wide open.

Japan still welcomes us, and we are still able to send missionaries and their families to this Land of the Rising Sun. We still have the men, and we still have the means to support the work in Japan in spite of the unusually high costs involved.

The book of Acts gives us many examples of how our ascended Lord guides his Church. It shows us that at times he sends his missionaries into areas that do not appear to be promising fields for evangelism. He once sent the evangelist Philip along the lonely road through Gaza, a place where there were few people, if any at all. There Philip met a government official from Ethiopia, as this African was riding along in his chariot reading the book of Isaiah. Through Philip the Lord brought this man to faith in Jesus. The conversion of this one man along this lonely road must have had its effect on the spread of the gospel in Africa in those early days shortly after the ascension of our Lord. Perhaps the Lord intends to use our seemingly little success in Japan in a similar way. We don't know whether this will be the case or not.

We do know that there is a group of people in Japan who have come to repentance and faith in the Savior through our mission efforts. Through the years, this mission church has demonstrated the sincerity of its people in countless ways. The

Fellow believers from various congregations as well as overseas guests gathered to celebrate the 25th anniversary of our Japan mission.

people of this church are asking the WELS to continue sending missionaries to serve them with the word and sacraments, to bring them to greater spiritual maturity, and to help them, in turn, bring the saving gospel to still more Japanese. May we continue to answer their call. May we continue to serve our Japanese fellow Christians as long as they need help and as long as our ascended Lord continues to make it possible for us to provide that help.

Mission Currents Four
The Hook of the Kafue

As a result of the synod's resolution in 1947 "that the General Board continue its investigation and explore the most promising heathen fields," Pastors Arthur Wacker and Edgar Hoenecke were called upon to undertake an exploratory expedition into Africa. We have already reported how these two men played active roles in the synod's decision to embark on an overseas mission project. As often happens, the strongest promoters of the program were subsequently enlisted to help carry it out.

To undertake this trip demanded major sacrifices of each of the men, and one can understand their reluctance to serve on this exploratory venture. Pastor Hoenecke's congregation in Plymouth, Michigan, was in the midst of a major relocation program and felt it was not the time to give its pastor an extended leave of absence. Pastor Wacker's wife had died a few years before this. For him this trip would mean placing his children in the care of others for five months. That the synodical leadership was less than enthusiastic in supporting their venture did not make the decision to go any easier.

In addition to these difficulties, the expedition involved costs that the general mission budget could not cover and that had to be taken care of by voluntary contributions. An itinerary had to be planned for travel on a continent where vast areas were still undeveloped. Considerable equipment, including the outfitting of a Dodge Power Wagon, had to be provided. Travel permits and arrangements had to be made. It wasn't until April 29, 1949, therefore, that the expedition finally left the United States. After three weeks at sea and another week of clearing customs and securing the necessary permits, the wagon with the two pastors began its trek from Capetown, South Africa.

The fascinating details of the Wacker-Hoenecke safari into Africa have been recounted by Pastor Hoenecke in a booklet entitled, *The WELS Forty-niners.* The picturesque scenery along the way was captured on movie film, which was later shown to congregations under the title, *Africa Still Calls,* generating publicity and funds to pay for the trip. Interviews with key personalities along the way were tape-recorded and presented along with the reports of the expedition to boards and committees.

How the two men ever managed to keep on going a distance of 4,000 miles through Southwest Africa, Angola, the Belgian Congo, and into Northern Rhodesia is a story almost as exciting as that of David Livingstone on his earlier treks through Central Africa. It meant crossing rivers on makeshift ferries, following roads consisting of nothing but deeply rutted trails, encountering mechanical problems with the vehicle that often defied repair, living in cramped quarters for long stretches in almost total isolation, yet somehow always managing to run across helpful people to assist

Pastors Edgar Hoenecke and Arthur Wacker about to set out on their extensive mission exploratory trip into Central Africa

in finding their way through deserts and forests until they finally arrived in Northern Rhodesia. There they could sit under a baobab tree and thank the Lord for leading them to the kind of place they had been looking for.

Northern Rhodesia was a British colony that seemed made to order for the opening of a mission. Located in Africa's central interior, it was relatively undeveloped. Its climate was moderate, much more healthful and comfortable than many other areas of Africa. Its government officials, especially influential men like Sir John Moffat, were encouraging mission development. One field recommended by the Secretary for Native Affairs was known as the Hook of the Kafue. People numbering in the thousands lived in this area, which covered hundreds of square miles and was bounded on three sides by the Kafue River before its confluence with the mighty Zambezi.

In retrospect, Pastor Hoenecke recently summarized his own feelings regarding this expedition as follows:

> We were weak pieces of clay in God's hands. Our success came only because we said frequently on the long trek itself, "Father, we are at our wit's end. We do not know where to go and how to proceed. But you said you would lead, so here we are; lead us." Both Art and I had no false ideas of our own sagacity. We saw only too clearly how stupid it was for our synod's mission board to insist on a wild goose chase through Africa's wilds, and for us to be dumb enough to go. Then it happened, and it seems we were led by the Lord to find the right field—to judge from results—after bumbling through about 4,000 miles of trails and deserts and forests with nothing to offer.

Unfortunately a travel delay made it impossible for Wacker and Hoenecke to report personally to the 1949 convention of the synod. For some reason their written report was not made available either. It was therefore not until 1951 that the synod could take any action regarding the matter. Although the report which became known popularly as the "Hook of the Kafue Report" engendered a lot of enthusiasm among the various groups which had been able to hear it, it met with a very cool reception from the special African Exploratory Commission appointed by President Brenner and chaired by him. This committee recommended "that we refrain from entering this particular type of mission work at this time." The "disturbed condition of the Church" and "the demands made by our mission fields which far exceed the monies on hand" were given as reasons for the negative report.

Prof. Conrad Frey, the committee's secretary, however, strongly dissented from the opinion of the others and gave a minority report, which was in principle accepted by the General Synodical Committee. In the previous "Currents" we reported on the favorable response of the 1951 convention to appeals to begin work in Japan. This same convention after hearing the report of the General Synodical Committee adopted the following resolutions pertaining to Africa:

1. We recommend that our Synod enter into foreign heathen mission work in the Northern Rhodesian field in Africa.
2. We recommend that the General Mission Board be authorized to send two missionaries to this field.
3. We recommend that the first year's cost of $34,810 . . . be taken from the Expansion Fund.

Because of delays mentioned above, plus a few other delaying factors, the prominently mentioned "Hook of the Kafue" area had to be given up as a choice in which to begin the work. The Gospel Light Mission, a small group from Australia, was favored by the Northern Rhodesian government with the assignment.

In October 1951 the General Mission Board elected an Executive Committee for Northern Rhodesia. Pastors Arthur Wacker and Arnold L. Mennicke and later Dr. Arthur Tacke became the members of this committee. It was only after nine calls had been extended that Pastor A. B. Habben of Hastings, Nebraska, accepted. Candidate Otto Drevlow who had just completed his studies at Bethany Seminary in Mankato, Minnesota, also accepted the call as a companion missionary to Pastor Habben. Mr. Paul Ziegler, a member of Pastor Habben's congregation in Hastings, was sent as technical layman to supervise construction and the physical operation of the mission. The choice of location in Northern Rhodesia was left to the missionaries. The Habbens and Zieglers arrived in Lusaka, Northern Rhodesia's capitol city, in June 1953, and the Drevlows in September of that same year.

Many people still associate our African work with the "Hook of the Kafue" since this catchy name was mentioned so frequently in the early reports. Perhaps it was just as well in the long run that the first center of the mission was closer to Lusaka, which eventually became its headquarters. Man proposes; God disposes. Somehow the Gospel Light Mission which began in the Hook of the Kafue region has passed out of existence.

While working in and near Lusaka may have been more difficult to begin with, it undoubtedly proved to have been an advantage in many ways. The story of the subsequent development of this mission will certainly show this to be the case.

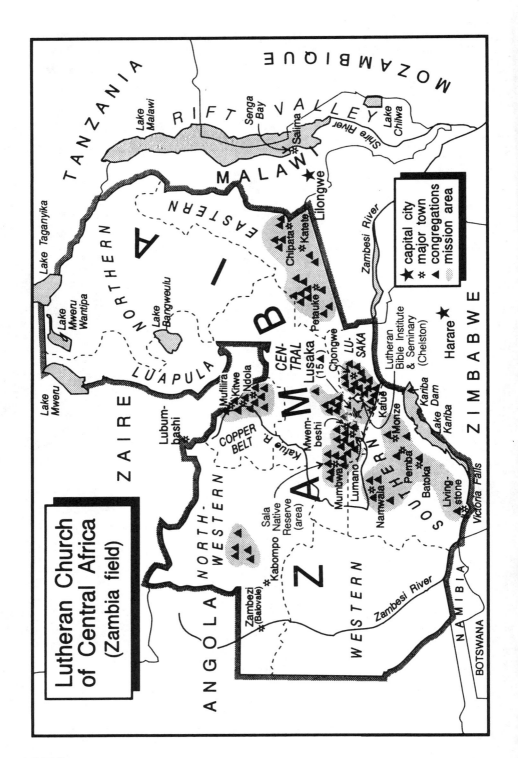

BLESSINGS BEYOND EXPECTATIONS
CENTRAL AFRICA

This account is first and foremost a history of the workings of God's grace these past forty years in the Lutheran Church of Central Africa. In part it speaks of men and their families leaving stateside homes to carry the gospel to another continent. It tells of the meeting of two cultures, of learning, growing, overcoming errors of judgment and technique, and the gaining of new insights. It is a story not lacking in friction and tensions such as must exist among honest men, a story of the forging of new friendships across seas and across national and racial and cultural lines.

At this moment the story cannot be complete, for it is told as seen through the eyes of a former missionary and thus is limited to what he has seen, experienced, and learned from others. Its more complete telling will have to await God's raising up of an African who will write it from the perspective of his people, one who better than any expatriate knows and shares their hopes and fears, their joys and expectations in Christ.

If the story as told here speaks more of the work of our missionaries than of the national workers, it is not that the contributions of the former have been greater than those of the latter. The Lutheran Church of Central Africa has been blessed with a large number of highly consecrated national pastors, evangelists, and lay people, who, with great zeal and with marked success, have spread the saving gospel in their land, and who increasingly have assumed responsible leadership of their church.

At its simplest and most profound, however, this is the story, often repeated in the history of the church, of men planting the seed of the word and of God giving the increase, *blessings beyond expectations.*

June to August, 1953

Our story begins inconspicuously enough in June 1953 with the arrival in Lusaka of Pastor and Mrs. A. B. Habben, accompanied by Paul Ziegler, a layman from their Hastings, Nebraska, congregation. Initially, they stayed at the Ridgeway Hotel in Lusaka.

Their first assignment was to find the most likely area in which to begin work. An executive committee report written several years later says of these first days: "When Pastor Habben and Mr. Ziegler left for Africa in 1953, the superintendent's attention was directed to five possible fields. The two made an exploratory trip of about 6,000 miles. Among the fields investigated was the one occupied by the Sala tribe."

Quite unexpectedly, our first contact was with European settlers of Lutheran background living in the Lusaka area. One day as Habben parked the mission truck with the words, "Lutheran Mission," on it on the streets of Lusaka, he was approached by a resident of the city, a woman of European background, with the question, "Are you really a Lutheran missionary?" Assured that he was, the woman asked if he would conduct services for a few Lutherans living in and around Lusaka and baptize their children. One of these families had traveled 1,100 miles one way to South Africa to have its children baptized by a Lutheran pastor. So it came about that on June 28, 1953, our mission's first service on Northern Rhodesian soil was held, not in an African village, but in the home of a European family by the name of Kleusch.

Ziegler's wife, Tilda, and their son, David, accompanied the second missionary pastor, Otto Drevlow and his wife, Elaine, arriving by ship in Capetown August 1. Ziegler came to South Africa to fetch his family, returning with them by train. The Drevlows, after some difficulty with their bill of lading, pulled their house trailer through South Africa and Rhodesia to Lusaka, arriving September 13. Drevlow's arrival completed the initial team of two missionary pastors and one layman as authorized by the synod. Drevlow had just graduated from Bethany Seminary, Mankato, Minnesota. He also came to the field as a licensed pilot with a light airplane. As it turned out, the plane was little used and later on sold.

The Drevlows, Habbens, and Zieglers arrived in Northern Rhodesia in 1953 as the initial team to Central Africa.

The Drevlows joined the Habbens and Zieglers in the Ridgeway for a day and then set up house in their trailer on the property of one of the European families worshiping with the mission. When Habben's and Ziegler's trailers arrived in mid-October, the missionaries relocated to a compound on the outskirts of Lusaka along the Great East Road.

The Land and Its People

In Central Africa the missionaries found a moderate climate, suitable and pleasant for people of European descent. Zambia for the most part is a plateau ranging from 3,000 to 4,000 feet above sea level and stretching westward from the escarpment of the Great Rift Valley of Tanzania and Malawi. This plateau is broken here and there by kopjes or small hills. In eastern Zambia the hot and tsetse-infested Luangwa Valley separates the Eastern Province and its principal city, Chipata, from the rest of the country. In the west and on the south the mighty Zambezi, climaxed by the incomparable Victoria Falls at Livingstone, forms a natural border with neighboring Angola and Zimbabwe.

Malawi, Zambia's neighbor to the east, into which our mission was to enter a decade later, is often referred to as the "Switzerland of Africa." The Great Rift Valley cuts though the country from north to south, leaving in its wake majestic mountains and valleys. Lake Malawi with its crystal-clear waters lies at the base of the valley and is one of its sparkling jewels. The Shire River runs southward from the lake to the Zambezi. The Shire Highlands in south Malawi rise to a height of 2,000 to 3,500 feet and offer an ideal climate. Here, where the city of Blantyre is located, we began our work in Malawi.

The African people of Zambia and Malawi are Bantus. "Bantu" is their common word for "people." The Bantu comprise the largest linguistic grouping in sub-Saharan Africa and include not only the Swahili in Tanzania and the Zulu, Tswana, and Swazi in South Africa but also the 72 Bantu tribes of Zambia and the 22 of Malawi.

In 1953 both Northern Rhodesia, as Zambia was then called, and Nyasaland, Malawi's name at the time, were British protectorates. In 1956 they were joined briefly with Southern Rhodesia (Zimbabwe) in the Central African Federation. Winds of change, however, were blowing throughout Africa in those post-World War II days, and after a short time the Federation was dissolved. Malawi and Zambia and ultimately Zimbabwe emerged as independent nations.

A word needs to be said about the circumstances that resulted in Lusaka being a Chinyanja-speaking area even though this language is native to Malawi. "*Nyanja*" is the word for "lake" and in Central Africa designates the lake, Lake Malawi. Chinyanja is the language of those living near the lake and is spoken not only there, but also in eastern Zambia. It also is the dominant language along the Great East Road that leads from Malawi to Lusaka.

During colonial days people traveled rather readily between Zambia and Malawi. Lusaka was an important center even in the earlier days, and people in substantial numbers came from Malawi to find employment. Their language became dominant in and around the city and thus also the main tongue in which our mission learned to work in Lusaka.

Joseph Mwambula, the first African convert of our mission, wrote in 1956 that "about three fourths of the Matero Evangelical Lutheran Church is comprise [sic] of members from the Eastern Regions i.e. Petauke, Fort Jameson and Nyasaland

(Malawi)." This movement of people along the Great East Road from Malawi to Lusaka ultimately was used by God for his purposes. It resulted in a common language on either side of the border, which in turn helped ease the passage of the gospel from the one nation to the other. Thus people in Zambia and Malawi were brought by God into one in the Lutheran Church of Central Africa.

The Early Years

The mission records of the first year and a half are sketchy. What can be patched together from later reports, however, gives us a clear outline of the beginnings of the work. The first African worship service was held December 6, 1953, in a rented hall in Matero, a suburb of Lusaka with a government housing project for African workers. One of those present was Benford Kawiliza, later to become one of the first pastors of the Lutheran Church of Central Africa. The choice of location was good, if only for the sheer numbers of people. Better than half of the estimated 25,000 Africans employed in Lusaka lived in Matero. Publicizing the work was done primarily by personal contact and word of mouth. Elaine Drevlow remembers making flyers with her husband for distribution in the compound. Joseph Mwambula, mentioned above, was instrumental in organizing the work and gathering the people. He also served as interpreter for the missionaries in the Lusaka area.

The Lord used a chance meeting of Sala Chief Shakumbila with Habben on Lusaka's Cairo Road to influence much of the early direction and activity of the mission. This meeting brought the mission into dealings with this shrewd and autocratic leader

Sala Chief Shakumbila (with fly whisk) wanted schools and a medical dispensary for his people.

179

of the Sala people. His tribe lived largely on the Sala Native Reserve about 35 miles southwest of Lusaka. Shakumbila wanted schools and a medical dispensary for his people, and in the Lutheran mission he saw the wherewithal to get them.

He invited Habben, Ziegler, and Drevlow to a September 21 meeting with the Sala Tribal Council at Lumano Village. At the meeting the Council granted the mission a 160-acre tract near Lumano for setting up a mission station. Two days later Shakumbila sent a message inviting the missionaries back, saying he had a better 160-acre plot to offer them. On this plot, the main station of the mission was built, a station that came to be identified by its stately twin palms. It was variously called Lumano for the village nearby, Sala for the tribal name of the people living about it, or Mwembezhi for the river that flows not far from it.

In April 1954 Habben and Ziegler moved their trailers under the twin palms on the Sala Reserve west of Lusaka.

The next day, September 24, the missionaries made a trip to the District Commissioner's office to confirm the land grant. In April 1954 Habben and Ziegler moved their trailers onto the newly acquired mission property. First services at Lumano were held Palm Sunday, April 11, 1954. It was the answer to many a mission prayer.

The urban work in Lusaka among both nationals and Europeans was carried on largely by Drevlow. By the time he left Africa in May 1954, services at Matero were drawing 100 to 125 people. Also, Drevlow was instructing some secondary students at Munali Secondary School and looked on them as future potential workers for the church. By now, 20 to 25 people were regularly attending English language services in Lusaka.

In February Drevlow had suffered a health problem that may have been brought on by stress factors relating to the work. As a result, he accepted a call to a stateside ministry in May 1954. He was replaced in October of that year by John Kohl, a man mature in judgment and with a heart filled with obvious love for the African people. Unfortunately, his African ministry, which was richly blessed, was brought to a close by dermatitis, so severe that it forced his return to the States in October 1956.

On arriving in the field Kohl found that during the vacancy a good number of people had drifted away. Among those remaining were Mwambula, who still was carrying on the work and became his trusted interpreter and assistant, and Timothy Tonga, who later became an evangelist at nearby Chunga Line. Timothy's two brothers, Yona and Akimu Tonga, later were instrumental in extending the mission to their home village of Kaluwa in the Eastern Province. Thus began what was to become a major area of our work in Zambia.

Mwambula became the mission's first convert, being confirmed on Sunday, November 27, 1955. December 4, a week later, Matero celebrated the second anniversary of its initial service with the baptism of a number of children and adults and the confirmation of a class of 22 adults. The following Sunday at Sala, Arthur Wacker, executive committee chairman, who had come to the field in August to fill in during Habben's furlough, confirmed his interpreter, Albert Muyangana, as the first convert at Sala. Later, Muyangana was the first Zambian national to become a Lutheran pastor. That service, Kohl records, provided the setting for the first celebration of Holy Communion where missionaries, their families, and interpreters received the sacrament side by side.

Other work initiated in Lusaka before Kohl left the field in the fall of 1956 included released time classes taught by Mwambula at the government school in Matero, work among the lepers at Lilanda Convalescent Hospital, regular hospital calls by Kohl and Mwambula as an evangelistic outreach, and classes taught in a number of the smaller African suburbs of Lusaka. Kohl continued the instruction work begun by Drevlow at Munali Secondary School, regarding its students as "the cream of the African youth," and a potential asset for the future of the church in Central Africa. He and Mwambula began collecting hymns for church use and produced "a literal translation of the greater portion of the chief doctrines of Holy Scripture as taken from our Catechism." Students from Munali

181

School translated Sunday school lessons into Chinyanja. In Matero a women's group was organized and met regularly for Bible study.

So we see that much of the basis for the type of work that was to characterize our mission in Lusaka and its environs was already in place by the end of 1956. Kohl and Mwambula also made several exploratory trips in response to requests for the gospel, including one to Monze in the Southern Province, where a preaching station was later to be established in 1969. Another trip was made to Mwambula's home area near Petauke in the Eastern Province, "in which," Kohl wrote prophetically, "we could expect the greatest degree of fruitfulness."

Meanwhile, at Sala, Ziegler's talents were being put to use, as he planned and supervised construction work at the mission station. In September 1955 the first permanent building was completed and dedicated, a residence for the Zieglers. By May 1957 we had two missionary houses at Sala, four houses for African staff, an office, a two-room school, workshop, pumphouse, and a temporary hostel for boys.

The building activity did not come at the expense of the spiritual work on the Sala Reserve. In spring 1955 Habben, assisted by Muyangana, was conducting services with reported attendances of 400 at Lumano, 200 at Katinti, 150 at Chiyaba and 250 at Shabasonje. Most of these were pupils of the schools we were managing, but included people from the surrounding villages as well.

Pastor Arthur Wacker had the privilege of baptizing Headman Lumano whom he had been visiting regularly on his sickbed. Two days later Lumano died, and on November 9, 1955, Wacker officiated at his funeral, the first Lutheran burial service in our Central African field of labor.

Without Chart or Compass

Habben's furlough and speaking tour in the United States began in August 1955. Scheduled to last six months, it was extended to February 1956 to make it possible for the executive committee to have a special meeting with him concerning the affairs of the mission.

It should be mentioned that Wacker had reluctantly asked leave of absence of his Scio, Michigan, congregation to go to Africa to replace Habben during his furlough. Once in the field, however, Wacker recognized as never before the need for the executive committee to have a firsthand knowledge of the work that it was to supervise. This experience led to the Board for World Missions' policy of making the regular field visitations that have become a systematic part of conducting our overseas mission work. Wacker, the reader will recall, six years earlier had formed part of the team of "Forty-niners" who had explored the southern part of the continent in search of a virgin mission field.

In a series of incisive letters written from Sala to his executive committee prior to his return to the States in February, Wacker not only rejoiced in the blessings of the mission but at the same time detailed problems he saw posing a serious threat to the work. The missionaries differed sharply as to basic mission philosophy and how the work should be carried forward. At the center was Habben's administrative style and a lack of communication between himself and the other men. Wacker proposed to remedy the situation by 1) an insistence on complete reports from the field on finances, policy, and procedures, 2) insistence likewise on regular monthly meetings of mission personnel to discuss matters of policy and procedures, and 3) clear definition by the Executive Committee of the individual responsibilities of the men in the field.

It should be mentioned that overseas mission work was something new both for the mission board at home and for the missionaries themselves. We had much to learn about world mission work. Few guidelines were given to the men sent out. It is not surprising that there should have been lapses or that there were honest differences of approach to the work.

Also, mission philosophy in general was in flux then even as now. Which approach to mission were we to follow? Up until the stirrings of independence in the post-World War II days, mission work in Africa almost exclusively followed the pattern of setting up a sizable mission compound in village and rural areas complete with missionaries' residences, staff residences, and possibly a school and medical dispensary. Few if any mission compounds of this sort are being built in Africa today. Already in 1953, the concept was being challenged. In the expansion of our work into Malawi in 1963, no mission centers of the traditional type were built.

In setting up a main station at Sala, Habben's mission philosophy was doubtless cast in the traditional mold. The way he went about his gospel ministry from this base has been described by some as a "give-away" program: free lorry trips for the people to and from Lusaka, grain handouts in time of hardship that struck some as "buying the favor of the people," and paying African workers excessive wages that were out of line with the economy of the nation. This was the nub of the problem, philosophically, that beset the mission in the early years. Habben countered that "you must earn the love and respect of the African before you can expect to win him with the gospel." This approach to missions was not at all unusual, even in the '50s. At the same time, the thought of developing an indigenous church, self-governing and self-sustaining, was not alien to Habben's thinking and finds frequent expression in his correspondence. Others, however, felt there must be a more immediate and a more direct path to that goal.

The Management of Schools

From the beginning in Central Africa, we were keenly interested in using schools as an arm of our mission. This was partly because missions in Africa traditionally operated schools and partly because of the historic commitment of WELS to parochial schools as an agency for training our youth. By the fall of 1955, the mission had secured the necessary governmental authorization to supervise schools in the Sala area. This approval became official with the notice of our authorization posted by the Education and Social Services Ministry in the January 13, 1956, issue of the *Northern Rhodesia Gazette.*

A bit of background is necessary to understand the rules governing the management of schools. By the time of our arrival in Zambia, it was no longer possible for a mission to set up its own schools. All schools operated under the Department of Education with the government furnishing 90 percent of the cost of buildings, 100 percent of the cost of equipping them, and 75 percent of the teachers' salaries. Also, it was stipulated that all teachers must have two years' training in one of the government's accredited schools before being certified to teach. Thus all schools were government owned and staffed, and the missions were simply given authority to manage them. With that much said, it should be stated also that the government gave assurances of no interference in the religious curriculum and required only that the secular curriculum conform to government education standards. To the government's credit, these assurances were kept.

In April 1956 the District Education Committee granted us the management of existing schools at Shabasonje, Lumano, Sala, Shamwete, and Katinti and of a new school to open at Kabile. The schools at Shabasonje and Lumano, previously managed by the Methodists, had been given back to the government with the stipulation that they would be withheld from any mission not holding membership in the World Council of Churches. Although this stipulation was directly aimed at our confessional stance, the government chose not to honor it and gave the schools to us. Once the transfer to our management was effected, the Methodists did not prove difficult to work with.

Different was the matter of the schools at Sala and Shamwete, which had previously been under the management of the Seventh Day Adventists. Here we experienced considerable and prolonged difficulties. It appears the problem was less with the Seventh Day Adventist faith than with the tribal consciousness of the Salas, who were prominent in these two areas and used the schools as a vehicle to assert their tribalistic feelings.

To meet the increased load brought with the supervision of schools, the executive committee determined to call a missionary pastor to replace Ziegler at the end of his tour in April 1956. Harold Essmann, a seminary graduate, was called as Manager of Schools and arrived in the field with his wife Ruth in September 1956.

The schools' management program, which began with 6 schools, about 600 students, and 13 teachers, grew until it involved 8 schools and more than 1,300 students taught by 26 teachers.

Through the years, however, it became increasingly clear that the entire program was not making the best use of our missionaries' time and energy. Dr. William Schweppe, veteran missionary of over twenty years experience in Nigeria, who in 1963 had succeeded Robert Sawall as Manager of Schools, pointed out some of the problems. It was difficult if not impossible to maintain discipline with the teaching staff. Schweppe mentions a teacher, who had joined our church, who was guilty of adultery and impenitent and yet could not be dismissed from his duties because of the peculiar arrangement of managing a school owned and staffed by the government. Apart from this, the time-consuming dealing with staff squabbles and demands, maintaining buildings, digging latrines, cultivating maize, collecting fees, and keeping books left the Manager of Schools little time for real mission work.

Initially, few could see any drawback to the schools management program as a mission arm. Many continued to feel that the only way to do effective mission work was to concentrate on the children as the foundation and future of the mission church. This shows how much we were the products of our own child-oriented Western culture. In a culture steeped in its respect for elders as in Bantu Africa, one does not easily reach the adults with the gospel through the children. The approach must rather be from the top down.

While this is changing particularly in urban areas, it was traditionally true that the conversion of a single grandfather or grandmother to Christ in Africa could make a great impact for Christ. By contrast, the Christian education of hundreds of children in our schools had, by March 1962, as noted in a report submitted by Manager of Schools Robert Sawall, produced only meager results. Apart from a few teachers whose Lutheran faith all too often was not highly evident in practice, there were only seven communicant members at Sala after eight years. In this report Sawall, reflecting the shift in the field's thinking, did a complete turnabout from his glowing report of six months earlier and argued persuasively for the relinquishing of the schools' management.

Already three years before, in a report of a February 1959 field trip, Executive Committee Chairman Arnold Mennicke with World Board member Ernst H. Wendland had perceptively raised the question "whether or not the management of schools is helping accomplish our aim of establishing an indigenous church."

In looking back, we can see that there was also a positive side to our involvement in the Sala area schools. In spite of the problems encountered with staff and students, our schools enjoyed a favorable reputation with the Ministry of Education. Several teachers remained faithful members of the Lutheran Church of Central Africa. The Lutheran Church gained name recognition in other parts of Zambia when school graduates moved to other areas and in some instances held important positions in business and in government. Neither should we forget that children in all grades at Lumano Martin Luther School received Christian training for at least a decade, resulting in the confirmation of many of the upper grade students.

Nevertheless, by the fall of 1964, it was clear what we needed to do in the long-term interest of our mission. Both the executive committee and the Board for World Missions resolved to relinquish the management of schools. The schools were formally handed over to the new Zambian government in July 1965. This move encountered no difficulties with government, since government policy after Zambia's independence favored such actions.

The Shaking of the Foundations

In March 1957 the second house was completed at the Sala Station and the Habbens were able to move out of the trailer that had been their home for three and a half years.

A month later Richard Mueller was welcomed to the field. En route he had been given the opportunity of an extended stay in Nigeria to observe the work of the mission there. Wacker had also visited there for two weeks on his return to the States in January 1956. Mueller's stay in Nigeria gained for him some valuable insights into the building of an indigenous church, and he was able to share these with the men in Central Africa.

In many respects Mueller became a field missionary par excellence, as this writer learned in working with him and seeing the groundwork laid by him and Raymond Cox for the work in Malawi. The first to master the language of the people, Mueller became a champion of the cause of missionaries learning the vernacular.

The work went on apace, a 1957 report showing 18 preaching stations, one organized congregation, and weekly attendance at services of over 1,000 people. The adult confirmed membership at this time though, apart from Matero with 65 communicants, was negligible. Those who look for more immediate tangible results, a Pentecost explosion of converts, need again to study the history of missions and see that early missions in Africa sometimes labored for over two decades before receiving their first baptized member. For those engaged in the work the progress must have seemed interminably slow, and expressions to that effect can be found in the reports of the executive committee. In retrospect, however, it can be said that our mission developed with unusual speed. Allowance had to be made for time to gain the confidence of the people.

In the meantime the personnel and policy problems continued to simmer. So acute was the disagreement that toward the end of 1958 it became clear that the executive committee would have to make an early visit to the field.

The visit took place in February 1959. World Board member Ernst H. Wendland accompanied Chairman Arnold Mennicke, since Wacker preferred to disqualify himself. The agenda was set to address concerns having to do with 1) unrest in the Matero congregation, 2) differences in policy among the missionaries, 3) a variety of smaller matters, and 4) demands of the chief.

Altogether, 51 hours were spent in meetings during their ten-day stay. Separate meetings were held with missionaries and teachers, three sessions with Chief Shakumbila, one with the District Commissioner, and one each with the Lusaka European and Matero congregations. Considerable progress was made on a number of fronts. This progress included a new perception of how ill-advised it was to tie our mission too closely to a single tribe, subject to the whims of the chief. On the issues dividing the mission staff, though some agreements were worked out, the basic problems of "how best to show our love to the Africans" remained.

The executive committee felt it best at this time to dispense with the position of superintendent and to assume a direct supervision of the field. The missionaries complied and agreed to communicate with the committee only jointly through their official Mission Council. This arrangement prevailed until the arrival almost three years later of Theodore Sauer and the return to the arrangement of having a field superintendent.

Ultimately the executive committee withdrew Habben's call and encouraged him to present himself for a stateside call. Habben reluctantly concurred but requested permission for a return trip to the field to gather his effects and prepare them for shipment home. The committee was not inclined to allow his request. In order to understand why, we must consider the situation in the field in mid and late 1959.

Chief Shakumbila understandably was squarely in Habben's corner and had written letters to the executive committee insisting on Habben's return from furlough, with thinly-veiled threats if he were not returned. In Shakumbila's point of view, Habben had provided help for his people. The other missionaries with their insistence on a strong indigenous church policy appeared to him to be wanting to take away that help and thus were forcing Habben out. The animosity of the chief was, therefore, directed at Essmann before he left the field in August 1959, not to return, and then was redirected at Greve, the only man left at the Sala Station.

The situation became tense when Habben was reluctantly permitted to return to the field to pack and ship his belongings. It reached a climax when villagers gathered to greet him and voiced complaints against the mission. The school children, defying the schoolmaster, left classes to "see Habben" and had a noisy and enthusiastic outdoor gathering in his support. This was Thursday, November 19.

Matters settled momentarily until Shakumbila appeared at the station Sunday afternoon to see Greve about the disturbances. Greve arranged a meeting with Shakumbila and the area headmen for the following Wednesday morning. When, by late morning, a large number of men had arrived and gathered under the large fig tree in the middle of the school compound, Greve declined to attend on the grounds that Shakumbila had agreed to meet with him in his home together with a small number of headmen. He felt nothing could be accomplished in that large crowd out-of-doors.

Thereupon, a three-hour demonstration was set off with the children shouting, "We want Habben." As a result of this disturbance, the children were sent home and the chief ordered the school to be shut down. Greve's ability to remain at Sala was seriously compromised. There were questions concerning his personal safety and that of his family, and he, too, was returned to the States. Unrest also surfaced at Matero when the congregation told Mueller they no longer wanted him to serve them. It seemed that our whole work was in jeopardy and that our stay at Mwembezhi was at an end. The missionaries appealed to the executive committee to send World Board Chairman Edgar Hoenecke to close the Sala Station.

The Habben Years: An Assessment

This much cannot be contested. There was continuing tension between Habben and his co-workers, and in the final analysis, his superintendency of the field became untenable.

On the other hand, the work he carried out among the people clearly had a positive side. Habben did not hesitate to mingle with the people and generally had a good rapport with them. Later missionaries often found, on coming to remote and widely scattered villages, that Habben had carried on work there. Hoenecke, in the field for an extended stay not long after Habben's leaving, received complaints from the villagers when "sermon boys" were sent around. They noted that in Habben's day "the missionary had come to serve the people." An African Catholic priest from the Southern Province told this writer at a religious history seminar in Lusaka in 1972 that back in the 50s "the Lutherans were the only people able to convert the Salas," a tribute to Habben's work.

When the smoke cleared from those initial years, however, the field had its casualties. Men whose subsequent ministries have been a blessing to the church had to leave the mission field either because of the personal differences on the mission staff or because of the animosity of the chief. What their future service might have meant to the mission or how much the spread of the gospel suffered as the greatest casualty of all, cannot be assessed.

It was not as if the work had come to a standstill. Even during the crisis year 1959, with all its uncertainties, for the most part the work itself went on. Progress was made toward setting up a medical program and the planning of a Bible institute. Souls continued to be saved. In the perspective of time and history, the difficulties of those early years will be reduced to a footnote, but they are chronicled here as a facet of mission history and as a powerful illustration of the grace of God at work. His grace overcame such serious difficulties as these in pouring out his unprecedented blessing on the Lutheran Church of Central Africa.

A Ministry of Mercy Takes Shape

Before the mission was granted its land by the Sala Tribal Council, Chief Shakumbila had expressed his desire to Habben that we provide his people with medical services. Without question, there was a dire need. Even the most basic facilities and supplies for medical treatment were lacking. Our missionaries' wives were besieged day and night with requests to tend wounds or to provide aspirins for a variety of ailments. Elaine Drevlow carried medications and wrappings for cuts and bruises on the regular Wednesday trips to Sala. Helen Greve, a registered nurse, used her home as a "virtual dispensary" and was credited by Hoenecke as one reason why the station at Lumano held together in the aftermath of the crisis of late 1959 and early 1960.

When Wacker filled in for Habben's furlough in the fall of 1955, his wife Hilda accompanied him to the field. As a nurse of considerable experience, who for a number of years had managed a hospital in Saline, Michigan, she was well qualified to assess both the medical needs of the people in the area and what, as a supporting church, we might be in a position to supply.

On the Wackers' return to the States they discussed these needs with world board chairman Edgar Hoenecke and his wife Meta, also a registered nurse, with fifteen years experience in public health.

Pastor Arthur Wacker's wife Hilda accompanied him on his 1955 visit to the field and was able to assess the medical needs of the people.

The matter was placed before the 1957 synod convention in the reports of the General Board for Foreign Missions and by the executive committee for our African mission. The convention delegates approved setting up a medical mission, both as a ministry of mercy and to relieve the missionary families of the strain of providing medical services for which they were generally unqualified. Support for this new work was to come particularly from ladies' groups throughout the synod.

Already in May 1956, the executive committee had resolved to survey how many women's societies could be counted on to support a medical mission on a regular basis. By the time of the 1957 convention, in excess of $8,000 in pledges had been made to start up the project. It was estimated that initially $7,000 to $10,000 annually would be required to support the medical mission.

In July 1957 the first formal inquiry was addressed to the Northern Rhodesian government authorities asking what we needed to do to receive permission to begin medical work. Perceptively, a letter written by Hoenecke at that early date expressed the thinking of the Medical Committee to carry on a medical program by sending two experienced registered nurses rather than a medical doctor. Although the whole matter of what type of medical program to set up was still to be thoroughly explored both at home and in the field, it is interesting to note that we finally ended up with just such a medical clinic staffed by two experienced American nurses.

The 1955 synod convention had elected Arthur Tacke, M.D., to the executive committee for our African mission. Following the 1957 convention, he was asked to appoint two other medically trained persons to form a Medical Mission Committee. Heinz Hoenecke, M.D. and Meta Hoenecke, R.N. were appointed. Their first assignment was to set up a blueprint or set of guidelines for medical programs in our world missions. In the fall of 1957, Tacke accompanied Mennicke on a field visit to Zambia and was able to gain a firsthand understanding of the medical needs.

The reply to our inquiry directed to the office of the Director of Medical Services in Northern Rhodesia did not come until October. Although the reply encouraged us in our aim to initiate medical services, it discouraged a medical program at or near the Sala station on the grounds that medical services were already available within a reasonable distance and that they did not "want to raise the medical standards of our area [Sala] too much above the others." Matters were left there for the next two and a half years, during which support for the medical project increased among the women of the synod. By February 1961, contributions for the project had exceeded $15,000. Fortunately, during the interval the attitude of government regarding the proposal to place the medical program near the Sala Station had changed.

The medical project made haste slowly and was marked by a careful gathering of information. Dr. Tacke wrote to Mennicke in February 1958: "I must admit that in spite of the Foreign Mission Board's great desire to establish a medical mission program, I myself am not fully convinced that we have a sound program to offer." It was deemed advisable to visit a number of different types of medical operations in Zambia and elsewhere on the continent and observe their programs before deciding definitely on the approach to medical work to be pursued. Opportunity for this came when the Hoeneckes made a trip to the field in February 1960. Hoenecke, newly elected to be full-time world mission chairman, made the trip at short notice to quiet the waters after the crisis accompanying Habben's departure from the field. Meta was able to go with him for the express purpose of exploring needs and options for the medical program.

In early April the Hoeneckes left Zambia on a special trip to visit the Synodical Conference Lutheran Hospital in Eket, Nigeria. On the same trip, they visited Dr. Albert Schweitzer and his world-renowned bush hospital at Lambarene, Gabon. On their return to Lumano, they visited a number of dispensaries of a more modest scale in the village areas of Zambia. Wherever possible, Meta donned her nurse's uniform and participated in the work for a period to get a feel for the program. All of this helped confirm the initial thinking of the Wackers and Hoeneckes in 1957 to provide "an emergency palliative and preventative health service rather than a full-scale medical or surgical program."

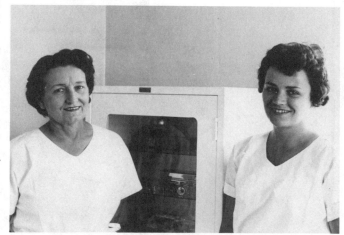

Edgar Hoenecke's wife Meta did much to organize the medical mission's program. Near the close of their 1961 visit to Africa, she helped orient Barbara Welch, Mwembezhi Dispensary's first nurse-in-charge.

The Hoeneckes left the field in May 1960 shortly after the arrival of Schweppe, who came from Nigeria to fill in temporarily at Mwembezhi for the furlough of the Greves. Greve did not return, and Schweppe's "temporary" stay lasted over a year until August 1961. The implementing of the medical program awaited the return of the Hoeneckes to Zambia in mid-September 1961 for a three month stay. Construction of the dispensary had begun under Schweppe and under Sawall, who had arrived at Mwembezhi a few months before. It fell to Hoenecke to complete the construction of the dispensary as well as to plan and build the nurses' residence.

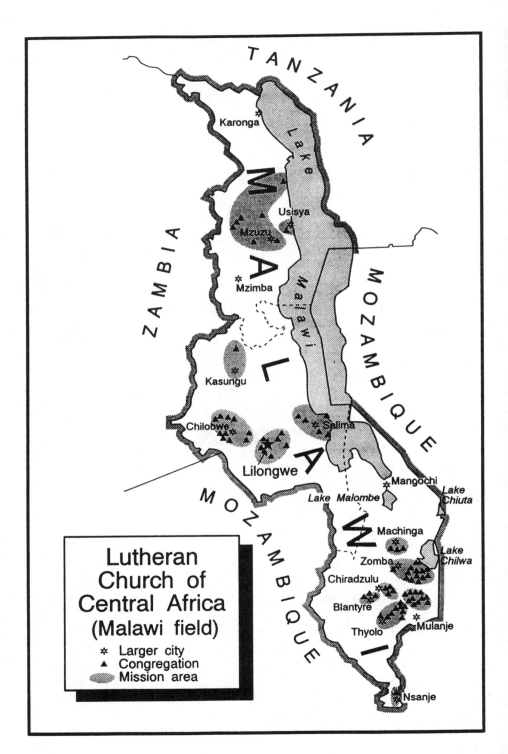

The distinction of being the dispensary's first nurse-in-charge falls to Barbara Welch. En route to Zambia, Welch was given an extended period of training at the Lutheran Hospital in Eket, Nigeria. Her arrival in mid-November still allowed a few weeks for Meta Hoenecke to orient her to the work prior to the Hoeneckes' return stateside.

On Sunday, November 26, 1961, Lumano Lutheran Dispensary was formally dedicated at outdoor services attended by 550 people. Missionary Sawall preached. Chief Shakumbila spoke words at the ceremony and also formally opened the doors of the dispensary. The case load during the first week of operation exceeded one hundred patients per day. Among the many national staff workers who have served through the years at Mwembezhi special mention must be made of the faithful service of Alfred Mkandawire who has served continuously at the dispensary from the beginning of its operation amid the constant rotation of nurses from the States. Sauer calls him "the stabilizing influence in the [medical] operation."

Alfred Mkandawire has served continuously as a stabilizing influence at the Mwembezhi dispensary from its beginning in 1961.

Medical Work in Malawi

The initiation of the medical work in Malawi came about in a different way. Although this is getting ahead of our story, by 1968 Raymond Cox and John Janosek were carrying on work primarily in Blantyre and in Malawi's Chiradzulu and Thyolo Districts with some contacts in Zomba, Lilongwe, and elsewhere. They had divided the work between themselves roughly along the line of Midima Road with Janosek serving to the south of that line and Cox to the north.

After Cox had made a trip to Lilongwe in the spring of 1968 to visit and teach contacts there, the District Commissioner sent us a letter informing us that we could not carry on mission work in any new area of the country where we were not previously at work. When we pursued this matter, we were asked what we as a mission were doing in secular areas such as agriculture, education, or medical work. We replied that, although we had no objections to taking part in these programs, at present we were not involved in them in Malawi. The ruling given to us was made to stand. This would have restricted our activities in Malawi largely to the Thyolo and Chiradzulu Districts.

Contact was pursued at various governmental levels to obtain the necessary permission to expand the work. At this point, a Lutheran Church-Missouri Synod layman, Jack Lesschaft, heard of our plight and offered his assistance. He was in the country at the time to help the Private Hospital Association of Malawi (PHAM) develop private hospitals to work under the Ministry of Health. His knowledge of Malawi's medical needs and his contacts with government officials proved invaluable. On his advice, the Missionaries' Conference and the executive committee resolved to set up a medical program in the Salima Settlement Scheme near Lake Malawi. A lakeside property was purchased near Salima at Senga Bay, and in March 1970 the Theodore Kretzmanns arrived to initiate and supervise the new program. They had come from Sala in Zambia where Kretzmann's work had experienced much blessing. Salimo Hachibamba once told this writer that there are many children in Sala named "Kretzmann" in love and respect for this man and his gospel ministry. Edith Schneider (Hintz), who had served two years as nurse at Mwembezhi, arrived a month later to assume the mo-

Missionary Theodore Kretzmann moved from Zambia to Malawi in 1970 to supervise the new medical program on Senga Bay.

bile clinic work. In 1982 the headquarters of the medical operation in Malawi were moved from Senga Bay to Lilongwe.

Blessings to This Day

It is a tribute to the ladies of the synod that they were able to assume the additional costs of the new work in Malawi and at the same time continue to support the entire medical program in Central Africa. This ministry of mercy is now funded generously and freely by the ladies of the synod to the amount of $150,000 annually.

We regret that a history of this nature does not permit the naming of all the nurses and national staff who have served in the medical mission through the years. One name that can be singled out is that of Linda Phelps (Golembiewski), who with Edith Schneider (Hintz) has the distinction of having served in both Zambia and Malawi and who has since served on the stateside Medical Mission Committee following its reorganization in 1983. Since the medical program involved a constant turnover of nurses serving in the field, mention should be made of Althea Sauer, R.N., who in addition to volunteer service in the dispensary provided valuable continuity and stability to the program while her husband was serving at Mwembezhi.

No discussion of the medical program would be complete without mentioning the names of Erna Speckin and Mrs. Arnold Mennicke. Mrs. Speckin was executive secretary of the Medical Mission from its inception until her retirement in 1983. She kept in constant communication with the nurses in the field and organized stateside contact women, conference by conference throughout the synod, to make sure that funding and necessary supplies were always provided. Mrs. Mennicke for two

Erna Speckin was executive secretary of the medical mission in Central Africa from its inception until her retirement in 1983.

197

decades processed and personally acknowledged all gifts to the Medical Mission.

How well has the medical program served its stated purpose as an arm of the mission? The program stands in its own right as a ministry of mercy and compassion. An older African one day told one of our nurses, "If you were not here, we would be dying like flies." As an arm of the mission the medical program has shown the love of Christ to the people and in this way has helped break down some barriers to the gospel.

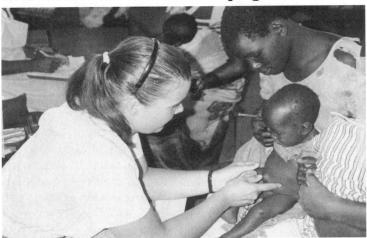

The medical program in Central Africa stands in its own right as a ministry of mercy and compassion.

Not to be forgotten is the direct gospel ministry carried on at the clinics through the daily devotions in God's word led by men like the now sainted Solomon Bimbe, the spiritual counsel for the ailing and their families, as well as the emergency baptisms of many babies at the clinics. A small chapel was set up in the Lumano Dispensary for providing spiritual counsel and comfort. The angels of heaven have been given good reason to rejoice at the healing of souls as well as of bodies that has occurred through the years in the medical mission program.

The Changing of the Guard

The year 1961 was a watershed in the history of the mission. At this critical juncture in the field's mission history, with the crisis of the Habben years just behind, the Lord of the church provided the mission with two key men, Theodore Sauer, called as superintendent of the mission, and Ernst H. Wendland, called the following year to organize and head the worker-training program. Sauer arrived in November 1961 and Wendland in September 1962.

One must realize the situation in which Sauer found the mission in late 1961 in order to understand the critical needs at that time. Although the turmoil connected with Habben's departure from the field and the years immediately preceding had now subsided, a residue of suspicion still affected relationships among the missionaries and between them and the executive committee. Sauer set to work quietly to promote unity of spirit among the men and to gain the confidence of the executive committee in the judgments of the men in the field. Changeovers in personnel that brought Sawall, Schweppe, Cox and Wendland to the field, made the task much easier. We had men here who, together with Mueller, were eager to turn the page on the past and get on with the mission of Christ.

Pastor Theodore Sauer arrived in Lusaka in 1961 as superintendent of the Central Africa mission. He and his wife Althea later served at the Mwembezhi mission station.

To address lingering problems of policies and relationships, Sauer, together with the mission staff, arranged a nine-day meeting in Lusaka between the Mission Council and representatives of the executive committee for April 22-30, 1963. A set of guidelines was prepared governing relations both on the mission field and between the mission and the executive committee. These were thoroughly discussed and approved. All of this helped immeasurably to lay the groundwork for the unprecedented blessing God was about to pour out on the Lutheran Church in Zambia and Malawi.

No set of policy documents is in itself going to rectify a difficult situation or solve all problems for all time. However, by bringing about a consensus in the field and between the field and the governing body in the States as to how the work ought to be conducted, Sauer quietly cleared away layers of misunderstanding and suspicion. The executive committee, in turn,

The early 1960s saw a "changing of the guard" in mission staff. Pictured above from left to right W. Schweppe, R. Cox, E. H. Wendland, R. Sawall, R. W. Mueller, and T. Sauer.

gained growing confidence in the men in the field and in the decisions that only they were in a position to make. All official correspondence with the executive committee henceforth went through the office of the superintendent, although individual missionaries were free to carry on direct communication in personal matters as deemed necessary.

The changing of the guard also brought to Zambia a humble, unassuming man of rich and varied mission background in Dr. William Schweppe. Schweppe was the veteran missionary who had gone to Nigeria in 1937. For many years he had served as superintendent of the mission and as president of the Lutheran Seminary in Nigeria before going to Ghana to pioneer Lutheran mission work there. The Lord brought him to Zambia in the early 1960s at a time when his wealth of mission knowledge could best be put to use in helping guide the mission on a sound basis.

The church suffered a tragic loss in Schweppe's death in a motor accident in July 1968 as he was returning from a missionary trip to the Southern Province. Schweppe was buried in the Lusaka cemetery in his beloved Africa. Greve, who worked under Schweppe in Nigeria, called him his "father who taught me all that I know about mission work." Mennicke wrote of him, "Being a veteran in the field of missions, Dr. Schweppe's counsel and advice was appreciated by both the missionaries and the executive committee. His good judgment on the field meant much, under God's blessing, for the development of our African work."

When one considers the caliber of men such as Dr. Schweppe and others serving our world mission fields through the years, one calls to mind the remark by Koehler in his *Wisconsin Synod History* to the effect that none but the very best of men should be sent into foreign work. With faithful wives working at their side, they have been used by God to bring the sound of the gospel and rich hope in Christ to people in places as remote as Africa's bush country and Java's cities and villages.

Ministry of the Written Word

In June 1964 a major two-day conference of the Mission Council was held in Chipata. Its main purpose was to study and expand the publications program of the mission.

From the early days of the mission, sermons had been written, translated, and printed for use by the lay leaders of the congregations. Sunday school materials and basic Lutheran doctrinal works such as the Small Catechism were also translated and distributed. Individual missionaries had done much of this early work on a hit-and-miss basis.

In 1960 Mueller initiated a formal mailing program in response to the many requests for spiritual literature and information about our Lutheran Church. He and his wife Irene sent out printed sermons and Sunday school materials on a regular basis. The mailing program was taken over by Ray and Lois Cox after their arrival in the field in 1961, and went with them from Zambia to Malawi in 1963. Although the field work in Malawi did not immediately mushroom, the mailing program did. From 1964 to 1966, prior to the calling of a full-time publications director and printer, the mailing program consumed much missionary time and energy. Cox recalls that, assisted by an American lay couple in Blantyre, the Gordon Nelsons, they mimeographed, collated, and addressed sermons, Sunday school lessons, and prayers every two weeks to a mailing list of over 3,000 names. A single month's mailing in 1965 involved 16,055 copies of printed materials.

Already by 1964, the Publications Committee was producing sermons, hymnals, liturgies, catechisms, adult instruction materials, Sunday school lessons, tracts, and various certificates and forms in English and four vernacular languages. Although the Chipata publications meeting did not as yet envision a separate publications director to head this program, the groundwork for an orderly program with procedures for the writing, review, revision, and translation of materials was laid in that meeting. Pending further study, it was resolved that larger productions should be done by contract printing. They were also to study further whether the publications program should be located in Zambia or in Malawi.

The 1965 WELS Synod Convention resolved that "a lay missionary be called to take care of the mechanical details and correspondence relative to the producing and mailing of literature." Elmer Schneider, a printer from Colorado, accepted the call as Publications Director and arrived in Lusaka in September 1966. Initially he continued printing by mimeograph in a room at the Bible Institute. In 1968 offset presses and printing equipment were installed in a new Lutheran Press building on the Chelston campus just outside Lusaka. This greatly enhanced and enlarged the publications program of the mission.

The Lutheran Christian, the new official periodical of the Lutheran Church of Central Africa, began publication in 1968 in English, Luvale, Chinyanja, and Tonga. This professional-appearing publication was sent out to all on the mailing list and replaced earlier publications such as the *Drum Beat* and the *Black Light,* which had largely been the product of individual missionaries.

One of the intangibles in evaluating the Lord's blessing on the Lutheran Church of Central Africa is the role the printed word and the mailing program have played. No one involved in the work would question that this role has been major in both the outward growth and the inner building up of the church.

A Worker-Training Program Set in Place

The training of workers received serious attention already in the earliest days of the mission. In 1956 the Mission Conference directed Habben to inquire of Schweppe in Nigeria as to the possibility of sending two promising Munali School students to Nigeria for seminary training. The conference also suggested that students interested in church work should first put in one year as "pupil teachers" in one of our schools in the Sala area. The minutes state, "In this way his character, ability, and worth can be more closely observed."

This move presaged later policy on the training of workers. In many instances a year of voluntary service as lay leader and

Sunday school teacher is asked of a man before he is recommended for the Bible Institute. Theological training in Central Africa is never purely academic. During the student days at the Bible Institute and Seminary, each student carries on a program of local congregational work in addition to his studies. Between Bible Institute and Seminary, the student is called to a period of full-time service as an evangelist. Those who qualify may then apply for seminary training. Seminary graduates serve a

Students at the Lutheran Bible Institute and Seminary carry on a program of local congregational work in addition to their studies.

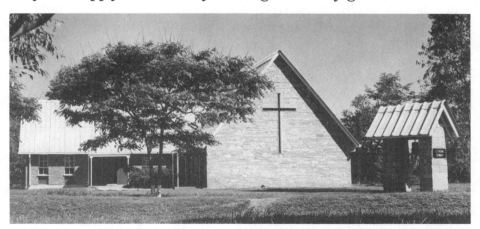

The Lutheran Seminary at Chelston was dedicated in 1971. All told, it takes at least nine years to train a man for ordination into the pastoral ministry.

two-year vicarship prior to ordination into the ministry. All told, it takes at least nine years to train a man before he is presented to the church for ordination and is called into the pastoral ministry. None of this training program, of course, was in place in the early days.

In 1958 Albert Muyangana and Lawrence Chipoya were sent to the seminary in Nigeria. Neither fully completed his studies, although Muyangana was assigned to work in the Northwest Province of Zambia on his return in late 1961 and was later deemed to have received a sufficient theological education to be ordained in 1967 as the first national pastor of the Lutheran Church of Central Africa. Chipoya initially was to begin work in his home area near Balovale, but was uncomfortable with the indigenous church policy as he had observed it in Nigeria and as it was being carried out in Zambia. He declined his assignment.

Interestingly, the work in the Northwest Province was the outgrowth of our mission efforts with the students at Munali School. One of those early students, Jim Konde, returned to his home at Kabompo in the Northwest Province and initiated the work there.

The WELS convention in 1959 approved the calling of a man to set up our own Bible institute in Zambia. The need for having our own training program for church workers was clear. What was not at all clear at this point was how to go about it, where to locate it, or even the fundamental question of how, specifically, it was to be used. Should it be used exclusively for the training of church workers, or should it include a training program for teachers in the schools we were managing?

One man was called to set up the school at Lumano and declined. By the time Sauer arrived in the field toward the end of 1961 that location had been set aside because it unwisely tied our mission to a single tribe. The church also considered it desirable to have the worker-training school in an urban rather than a rural setting. From the very beginning, the executive committee considered the establishing of a Bible institute as a step toward developing a seminary program. Our commitment throughout has been to a full theological training.

Sauer's call in 1961 was to serve as superintendent of the mission and at the same time to start the Bible institute. Once in the field, it became clear to Sauer that organizing the mission, addressing policy and personnel matters, and setting a forward-looking program in place would consume his total energies and leave little time to devote to setting up a Bible institute.

All this was the Lord's way of providing another key man for the field in the person of Ernst H. Wendland from Benton Harbor, Michigan. Wendland, called to the field with the sole responsibility of setting up the Bible Institute, arrived in September 1962. Wendland favorably complemented Sauer in forming a mission team that quickly gained the full confidence of the executive committee. The students soon learned to appreciate and respect this man whom God had placed in charge of the worker-training program.

The writer recalls a student strike against the work program when Wendland was gone for a weekend. While the acting principal was considering how to deal with the problem, Wendland returned on Monday morning and gathered the student body in the chapel. Pacing back and forth in front of them momentarily, he paused to glare at them over the top of his glasses and then asked: "Now what's this all about?" That ended the matter.

Ernst H. Wendland, called to set up a worker training program in 1962, returned to the field in 1989 to serve in this program under former student Hachibamba.

Within a few weeks of Wendland's arrival in the field, he and Sauer made an information-gathering trip to mission schools in Southern Rhodesia, stopping at the Baptist mission at Gwelo and the Swedish mission at Mnene, as well as at a Catholic seminary they happened to see en route. Wendland, as characterized by Sauer, had the ability to absorb ideas from others, to sift and sort and come up with the best of what they had to offer for our own use. They also visited a Bible school in Chizera in the Northwest Province. Correspondence was carried on with Nigeria to learn about the program there.

Much of our approach to setting up our Bible Institute was gleaned from these contacts, such as the size of property needed and whether or not to teach secular subjects. To avoid governmental entanglement, it was determined not to teach secular subjects. A comment by the head priest at the Catholic seminary in Rhodesia had made an impact. He was emphatic in pointing out that they used no shortcuts in their program of theological education, but gave their students a training fully equivalent to that offered at Roman Catholic seminaries anywhere else throughout the world. Thorough theological education became an earmark of our worker-training program both at Chelston and later also at Lilongwe, Malawi.

As a direct outcome of visiting these other schools, the missionaries decided to set up a proper physical plant before starting classes. A property on Burma Road in Lusaka, which had been secured in February 1961 as a site for the Bible Institute, was reevaluated and rejected as being too small to allow for student garden plots, which would give the school a measure of self-subsistence. This decision led to a second look at a plot of land in Chelston Township that had earlier been offered to us by Ervin Volker, one of two brothers who belonged to the Lusaka congregation. Chelston was located on the Great East Road about eight miles from the center of Lusaka. When the Volkers had first made their offer in the fall of 1959, the government had rejected use of the property as a site for a school. Also, the executive committee had been cool to the idea of building that far outside the city.

The second time around, however, the forty acre property was approved by both the government authorities and the executive committee. The principal's residence, the initial classroom unit, and student living quarters were built, and classes began in fall 1964. Eight students were enrolled that first year. The following year there were eleven, seven in the first-year class and four in the second.

The worker-training component of God's plan for the great outpouring of his grace in the Lutheran Church of Central Africa was now in place. At this point the mission was still quite small. It consisted of 225 communicants served by seven missionaries and ten national workers in seven organized congregations and ten preaching stations.

The Advance into Malawi

As early as 1959, Mueller had conducted an extensive survey of the Copperbelt 200 miles north of Lusaka, although no follow-through was made at that time. By 1962 the almost entirely new contingent of missionaries in the field felt that the Copperbelt ought to be explored again. Neighboring Malawi was also to be visited. Mueller and Cox were asked to do these surveys. They visited all the major cities of the Copperbelt and met with the District Commissioners. In October 1962 they made an exploratory trip to Malawi. Blantyre, the principal city of Malawi at that time, was 700 miles from Lusaka. The road at best was gravel except for a short tarred stretch extending out about 20 miles from either city. These were not entirely virgin fields. Through the mailing program, we had developed extensive contacts both in the Copperbelt and in Malawi. Also, a good number of our members, especially in Matero, had relatives and friends in Malawi. Some had moved back there. Their letters called us to Malawi.

The survey team came back with a thorough report. They recommended that we enter both fields. The Mission Council, however, in the light of the manpower situation, thought it wise to enter just one or the other. Malawi was favored. The Copperbelt, it was felt, could limp along with whatever service the skeleton staff left in Lusaka could provide.

The executive committee and World Board were uneasy with this major expansion of the work and felt the field had overstepped its authority even in exploring what appeared to them to be a new world mission field. Although the missionaries, too, felt a measure of apprehension at so large a step, both Sauer and Cox recall that when the survey team report was completed, Bill Schweppe said simply and quietly, "The Lord is calling us into Malawi." And that settled the matter. Sauer calls Schweppe's remark one of the great understatements of our work in Central Africa.

In conjunction with their April 1963 field visit, executive committee members Mennicke and Waldemar Hoyer accompanied the missionaries on a trip to Malawi and came away believers. Their report of that visit states: "We recommend that Pastors Mueller and Cox move to Nyasaland as soon as arrangements for their moving can be made." Lending urgency to the expansion was the imminent breakup of the Central African Federation and the need to establish our mission in Malawi while it was politically feasible. Both Zambia and Malawi gained independence in 1964, Malawi in July and Zambia in October.

Mueller and Cox arrived in Blantyre on June 16, 1963. On Sunday, June 23, 1963, almost ten years to the day from the first Lutheran service in Zambia, the first Lutheran service of worship on Malawian soil was held in Mueller's home. Twenty-six people were present, ten of them nationals. Included among

Missionaries R. Cox and R. Mueller (pictured to the left above) spearheaded the advance into Malawi (formerly Nyasaland) in 1963.

the nationals was Deverson Ntambo, later to become the first Malawian Lutheran pastor and a respected leader in the Lutheran Church of Central Africa.

The missionaries in Malawi made as many contacts as possible with people with whom they had corresponded from Lusaka. These included Cylice Bowman of Chiradzulu, who later became a full-time evangelist of the church. Contacts were also made in the Thyolo District. In this time just prior to independence, locating individuals in the villages was not always an easy task. Often our two missionaries were suspected of being agents of the colonial government and sometimes met outright hostility.

Initially, Mueller and Cox followed the mission strategy of starting a few strong congregations before beginning to spread out in the country. With this approach, they as missionaries would plant the word and then as quickly as possible encourage those taught to be on their own in carrying it to others. They focused on the groups led by Bowman in Khanyepa Village and by Ntambo in Blantyre.

Bowman became virtual pastor of the Khanyepa Church, which grew by leaps and bounds under his leadership. But after Cox's return from furlough in late 1964, he found the knowledge of the faith among the people at Khanyepa to be woefully inadequate. Bowman had been brought forward too fast. He was given opportunity to attend the two-year Bible Institute course in Chelston and for many years after his return served faithfully and effectively as evangelist in Chiradzulu and Thyolo.

Following his furlough in 1965, Mueller was reassigned to Zambia. After almost a year of serving alone in Malawi, Cox was joined in May 1966 by John Janosek, a seminary graduate who had served his first year in Africa at Mwembezhi. Janosek, like Cox and Mueller before him, became a missionary of the first rank. He is fluent in the language of the people and in his more than 25 years in Blantyre has personally experienced the remarkable growth of the mission in Malawi from a few hundred members to the more than 18,000 baptized members today.

In his more than 25 years in Malawi, Missionary Janosek has experienced the remarkable growth of the mission there.

The near shutdown of our mission expansion in Malawi in 1968, detailed in our account of the start-up of the medical work in Malawi, caused the men to reassess their philosophy of starting with a few strong churches. At this point, they decided to establish congregations quickly in every area where we had made some contacts, so as not to limit the places in which we would be permitted to labor. So the mission spread rapidly, often by means of isolated outposts. After eighteen months of labor by Cox and Ntambo among the Moslems in the Ntaja area, one man arose during a Bible class and asked, "Can I be baptized in the name of the Lord Jesus Christ?" That man was Kalungu Mwepeta, still a leader of our church at Nachuma.

The stage was set for the beginnings of an explosive mission growth in Malawi, which has continued unabated to the present. We will return to that story later.

Further Steps Toward a Truly Indigenous Church

When Sauer did not return to the field from his furlough at the end of 1964, the executive committee asked Wendland to become the acting superintendent of the field while still continuing to head the worker-training program. The Bible Institute had just begun its first year in September. Classroom texts in simplified English on doctrine, church history, homiletics, pastoral theology, and exegetical studies suitable for use in Central Africa were non-existent.

A marked expansion took place during the 1960s when many villages began to appeal to the LCCA to establish preaching places.

Wendland had to produce much of this material on the run. He became the principal and almost exclusive writer of the textbooks for the two-year course at the Bible Institute. He produced hundreds of pages of text material. In addition to the many administrative tasks that fell to him as principal of the Bible Institute, he was the only full-time instructor, taught most of the classes, supervised the afternoon study periods, administered the work program and food rations for the students, maintained with student help the forty-acre Bible Institute site (which was neatly landscaped and well-kept, including a citrus orchard), and supervised the work in six congregations and preaching stations. Planning, organizing, and writing textbooks for the three-year Seminary program loomed on the near horizon. Without the total cooperation of his wife Betty, who served as his secretary and also taught classes in singing, English, and literacy at the Bible Institute, his workload would have been impossible to carry.

Assuming the acting superintendency at this point was in itself no small undertaking. In a relatively short period of time, substantial progress was being made toward the orderly transfer of leadership to the nationals.

The first representative convention of the fledgling body was convened in August 1964 under Wendland's leadership. A year later a second convention was held. Articles of organization were adopted, and a synodical council was elected, which consisted of five men: the superintendent of the mission, two called national workers, and two lay delegates. The secretary and treasurer, also elected by the synod, together with the remaining expatriate missionaries, served in an advisory capacity. These were heady times of political independence. The actions that led to the transfer of leadership of the church required the utmost care and negotiating skills, for fear that we move too quickly and lay on the nationals too much responsibility too soon or move too slowly and lose everything.

When Sauer returned to the field in October 1970 and in the following year reassumed the superintendency of the field, he was amazed at the progress that had been made in the organization of the national church. A marked expansion had also taken place. When Sauer had left the field in 1964, the Lutheran Church of Central Africa consisted of seven organized congregations and ten preaching places with a communicant membership of 225. By 1970 this had become 46 congregations and preaching places with a communicant membership of 816. What had been a loosely structured organization was now marked by regular conventions of the church, with nationals becoming experienced in their roles of leadership on the Synodical Council.

During the second Sauer superintendency, the years were marked by the beginnings of a rapid growth of the church, particularly in Malawi. The first seminary class of Salimo Hachibamba, Benford Kawiliza, and Lot Lubaba was graduated in 1972.

The August 1974 convention of the Lutheran Church of Central Africa (LCCA) adopted a formal constitution to replace the 1965 Articles of Organization. This was a landmark occasion with far-reaching implications for moving toward the goal of a truly indigenous church. The convention elected a full set of officers and all the boards and committees needed for the synod to function. For the time being and with the full approval of the national church, the chairmanship of the LCCA remained in the hands of the superintendent of the mission. Hachibamba was elected vice-chairman, Ntambo secretary, and Benson Mavika treasurer. These three nationals with Sauer as chairman made up the Chairman's Advisory Council. Now it was just one expatriate sitting with three nationals on a council making important decisions.

In August of the same year, 1974, the first three graduates of the seminary program completed their two-year vicarship and were ordained into the holy ministry: Kawiliza as pastor of Matero Lutheran Church, Hachibamba as instructor at the Bible Institute and Seminary, and Lubaba as supervising pastor in Zambia's Southern Province.

Taming the Babel of Tongues

When Wendland's oldest son, Ernst R. Wendland, graduated from Northwestern College in the spring of 1968, the Executive Committee for the Lutheran Church of Central Africa asked him to serve for a year as a teaching assistant at the Bible Institute, this arrangement to be renewable for a second year subject to funding. Wisconsin Lutheran High School in Milwaukee helped finance this program. In this role, the younger Wendland was to oversee the property maintenance and the student work and food rations programs, as well as to teach classes. At this time the senior Wendland was still wearing his double hat as superintendent and principal of the Bible Institute, and was only a year away from initiating the first seminary class, so the help provided by the younger Wendland was a godsend.

In this way the Lord was also preparing an exceptional worker for the Central African field. Highly energetic and methodic in his work habits, Wendland has provided an unparalleled service through the years in language and translation work. Theodore Sauer, newly returned to the field in 1970 after his six-year stateside ministry, recognized Wendland's developing linguistic interests and skills. He encouraged the executive committee to extend a call in language work that would keep Wendland in the mission field.

The committee, therefore, created the new position of Language Coordinator for Publications, to which Wendland was

As Language Coordinator, Dr. Ernst R. Wendland has provided unparalled service in language and translation work.

called in the fall of 1971. Supervision of the translation of the weekly sermons and Sunday school lessons, instruction books and Lutheran doctrinal materials such as the Catechism, and hymnbooks, all fell to the newly-created office. The position of Language Coordinator in Central Africa is unique in WELS world missions. But Central Africa is also unique among our world fields in terms of sheer numbers of languages to deal with. While we continue to do the majority of the language work in Chewa (Nyanja) and Tonga, we are also translating works into Bemba, Luvale, Tumbuka, and Lunda. Lunda is also the language of a potential new mission field in neighboring Zaire.

Wendland's linguistic skills have been recognized outside the mission. His entry into the field of Bible translations in the mid-seventies led to his being named "Honorary Translations Consultant," an unsalaried position for the United Bible Societies (UBS) in Central Africa. In this position, he oversees Bible translation projects in a number of African languages. He is assisted by Salimo Hachibamba, coordinator for the Tonga work, and Daison Mabedi, one of three reviewers for the Chewa translation. In addition, Wendland is responsible for all other UBS projects in Zambia, which at present include the Nkoya, Mbunda, Lala, Lenje, and Bemba languages. Through the years many Bible Institute and Seminary students also have assisted in translating and reviewing LCCA materials and Bible translations.

It would be difficult to overestimate the blessing that has come to our gospel ministry through the efforts of these men. Our language coordinator and those who work with him have made it possible to bring the word of God both to our members and to many others in the languages they understand best and revere most.

Expansion into All the Land

In 1975 Cox was appointed assistant superintendent of the mission. The following year when Sauer asked to be relieved of his office, Cox succeeded him as superintendent. Cox brought to the superintendency his own brand of practicality and solid credentials as a field missionary. In 1982 the mushrooming growth of the church in Malawi brought Cox back a second time to the field he had been instrumental in opening in 1963. By 1982 the communicant membership in Malawi exceeded 3,000 and had grown to almost twice that of Zambia. Although the purpose of Cox's move from Zambia to Malawi was to increase the staff there, the return of Malawi Missionary John Kurth to the States at that time left the total number of workers the same. Only Cox and Janosek were left to care for the more than 2,000 communicants scattered over the southern region of Malawi. Cox had to serve as superintendent of the entire mission as well. At the same time, new work was reaching down the escarpment into the lower reaches of the Shire River among the Sena people.

People frequently ask what accounts for the much more rapid growth of the mission in Malawi than in Zambia, by ten

In a centennial thankoffering a congregation in Wisconsin provided the funds for this fine chapel in Lilongwe, Malawi.

years the older of the two fields. By 1990 more than two thirds of the membership of the Lutheran Church of Central Africa was in Malawi.

A number of reasons for the disparity in growth are suggested. The greater density of population of Malawi with 60 people per square mile as opposed to 16 per square mile in Zambia has contributed to the building of some sizable congregations in Malawi. Zambia has more congregations for its fewer than 4,000 communicants than Malawi has for its nearly 10,000 communicants. From the start of the work, virtually every missionary in Malawi was able to devote his energies to learning the language and carrying on a program of field missionary work. This was not the case in Zambia, where the missionaries have been deeply involved in the worker-training program, which until 1981 was carried on entirely in Zambia. Doubtless, other factors have played in, such as the general unrest in southern Africa, which affected Zambia more than Malawi. Perhaps it is less important to analyze the blessings of God than to rejoice in them and take full advantage of them by strategically deploying our mission manpower where the Lord is pouring out his blessing.

Although surveys of the Copperbelt of Zambia, some 200 miles north of Lusaka, had been made as early as 1959, earnest requests for a resident missionary for this area with an estimated population of 800,000 were not made until the beginning of the 1970s. By that time we had two small established congregations in the Copperbelt, one at Kitwe and the other at Ndola. It was difficult to care for them from 200 miles away at Lusaka, and a once-a-month visit was all that could be made. A resident missionary in the Copperbelt would also be that much closer to the Northwest Province, which was 500 miles from Lusaka. When Muyangana, who served the area for a number of years, resigned in 1973 for personal reasons, the need became even more acute. This need was finally met with the placement of a missionary in Ndola in 1974. He was joined by a second man in 1978.

The Eastern Province of Zambia was served through most of the 1970s from Blantyre, Malawi, a distance of 350 miles. It was about the same distance from Lusaka. You will recall that it was the Tonga brothers, Yona and Akimu, whose efforts had led to the founding of the first LCCA congregation in this part of Zambia.

In August 1987 the first resident missionary was placed in the Eastern Province. He was joined shortly thereafter by Benford Kawiliza, formerly pastor of Matero Church, who accepted the call to Chipata as the first national missionary of the LCCA. A second expatriate pastor was then assigned to Chipata, realizing the plan set in motion in early 1987 for a three-man pastor team to serve the Eastern Province.

In October 1987 Ray and Lois Cox moved to Mzuzu, where he became our first missionary to live in Malawi's Northern Province. Prior to that the congregations of the area had been served by missionaries from as far as 470 miles away. He remained there until early 1991, when he accepted a call as principal of the Bible Institute at Lilongwe.

More recently there has been contact with a Rev. Babungi Nkufulu-Lutulu from Kananga in Zaire to the north of Zambia. He serves 11 congregations with a membership of about 1,000 souls. This contact once more underscores the unlimited possibilities for winning souls for Christ that God continues to set before the Lutheran Church of Central Africa.

1991-'92 staff at the Lilongwe, Malawi, Bible Institute, Pastors Daison Mabedi and Raymond Cox

Toward Greater Self-Determination

By the end of the 1970s, the growth of the field in Malawi had reached the point where its own worker-training facility in the form of a Bible institute became necessary. The school was opened in Lilongwe in 1981 under the principalship of Walter Westphal. Deverson Ntambo was called as part-time instructor in addition to his pastoral responsibilities in a nearby congregation and, in 1984, he became Dean of Students.

Originally set up along the lines of the Chelston Institute, the Lilongwe school in 1987 introduced a modular system of teaching. In place of the two-year in-residence course, from which the student on graduation qualifies for service as an evangelist of the church, the modular program brings qualified lay leaders to the Bible Institute for four one-month intensive study sessions. The men come to the Bible Institute without their families and return to their villages after each session.

A select number of these students is permitted to enter the second year as preseminary students, who come with their families for a full year of in-residence training. The preseminary students then return to the field and serve their village congregations, in most instances in the local area from which they have come. If they are not selected for seminary training within a period of five years, their subsidy from the LCCA is discontinued, although the local congregations may support them as they are able.

Students of missiology will recognize some of this thinking as originating in the Theological Education by Extension (TEE) literature of the early 1970s. The modular approach to theological education holds promise of help along the path to self-support for the church in Central Africa. The Bible Institute in Zambia has also adopted a modified form of the modular program. First-year Bible institute students are being instructed while still at home, making use of specially prepared study materials. Area missionaries assist in supervising this self-study program. Seminary students from both countries are still being trained exclusively in Chelston, although it may not be too long before Malawi has its own seminary.

By the mid-80s, it was felt advisable to administer the mission programs in Zambia and Malawi separately. While Cox remained superintendent of the entire field, Assistant Superintendent Mark Krueger was given almost full administrative authority in Zambia. In 1986 the mission administration was completely separated, with a three-man Mission Council headed by a Mission Coordinator in each country. Although the Lutheran Church of Central Africa presently continues to operate as a single synod with two conferences, one in each nation,

The Bible Institute in Lilongwe, Malawi, was begun in 1981. Under its modular system qualified lay leaders are brought to the school for intensive study sessions.

plans are underway to give the various boards and committees of each conference greater autonomy. Difficulties in travel from one country to another may necessitate further reorganization.

At the same time the way was being paved for one of LCCA's own pastors to assume the chairmanship of the church. In a giant step toward self-determination in 1988, the Lutheran Church of Central Africa elected the first national, Pastor Peter Chikatala, as chairman.

The reader will recognize by now that we operate with two separate organizational structures in Central Africa. The one is the Lutheran Church of Central Africa. This group is the national church body that is governed under its own constitution. The other is our WELS mission in which our missionaries serve under the direction of the WELS Board for World Missions and its Executive Committee for Central Africa.

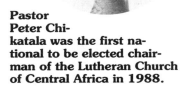

Pastor Peter Chikatala was the first national to be elected chairman of the Lutheran Church of Central Africa in 1988.

In 1987 another major step forward was taken when Salimo Hachibamba was called to head the Bible Institute and Seminary in Chelston. The ability of a national pastor to assume the challenge of this position is a measure of the maturing of the church. In 1988 Daison Mabedi was called as Dean of Students to the Bible Institute in Malawi, replacing Deverson Ntambo, who accepted a call to a congregation in Zomba. Pastor Mabedi is also the chairman of the Malawi Conference of LCCA. In a unique ar-

Salimo Hachibamba, one of the first students at the Chelston Bible Institute, now heads the Bible Institute and Lutheran Seminary there.

rangement, our missionaries serve as pastors of and have full membership in LCCA.

There was a setback in the early 1980s, when a number of LCCA members in Malawi withdrew to affiliate with the Lutheran World Federation. They charged, among other things, that the missionaries were dealing unfairly with the national workers and pointed out that the national workers are supplied bicycles while the expatriate workers are given automobiles. They failed to recognize that LCCA receives a substantial annual subsidy from WELS and that it is LCCA that determines how the subsidy is used. WELS missionaries, on the other hand, are supported directly by the Wisconsin Synod according to policies set by the synod in convention and administered by the Board for World Missions and its executive committees.

It is inevitable that, with the cultural differences between Westerner and African and with the delicate nature of the transfer of power, some will from time to time misunderstand the intentions and purposes of the mission. But overall, despite occasional difficulties and misunderstandings that have arisen, one has to marvel at the wisdom and patience the Lord has given both nationals and expatriates for bridging cultural gaps and working out a careful step-by-step program to bring the Lutheran Church of Central Africa to full maturity.

An important step forward was taken at the 25th anniversary LCCA Convention in 1978. This convention took note of the quarter century of work that began with the arrival of Habben and Ziegler in Lusaka in June 1953. The convention took "Stewardship" as its theme. For the first time in the history of the LCCA, each congregation was given responsibility for setting the salary of its worker. Previously, salaries had been determined at first by the mission and then by LCCA itself. If the congregation was unable to raise the entire amount, it could request a subsidy, the amount not to exceed the support previously supplied through LCCA. The administration of this subsidy is governed by the national church. Although the dollar amounts of support for the national workers are small by American standards, the principle established by the 1978 convention is one more important step toward the development of an indigenous church.

Blessings Beyond Expectations

Through the past two decades, the rapid growth and expansion of the Lutheran Church of Central Africa has continued without a pause. Beginning with 1970, the growth of the church continued at a consistent and phenomenal average of 12 percent per year.

By the end of 1976, when Sauer relinquished the superintendency to Cox, LCCA listed 5,555 baptized members, 2,740 communicant members, and 6,611 souls under its care in 101 congregations and preaching stations. In the six years of Sauer's second superintendency, the number of communicants had more than tripled and congregations more than doubled. But this was only the beginning of the harvest. The solid groundwork laid in the worker-training program, the patient development of policies governing the work, the language mastery, the extensive mailing program, the ministry of mercy in the medical program, the grooming of nationals for leadership in the church, and the learning of effective ways of carrying out field ministry, all have continued to bear ever richer and more abundant fruit.

As of the end of 1991, the Lutheran Church of Central Africa numbered 26,833 baptized and 13,555 communicant members in 150 organized congregations and 14 preaching stations. Of these more than 18,000 baptized and nearly 10,000 communicants belong to the Malawi field. A special joy in May 1991 was the graduation of ten men from the theological seminary in Chelston. Truly, *blessings beyond expectations!*

A special joy in 1991 was the graduation of ten men from the theological seminary in Chelston.

What lies ahead? No one would have believed two decades ago that the 12 percent annual growth rate of the Lutheran

Church of Central Africa would have continued unabated for fully twenty years. Dare we hope and pray for the same in the coming two decades? Anyone with a pencil and paper can quickly calculate that a sustained 12 percent growth rate would provide a church in Central Africa of over 220,000 souls by the year 2010. Are we prepared for the blessing? If the unprecedented blessings of God in Central Africa to this date have taught us anything, it ought to be that we do not underestimate the grace of God and the power of his word.

Postscript

Rev. Arnold L. Mennicke

A resolution of the 1981 WELS Synod Convention gave thanks to a gracious God for thirty years of uninterrupted service provided by Arnold Mennicke as a member and chairman of the Executive Committee for Central Africa. Mennicke was a member of the executive committee from its inception in 1951 and its chairman from 1956 until 1981 when he chose not to stand for reelection. Through the turmoil of the early years to the rapid growth of the later years, Mennicke stood at the helm of the mission organization governing the mission in Central Africa. Blessed with an extraordinary measure of patience and calm, Mennicke's was a steadying influence through troubled times and, throughout, a positive and encouraging voice in the synod in the interest of world missions. Mennicke was well known to the members of the Lutheran Church of Central Africa through his several visitations to the field. His stepping down marked the end of an era.

Pastor Arnold Mennicke and his wife Thea were recognized for their 30 years of uninterrupted service to the Central Africa field in 1981.

MISSION CURRENTS FIVE
MISSION GOALS, POLICIES, STRATEGIES

John Brenner, the man who succeeded Bergemann in 1933 as president of the Wisconsin Synod, ended his years in office in 1953. He is remembered as a man with a strong personality, who took over the leadership of a debt-ridden church body, guiding it with a firm hand through another world war crisis into a time of doctrinal and fiscal stability. One never had to wonder where he stood. No doubt his struggles during times of fiscal crises had much to do with his extremely cautious attitude toward appeals for expansion of the synod's work. But one can never question his strong concerns about the church getting out with the good news of the gospel, as stated by him frequently in addresses and reports to the conventions of the synod. Consider the words in his presidential report to the 1943 synod convention:

> Wisdom demands that we hold fast the Gospel as our most precious possession and permit no one to take it from us. . . . The Lord is also still continuing the existence of the

world only for the sake of the preaching of the Gospel, which is therefore the most important thing in our life. . . . We cannot be neglectful of the souls of others. This is still the time of grace for the entire world.

It is also true that toward the end of the Brenner years a breakthrough had been made toward greater world outreach,

One can hardly imagine a leader with a greater heart for world missions than Oscar Naumann.

both in the direction of the Orient as well as Africa. Brenner's successor, Oscar Naumann, guided the synod's work for the next 26 years (1953-1979), and one can hardly imagine a leader with a greater heart for world missions.

In the year of transition from Brenner to Naumann, the synod voted by an overwhelming majority to divide the mission administration between "The General Board of Home Missions" and "The General Board for Foreign and Heathen Missions." World mission reports received special billing at synod conventions. World missionaries were presented to the delegates and given the opportunity to speak of their experiences. The synod was ready to lift up its eyes to the world as its field.

Each board would have its own chairman. The Board for Home Missions would consist of a chairman and members of the various district mission boards. The Board for Foreign and Heathen Missions would be made up of a chairman together with members of the executive committees designated by the synod for the various fields. Basically this mission setup has remained much the same, except for the addition of a number of full-time administrative positions to each board.

In 1955 Pastor Edgar Hoenecke was elected as chairman of the Board for Foreign and Heathen Missions. Again, the congregation at Plymouth, Michigan, was asked to make a sacrifice for the cause of missions by sharing its pastor with a very time-consuming synodical office. Under Hoenecke's leadership, the board began to formulate its general policies and objectives.

Many of these guidelines still form the basis of the principles and objectives that the Board for World Missions follows today. They relate to matters of organization, support of foreign fields, qualifications of missionaries. They address training of nationals, carrying out indigenous principles, establishing limited medical services. They deal with matters pertaining to the relationship between the Board for Foreign Missions and the other departments of the synod. They are scripturally based throughout, looking to the Lord for his mandates and his promises. These guidelines were all adopted by the 1957 convention of the synod.

When asked recently where he got his ideas for all this, Pastor Hoenecke replied:

> I read extensively. . . . I had a very good "*Anschauungsunterricht*" (loosely translated, "hands-on learning experience") on how not to do heathen mission work through my years of administering the Apache mission. . . . The policies were also the product of sheer necessity. I simply had to prepare carefully and propose a program which gave every reason to hope that the synod would not be saddled with mounting costs and minuscule returns. I also did not want to see the synod stalled in one field, but wanted our people to be encouraged by their experience to push forward to ever new fields in the world. . . . And last, but actually first of all, I wrote the early policy statements because they came as an answer to my prayer that God should consider my abysmal ignorance in the business of administering the world mission field and give me the guidelines which would bring about his will in the matter for which we had fought so hard. That, and especially that, lies at the bottom of the whole matter of our success! This is not the work of an individual or even of a number of individuals; this is plainly and positively the handiwork of our God who promised to crown our weak ventures with the rescue of lost souls. Isaiah 55!!

Those who were privileged to participate in some of the early organizational meetings of the Board for Foreign Missions will remember the exciting experience under Hoenecke's tutelage of studying various books like Roland Allen's, *Missionary Methods: St. Paul's or Ours,* or T. Stanley Soltau's, *Missions at the Crossroads.* For many, these were new vistas, new worlds to conquer.

When in 1959 the synod decided to declare both the office of synod president as well as the chairmanship of the Board for Foreign Missions to be full-time positions, Pastor Hoenecke accepted the call to direct the world mission program. Quite evidently by this time, such a step was necessary to carry out the expanding work of world missions effectively and also to have an open eye for new opportunities. For reasons relating to his wife Meta's health, Hoenecke was granted permission to live in the southwestern part of the United States.

The creation of the two above-mentioned full-time offices contributed greatly to the further development of world missions. Pastor Hoenecke writes of his association with President Naumann:

> President Naumann was not only personally dedicated to the new global outreach of his synod with the gospel, but he inspired and encouraged all of us, especially those who were entrusted with the administration of the world mission program. Many appeals reached his desk from all over the world for help in proclaiming the pure Word. These appeals he not only forwarded to my desk, but urged me to follow up on them, and whenever he could, he personally accompanied me on visits to new fields.

President Naumann added a personal touch to world missions as typified by the following vignette: While this writer, his wife, and six children were in a departure lounge at O'Hare field in Chicago for their first mission trip to Africa, things were seeming rather lonely. Who should unexpectedly enter but President and Mrs. Oscar Naumann for a word of encouragement and farewell! Here this busy man drove all the way from Milwaukee just to say goodby. What a boost for all of us for the long trip ahead into a totally new area of life and work!

During these same years a vexing concern confronted the synod and took up much of its discussions. Deteriorating relations with the Lutheran Church—Missouri Synod, chiefly over questions relating to the principles of church fellowship, finally led to the severing of relations between the two synods. The break occurred at the Milwaukee convention of the Wisconsin Synod in 1961. Some feared that this step would harm world mission outreach, especially since both synods were associated in mission work in Nigeria. Actually, however, it strengthened the Wisconsin Synod in its resolve to stand on its own confessional feet and to reach out to others at home and abroad accordingly.

Although much of the interest at the 1961 synodical convention was centered in matters relating to church union, Chairman Hoenecke took occasion to present to the convention the concept of a "Christian Missioners' Corps." Briefly, a team of missionaries would be trained and sent to centers of influence in the world with instructions to help build indigenous churches there. The program was designed, with a minimum outlay of men and money, to establish Christian nuclei in centers of population. The convention endorsed this proposal and voted the sum of $25,000 to test it.

While these developments were going on within the synod and the Board for World Missions, the Lord of the church was gradually opening the door to vast new mission opportunities to the south. The "Happy Convention" of the synod at New Ulm in 1945 led not only to a greater awareness of mission fields in Africa and Japan. There were good neighbors much closer by, yes, right at our very doorstep and even within our own borders, in desperate need of help. These good neighbors happened to be Latin Americans.

Sometimes mission interest has a way of looking toward places in far-off lands while overlooking the people right next door who are equally a part of Christ's Great Commission. Some among us, however, as far back as 1945, called attention to this need through a project that was begun among Spanish-speaking people in Tucson, Arizona. This initial work among Latin Americans in the United States, modest as it was, grew into an awareness of the need for work among Latin Americans elsewhere. When the opportunity arose to put the exciting concept of a Christian Missioners' Corps into practice, the Board for World Missions recommended Puerto Rico as the site for this program to receive its first test. In 1964 two missioners were sent by our synod to this Caribbean island, and by 1965 the increased mission activity among Latin Americans in our synod brought about the establishment of an Executive Committee for Latin American Missions.

How this all came about, ever so slowly and gradually, makes for an interesting and important episode in our synod's world mission history.

A GROWING AWARENESS OF LATIN AMERICA
Tucson, Mexico, Puerto Rico

Did those delegates even begin to realize where their resolution would lead? It was August 6, 1945, the last day of the 28th biennial convention of the Wisconsin Evangelical Lutheran Synod, the same day the horrible mushroom cloud of nuclear death and destruction rose over Hiroshima, Japan. It was the "Happy Convention" previously referred to. In New Ulm, Minnesota, God-fearing delegates resolved "that the president appoint a committee to gather information regarding foreign fields that might offer opportunities for mission work by our synod." It was high time, they indicated, for our synod to renew efforts to bring the gospel to souls headed for even greater death and destruction.

From that resolution came our work in Latin America. Right outside the doors of our country resided the people of Latin America, already then one of the fastest growing regions of the world and today numbering more than 400 million. Right inside our doors in the Southwest was a segment of that population, already then one of the fastest growing minority groups in our land and today numbering more than 16 million.

Tucson

In 1948 our synod through its mission board called Pastor Venus Winter of Flint, Michigan, to begin Spanish work in one of the cities of the Southwest. On December 5 he conducted his first Spanish service at Phoenix, Arizona. After a short period of testing, he shifted the work further south to Tucson because of the greater concentration of Hispanics there.

What a challenge Missionary Winter faced! He had no nucleus of people, no list of prospects, but he did have a great love for Spanish-speaking people. He had no model to follow, no guidelines as to where or how to begin, but he did have God's word with its message and promise. In that first year of work, for as many as 16 consecutive Sundays, the missionary himself was the only soul present in the rented building. "On those trying Sundays," he wrote, "when he had no one else to preach to, your missionary preached to himself by memorizing Bible verses and hymns in Spanish, for he still hoped to have an audience to whom to apply those precious verses and hymns."

It soon became apparent that the initial work lay with the children. After nine months, a Sunday school was opened. When this handful of little ones agreed to stay for church, worship services were also started. In 1949, early Sunday morning radio services were also begun. From these gospel broadcasts came about 75 percent of the membership of San Pablo (St. Paul) Spanish mission.

Pastor Venus Winter was the synod's first Latin-American missionary.

At first this little congregation worshiped in rented quarters. Then in 1955 an attractive combination chapel-school was built,

San Pablo chapel and school, Tucson

and in 1957 San Pablo Christian Day School was opened, with Pastor Winter teaching all the classes. During the years of its existence and under the faithful work of various teachers, this school served as a steady feeder for our Spanish mission.

Slowly, unspectacularly, the work of sowing the gospel seed continued. "In these years our success was not what many would consider sensational," Pastor Winter reported. "And yet to your home missionary in the field every convert was a sensation, a miracle of God. With the pressure of Rome against us, and its Sunday school buses operating right around our chapel, and with sects like Mormons and Jehovah's Witnesses working overtime in our area, we at times lose some whose confidence we thought we had won but who were not yet well grounded in the faith. But the Lord was with us so that we'd always gain some from year to year."

Until his retirement in 1981 the veteran missionary worked faithfully with the word, which God himself described as "his power for salvation" and of which he declared that "it will not return to me empty." And the mission grew to over 100 souls.

Though our first Spanish mission closed its doors in March 1988, because both the field and circumstances had changed, the beachhead had been established. "*Si, Cristo Me Ama.* . . . Yes, Jesus loves me," precious souls had been taught to sing. Spanish-speaking people, both young

A Spanish-speaking child learns, "He died for me."

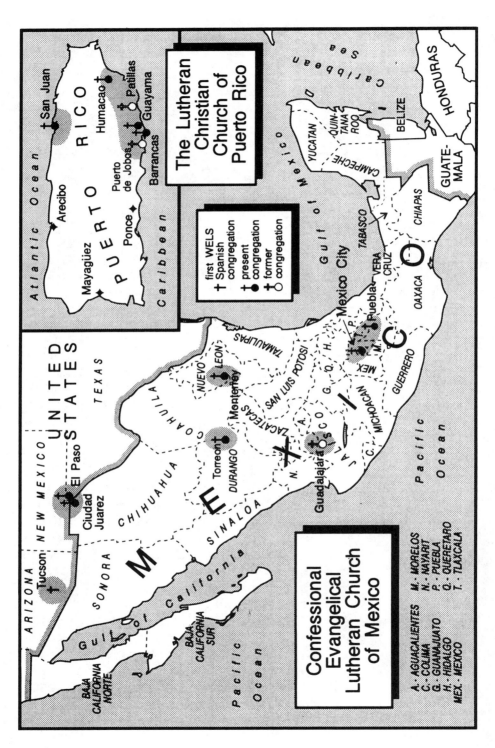

and old, were learning that Jesus loves them . . . loved them to death!

Across the Border into Mexico

What had begun at Tucson was not to end there, though years passed before expansion in our Spanish work would come. Already in 1960 the Board for World Missions had planned to expand the work into Mexico, second most populous nation in Latin America and our immediate neighbor to the south. A team of men had been sent to explore possibilities but returned with a negative report because of the difficulties imposed by Mexican law on mission work by foreigners. Non-Mexican pastors were not allowed to reside in the country and were even restricted in the church work they could do when invited in as temporary guests by a national church body.

So the board sought another way to reach at least somewhat into Mexico. In 1966 the Latin American Committee commissioned Ernest Zimdars, a graduate of our seminary, for work at El Paso, Texas. Among its large Spanish-speaking population, he would seek to gather a flock and also would try to reach across the Rio Grande River to El Paso's sister city, Ciudad Juarez, in the state of Chihuahua, Mexico.

In El Paso, through the faithful preaching of the word by various missioners over the years, souls were gathered and San Juan (St. John) Congregation established. Across the border in Juarez, through the use of radio broadcasts, contacts were also made. Though the missioner could not hold public worship services, Mexican law did permit him to visit people and conduct devotions in their homes. As a result of such work, a group of people was eventually gathered under the name of *Cristo Redenter* (Christ the Redeemer) Congregation, and in 1973 a chapel was built. Mexican students, studying at our Spanish seminary in El Paso, assisted in this work, and today one of these graduates serves as pastor at Cristo Redenter. But that's getting ahead of the story.

In 1964 President Oscar Naumann of WELS received a letter from Mexico City, dated November 24. In that letter a Mexican pastor who was also a seminary professor wrote:

> I am the president of the Mexican Lutheran Church, a group of 15 congregations in the Republic of Mexico, filiated with the TALC (The American Lutheran Church). Through the time, reading the news in the Lutheran papers and in

some books like *Popular Symbolics* I have learned about the firm standing of the WELS in such matters like the unionism and its adhesion to the right doctrines of the Lutheranism. So I would appreciate very much, if you could grant more information about the tenets and characteristic usages of the church, whose president you are. I am sure the information you would grant us would be very useful in order to get the right vision of what the true Lutheran church must be.

The letter was signed, "Rev. David Orea Luna."

Man's plans so often do not work, and human timetables so seldom are right. But not God's! Here, at his own wise time and in his own gracious way, God was offering WELS what it had not gained for itself—the opportunity to preach the Bible truths, restored by Luther, in the country of Mexico.

President Naumann replied at once, but three years went by with no further contact from Pastor Luna. During those years, God was at work through his word as he always is. Though Dr. Luna was not successful in warning his church body against its liberal and unionistic tendencies, he did grow in his own knowledge of and concern for the truth. Consequently, at the end of 1967, he and one of his former students, Pastor David Chichia Gonzales, withdrew from the Mexican Lutheran Church "out of love for the truth and for confessional Lutheranism."

Shortly before this time, Dr. Luna had again contacted President Naumann with a request for more information and for an interview to clear up points of doctrine. In March 1968 a formal colloquy, or oral examination, of both Dr. Luna and Pastor Chichia was held, and both men were declared to be in doctrinal agreement with us. As a result, fellowship ties were established, and the door was opened for our gospel work in Mexico.

All was not rosy, however. Over sixty members of Pastor Luna's congregation had remained loyal to their faithful shepherd. For them this

It was through Dr. David Orea Luna that the door was opened for our gospel work in Mexico.

meant losing the use of their church building and not being able to gather again for public worship for two years until a new chapel could be built. Mexican law required that buildings erected or used for worship purposes be "nationalized," that is, turned over to the government. The government then holds title to the building, but assigns it to the congregation for use as a worship facility. Under such conditions it is almost impossible to find rented facilities, or dangerous to use one's own home for worship. Who would want to run the risk of having his property nationalized?

WELS, meanwhile, was suffering its customary shortage in the operating budget. Nevertheless, the Lord provided, as he always does. When Executive Secretary Hoenecke reported the news of the successful colloquy to the WELS Synodical Council at its May 1968 meeting, a spontaneous offering was gathered to thank God, whose word does not return empty. From that offering came enough to support this fledgling mission for two months. Other gifts quickly followed and supplied the money and facilities needed to keep this young church going until WELS in 1969 funded the Mexican Mission as part of the ongoing work of its Latin American Committee.

Organizing the IELC

The year 1970 was special for the Mexican Mission. In July of that year, Pastor Luna's small group, held together by private devotions conducted by their pastor in their individual homes, dedicated their new church building in Mexico City. Their offerings paid for furnishing the interior, while gifts from the WELS covered the rest. Once again they could raise voices in praise to their gracious God and hear his word faithfully proclaimed for the nourishment of their souls. What must Pastor Winter have thought as he recalled those first lonely days in Tucson and now stood in the pulpit of Cristo Resuscitado (The Resurrected Christ) Church on that dedication day and preached to God's flock about their heavenly Shepherd on the basis of Psalm 23!

Also the same year, "The Message of Salvation" was beamed over the airwaves in Mexico. This program would eventually be heard over a radio network in eight major cities. Moreover, in November of that year, the Confessional Evangelical Lutheran Church of Mexico (IELC) was formally organized, with Dr. Luna as its first president.

Pastor Luna understood the value of the printed word. He was a gifted writer and had earlier begun publication of the magazine *El Amanacer* (*The Dawning*). In 1970, after a gap of three years, this magazine again appeared. Today what he started lives on in the form of a bi-monthly publication entitled *El Mensajaro Luterano* (*The Lutheran Messenger*). Its 3,000 copies serve our congregations and preaching places in Latin America. This magazine, under the editorship of our staff at El Paso, also reaches out to nearly every other Latin American country as well as to Spain.

From the beginning, Dr. Luna recognized the pressing need to train Mexican men as pastors for the emerging church. As little groups formed in the cities of Guadalajara, Puebla, and along the border in Juarez, this need for national workers increased. The "Martin Luther Theological Institute" was begun in Dr. Luna's home in Mexico City, with two students enrolled. Occasionally our men from Tucson and El Paso would visit and present lectures. Because of legal prohibitions, however, their visits could not be on a regular basis or for any longer than one week.

As the work in Mexico advanced, the Latin American Committee felt the need for someone to serve as its Friendly Counselor to the mission. In 1971 Rupert Eggert, one of our first two missioners to Puerto Rico, answered their call and moved to El Paso. Again, regulations in Mexican law would not allow him to live directly on the scene in Mexico. He was also called as director of the Latin American seminary, which was to be located in El Paso and serve the entire Latin American field. Very shortly a tragic loss would make the need for this seminary painfully clear.

Progress in Spite of Loss

On March 7, 1972, Dr. Luna died suddenly and unexpectedly. The loss to the IELC was tremendous. Gone was their respected leader, their mission planner, their trainer of future workers. But the work goes on. The Lord always knows what he is doing and always plans his actions for the best of his kingdom. The theological training effort was shifted entirely to El Paso and placed under Missioner Eggert's leadership and care. The seminary program continues to be carried on there in the simple, but attractive building that it shares with San Juan Congregation. From these efforts have come two of the present three Mexican pastors. One of the two students presently enrolled in our seminary and currently vicaring is the youngest son of Dr. Luna.

Ups and downs are visible in the twenty-some years since that eventful colloquy of 1968. Chapels have been erected at Mexico City, Guadalajara, Puebla, and Juarez. Successful vacation Bible schools have been held in the summers. Defections, both of pastors and people, have occurred. Government restrictions have brought the radio broadcasting to a complete halt. Changes, often involving long vacancies, have taken place in our three-man expatriate team.

Paul Hartman from Puerto Rico replaced Eggert as Friendly Counselor, while James Connell from Colombia took over Mark Goeglein's position as Mass Communications Director. Connell's task is to coordinate the planning and production of Spanish material for all our Latin American fields. Some of the results have been the production of Sunday school and vacation Bible school materials, the publication of *El Mensajaro Luterano,* and the translation into Spanish of various volumes of the popular WELS Bible study series, *The People's Bible.* Who but the Lord can accurately measure the progress made and souls reached through the varied efforts among our neighbors to the south!

Early on, the Mexican pastors and vicars were included in the Latin American conferences, scheduled every two years. Begun in Puerto Rico in 1964, these meetings bring together the Spanish-speaking workers from our various

Pastors Jose Lorenzo Perez, Josue Saucedo, Daniel Perez, Vincente Guillen, and David Chichia meet in Mexico City, 1983.

fields for study of doctrine, discussion of mutual concerns, and coordination of efforts. Lay members of the IELC have attended the WELS Latin American Lay Delegate Conferences, begun in

1986 and held every two years. At these meetings, lay leaders from our far-flung Spanish fields share mutual joys and concerns and are given opportunity for fellowship and growth.

The story of Santa Cruz (Holy Cross) Congregation provides a fitting close to the account of our gospel work in Mexico. Begun in 1941, this larger congregation had been affiliated with the Lutheran Synod of Mexico as part of the mission program of the Lutheran Church—Missouri Synod. On March 30, 1984, after lengthy discussions on matters of doctrine and practice, Santa Cruz Congregation applied for membership in the IELC and is now served by one of its national workers.

On the cover of his magazine, *El Amanacer,* Dr. Luna regularly printed the words of Romans 13:13, "The night is nearly over; the day is almost here." By God's grace, his hope for the dawning of a truly confessional Lutheran Church in Mexico is turning into a new day.

Missioners to Puerto Rico

For some paragraphs now the discerning reader has noticed the term "missioner" used. This term came out of new thinking on the part of our Board for World Missions. Faced with spiraling costs in its mission fields and with the need to manage limited resources as effectively as possible, the board in the early '60s initiated the Christian Missioners' Corps program as a possible way of entering new areas. As mentioned in the previous chapter, this concept was to send out men in teams of two, just as Paul and Barnabas were sent out by the early church. These teams would seek to train leaders among the early converts and help a national church develop that could stand on its own feet as soon as possible. The men on these teams were called "missioners."

As a test site for this new program the Board for World Missions chose the island of Puerto Rico. This island, discovered by Columbus in 1493, ceded to the United States in the late 1890s, and granted commonwealth status in 1952, was a good choice. With some 3,300,000 people in a land area nearly the size of Connecticut, Puerto Rico is the most densely populated nation in the Western Hemisphere. Because of its unique relationship with the U.S., its usage of both Spanish and English, its freedom of religion and stable government, Puerto Rico offered opportunity both to implement the Christian Missioners' Corps program and to expand our efforts in Latin American missions.

The 1963 synod convention reacted favorably and authorized the calling of two "missioners" for Puerto Rico. By August of that same year, Rupert Eggert had accepted the first call and, by June of the next year, Roger Sprain followed suit. Our first missioners settled in the capital city of San Juan and spent months learning the language, becoming acquainted with the people and their culture, and planning their outreach. They chose the radio as one way to reach the people of Puerto Rico, both in the city of Humacao on the eastern side of the island and in Guayama on the southern coast. Coupled with the radio was a community-wide canvass in both areas. By October 1967 Missioner Sprain moved to Guayama, a community of 45,000, while Eggert concentrated on Humacao.

Missioners Roger Sprain and Rupert Eggert pioneered the work in Puerto Rico.

The first confirmations did not come until the spring and summer of 1970, six years after the missioners arrived. In Guayama the Lord led Sprain to a collection of humble homes built out of scavenged wood and tin along the train tracks leading into a nearby sugarcane field. Called *Gran Stan Bran* (Grand Stand Branch), the community housed the poorest of the poor. Nearby under a tree in a field, the missioner conducted Sunday school for the children he had gathered by playing baseball with them. One day as class was in session, a lady from one of those homes rushed out to invite them into her small back yard. This was Doña Josefa, a modern day Lydia, who became a pillar in the mission. Soon friends and neighbors, invited by her, brought their wooden chairs to her backyard where they sat along that sugarcane railway, learning of the one way to heaven. The confirmations followed.

So did the desire for their own house of God. For the price of $145, with $20 down and the promise of monthly payments,

Missioner Charles Flunker and members of the Barrancas congregation. Flunker moved from Puerto Rico to Brazil in 1986.

that little group bought an old building, last used as a chicken coop. Joyfully and proudly, they came the night before dedication with their cleaning supplies and pails of whitewash to adorn their house of God. Need we ask who regularly swept that little chapel after its dedication? Why, Doña Josefa, of course.

In 1972 the government relocated the Gran Stan Bran community to Barrancas, fifteen minutes south of Guayama, on the sea. There, the small group of communicants labored to build a 25 by 40 foot cement block chapel. Reporting on its dedication on June 3, 1973, the missioner wrote,

> The total cost of the building was under $6,000, half of that amount on loan from the Church Extension Fund of Puerto Rico. Borrowed or donated tools, hand-mixed cement, and homemade blocks, along with individual gifts by friends both local and stateside, helped make this church a reality.

Motivated by their faith, believers stepped forward to put up their house of God without depending on the mother church. This little congregation paid back its loan and elected a church council. It owns and maintains a passenger van to transport its members to worship services, and meets its own monthly expenses.

Their faith moved them not only to build a church, but also to witness to others. In the fall of 1975 one of the missioners joyfully wrote:

Our present communicant membership is scattered in areas offering as much mission potential as our manpower can handle. There are prospective members beyond the Guayama area in such places as Puerto do Jobos and Patillas. . . . For example, Mrs. Maldonado of Blondet, in whose home we conducted adult information classes and still do, invited her neighbor lady, Antonia, who came for five lessons in the middle of the course before moving away to Puerto de Jobos. Another prospect lost? No, Antonia invited her next door neighbor's children to come to Sunday school with her children (we pick them up at present) and another friend's children from around the corner. She has asked for instruction classes to continue for herself, her sister-in-law, and her husband who just last week returned from the United States. . . . Mrs. Maldonado is one of several who has taken the Lord at his word and is telling her friends and neighbors "what great things God hath done for her." Lord, help us to do the same.

As doors were opened to the missioners, the work spread. The year 1981 saw the start of a daughter congregation in the Dorado subdivision of Guayama. In 1989 this group, now organized as a congregation, dedicated an adequate worship facility. A third congregation on the island, organized in 1987 in San Juan, meets in the missioner's home and pays rent for this space. In Humacao there is a preaching station where a modest-sized group rents a room for worship services. All three congregations and the preaching station regularly contribute a portion of their offerings for foreign and domestic mission work. Commenting on the 25th anniversary of our work in Puerto Rico, the missioner wrote, "Noteworthy is the fact that the 200 baptized members of the church are made up of families. The men—young, middle-aged and older—take an active part in leading the church."

Chapel at Dorado. Dedicated 1989

Ralph Martens, missioner in Puerto Rico from 1972 to 1991

Over the years missioners have come and gone: Eggert and Hartman to El Paso, Sprain to Colombia, Flunker to Brazil. In their place the Lord has sent men with names like Ralph Martens, who served on the island from 1972 to 1991. John Strackbein, Ronald Baerbock, and Timothy Satorius, as of this writing, constitute our three-man team of missioners to Puerto Rico.

Though for some reason known only to him, the Lord has not yet provided native Puerto Rican missioners or pastors, several men are receiving pre-theological training. If successfully completed, this effort will be followed by four years of seminary training and, we pray, national pastors.

The vicar program in Puerto Rico, initiated in 1971 and for many years supported totally by special gifts from interested WELS members, has given valuable training to a number of young men from Wisconsin Lutheran Seminary at Mequon. It has also helped to heighten the awareness of Spanish mission work in our circles and yielded a number of men for worldwide mission service. Included are Carl Leyrer and Philip Strackbein in Colombia, James Connell in El Paso, and Robert Meister in Taiwan.

Almost thirty years ago, the Lord called two men to work together with him in the Christian Missioners' Corps program in Puerto Rico. For purposes of uniformity our world mission board decided in 1989 to discontinue the use of the term "missioner." Whatever the title of the workers, Puerto Rico was to serve as the training school for this new concept and, we hoped, a stepping-stone to work in South America. It has been, under God's guiding hand. Even more so has the Lord turned the island into a mission field, where together with our "missioners" he has shared the good news of the one way to heaven, our Savior Jesus Christ.

MISSION CURRENTS SIX
ORIENTAL OVERTURES

Addressing the Forty-Eighth Convention of the Wisconsin Evangelical Lutheran Synod in 1985, Pastor Theodore Sauer pointed out how world missions begin in various ways. One way is "taking the initiative and looking for places in which to do mission work". This was the way in which we entered Apacheland, Central Africa (Zambia), and Puerto Rico. A second way is "spreading out from existing stations," as happened in the case of Malawi, which grew out of Zambia, and Taiwan, which developed out of Hong Kong. A final way is "responding to appeals." These appeals, as Pastor Sauer explained, "generally come from individuals or groups which are already involved in church work and often arise out of confessional concerns."

While, as a matter of policy, the Board for World Missions prefers to begin work in a new field by taking the initiative, it cannot disregard appeals from those who for confessional or other reasons plead with us to help them bring the gospel to their countrymen. It is also a fact of life that a church body from America simply cannot legally enter many countries these days except through nationals who have already organized in their own land.

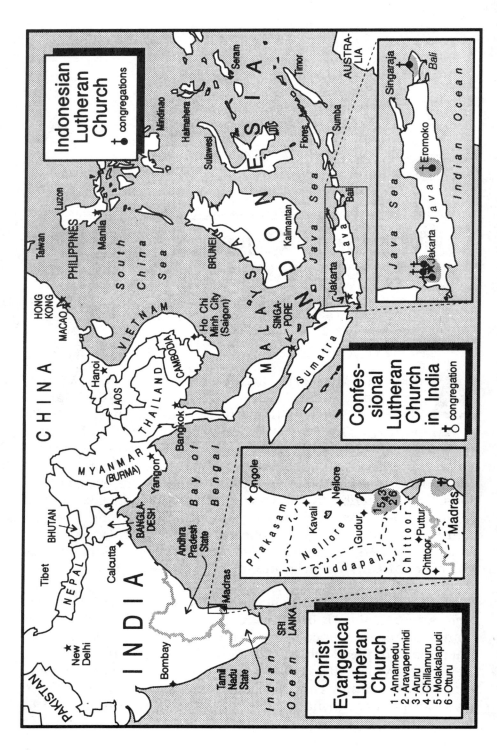

"Responding to appeals" seemed to be the way to go during the 1960s. As Pastor Sauer explained in his presentation to the synod, "It is in response to direct appeals that we began work in Hong Kong, Indonesia, Mexico, India, and Cameroon." We note that much of our work in southern and eastern Asia began in this way and had its beginnings in the 1960s.

In 1960 Peter Chang, in the name of the Christian Chinese Lutheran Mission (CCLM), appealed to our synod for the first time for support. Chang's appeal was later renewed and, as we shall see, eventually led to our synod's decision to enter Hong Kong in 1965.

In 1968 a pastor from the island of Java, Martinus Adam, appealed to various Free Churches in Europe to help his struggling Confessional Lutheran Church of Indonesia. In a roundabout way, this appeal came to the attention of our synod. After an investigative visit to the field in 1969, the synod resolved to declare fellowship with this young church body and to assist it in its work.

One more opportunity to work in Southeast Asia presented itself in the 1960s, again by way of personal appeal. Mr. T. Paul Mitra, living in Madras, India, had for some years been serving a small group of Lutherans living in extreme poverty and isolation. Again, after considerable correspondence and a visit to the field, the 1969 synod convention resolved "that we enter this field in India if further study by the Board for World Missions finds all things acceptable."

As we review the beginnings of our synod's work in these areas, we encounter some interesting stories. But we also run into a host of unforeseen problems. What was begun in good faith often turned out to have negative side effects. Frequently the thought must have occurred to both missionaries as well as mission executives that it might have been far better to have entered such places completely on our own and on the basis of our own exploration.

It should be stated again for the record, however, that starting "on our own" in most countries of the world today is no longer possible because of governmental restrictions. Either we accept the invitation of an existing national church body—or we stay at home. The synod can be thankful that these beginnings were made when they were, even under tenuous circumstances at times. Without these beginnings, it is doubtful that we would be working in these fields today.

Something else should be stated at the outset of this section dealing with East and Southeast Asia. Although each of these ventures reached out to a small confessional group, in every case the vision of an open door to millions of others was never lost sight of. Reports of this work appearing in official proceedings, publications, and publicity materials speak of people in terms of "Hong Kong's five million," "Taiwan's 20 million," "Indonesia's 100 million," and the "countless millions" living in China and India. In fact, in the case of China we are speaking in terms of one billion, no less!

Is it unrealistic even to think in these terms? The words of Pastor Raymond Zimmermann, chairman of the Board for World Missions, to the synod in 1970 reflect the sentiments of the board when he states:

> The task of our synod, as defined by our Lord, is fantastic in its extent. "Go ye into all the world and preach the gospel to every creature." The world is so very large. There are so many—so tremendously many—people in the world. How can a comparatively small church body such as ours make even a dent in this challenge? Rather than to let ourselves be awed into a complacent kind of inactivity by the immensity of our task, let us rather follow the example of the apostles, who had an even greater task, and go to work!

It was in this kind of spirit that East Asia was entered.

OPENING DOORS TO THE FAR EAST
SOUTHEAST ASIAN MISSIONS

HONG KONG

A Call For Help

The first appeal leading to our synod's involvement in mission outreach in Southeast Asia came from Hong Kong, a British colony since 1842. Located on the southeast coast of China, its 400 square miles, only one-seventh of which are arable, are home to over five million people. Within the past decade or more, hundreds of thousands of refugees have streamed into the city from Viet Nam and South China. Although still a free port and one of the greatest trading centers of the Far East, Hong Kong's ninety-nine-year lease from mainland China expires in 1997, and it appears that the "landlord" is not about to renew it!

In 1960, however, when a call for help from Hong Kong first came to our synod's attention, the threats of a takeover by the People's Republic of China still seemed rather remote. The call

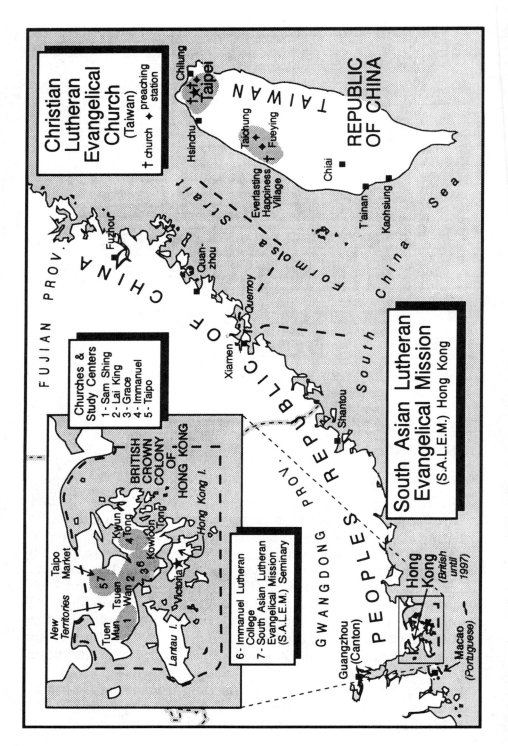

The appeal for help in bringing the gospel to Hong Kong came from Peter Chang.

came from Peter Chang, who later was to become president of the Christian Chinese Lutheran Mission (CCLM). It wasn't until 1965 that our synod in convention voted to assist CCLM with "support, guidance, and friendly control." A glimpse into Chang's background will offer some indication, at least, of some of the problems that later surfaced in connection with the beginnings of this mission.

Through the influence of deaconess Gertrude Simon of the Lutheran Church—Missouri Synod, Chang became a student of that church body's Bible institute in Hong Kong. As a student he served a rooftop Sunday school in one of the city's hundreds of huge tenement buildings known as resettlement blocks. Often these tenement blocks housed tens of thousands of people. Already at that time, Chang gave evi-

Many of the Lord's little ones first heard about their Savior in the rooftop schools which are perched on top of teeming tenement buildings.

247

dence of entrepreneurial tendencies. Independent of his parent body and encouraged by Simon, he expanded his work, organizing a primary school for refugee children. He

Occupying part of the first floor of a crowded tenement building, Immanuel Lutheran English Middle School served as an agency to bring the gospel to the young.

helped support this and other similar undertakings with handicraft projects as well as funds solicited from church bodies in other countries. In this way, one of his appeals came to the attention of our synod in 1960.

WELS officials at the time properly referred Chang's appeal to the body with which he was affiliated. Although both Chang and Gertrude Simon were directed by his supporting church body to give up their independent activities, they were reluctant to do so. Instead, Chang enrolled in a Bible institute of another Lutheran church body in Seattle, Washington. In his absence, his work in Hong Kong continued under the banner of the Christian Chinese Lutheran Mission.

Chang's studies in Seattle were short-lived. After six months he enrolled at the seminary of the Evangelical Lutheran Synod (ELS) in Mankato, Minnesota. There he became close friends with fellow student John Schwertfeger, an alliance that was to develop further in Chang's later activities.

Chang returned to Hong Kong in 1962 with no assurance of outside help. The ELS indicated that it was "not in a position to guarantee all [Chang's] financial needs." Yet Chang kept moving forward. He reactivated a Voice of Salvation radio broadcast that was beamed into mainland China. He founded Grace Lutheran Bible Institute with 33 students and seven teachers. He assembled 250 pupils in the Immanuel Lutheran English Middle School (ILEMS), enlisting Ruth Ruege, John Schwertfeger, and Rev. Kenneth Seim from WELS congregations in the United States as helpers. His goal was the development of an educational system from primary school through Bible school and seminary.

In spite of poor facilities, the enrollments in Chang's school system thrived. Partly through the use of funds from the family of his wife, Bernice, he had managed to purchase a series of ground-floor shops, joined them by means of a central hallway, and supplied light and air by means of shafts open to the sky. Unfortunately, tenants on the upper floors found these shafts to be handy disposal places for all manner of garbage. To many students, however, Chang's schools were veritable havens when compared with "homes" perched precariously on the hillsides of Kowloon and made of cardboard boxes and shipping crates.

From CCLM to CELC

Although a limited fee system was inaugurated in Chang's schools, clearly additional money and manpower would be urgently needed to carry on this expanded program. The situation became all the more critical when in 1963 a seminary was added to it. Once more Chang appealed to WELS for help. WELS responded by sending a delegation to Hong Kong to see the work at first hand before making any commitment.

The visitation was carried out in 1964 by Edgar Hoenecke, Executive Secretary of the Board for World Missions; WELS President Oscar J. Naumann; and Pastor Leonard Koeninger, WELS Relief Committee Chairman. One observer describes the mode of communication used at the subsequent meetings as a type of "Chinglish" translated into "English" and vice versa. In other words, there were communication difficulties. In any case, the discussions satisfied the visitation committee that a basis for fellowship between WELS and CCLM existed.

Emergency methods of support were planned to fill the gap, until the synod could meet to take whatever action it deemed necessary. A film entitled *Hong Kong—An Open Door* was shown at WELS district conventions. Mission weekends were organized in the Michigan District with 56 congregations participating. Nearly $20,000 was gathered for CCLM'S work. Rev.

Conrad Frey, president of the Michigan Lutheran Seminary, was granted a year's leave of absence to continue monitoring the situation and to serve CCLM as resident seminary professor. In May 1965 Pastor Marlyn Schroeder of Arlington, Wisconsin, replaced Frey as "interim counselor."

In August 1965 WELS in convention officially committed itself to assist CCLM with "[financial] support, guidance, and friendly control." The following steps were enacted: *Guidelines for Cooperative Work in Hong Kong* were set up; an executive committee for Chinese missions was established; the position of a resident Friendly Counselor was created to serve as liaison between the church in Hong Kong and the Board for World Missions and its newly established executive committee.

Rev. Leonard Koeninger was appointed as the first chairman of the Committee for Chinese Missions. Missionary Richard Seeger, after nine years of fruitful service in Japan, accepted the call as Friendly Counselor. The efforts of Frey and Schroeder were not without results. Not long after Seeger's arrival two seminary graduates, Stephen Chu and Timothy Lee, were ready to be assigned as pastors. There was reason to hope that the work would proceed in a satisfactory way.

Unfortunately, this was not to be. Previous misgivings concerning certain aspects of Chang's activities began to surface. All of us are aware of the difference between "hindsight" and "foresight." Several had noted that Chang's lifestyle was considerably above that of his fellow workers. Others had sensed an undercurrent of tense unrest between Chang and the Hong Kong seminary students.

Seeger soon found himself on a tightrope between censuring some of Chang's actions or following a more conciliatory approach for fear that the national church be alienated. Seeger and the executive committee were at an impasse as to which course to take. Eventually, Seeger accepted a call to a congregation in Milwaukee in 1967. The Schwertfegers left soon after, to be replaced by Teacher Howard Festerling. For a time an atmosphere of political uncertainty also hovered over Hong Kong, brought on by communist terror squads. A bomb placed at the entrance of the Festerling apartment building and another on the doorstep of the Immanuel Lutheran English School raised serious questions about security and safety.

Affairs began to settle down a bit with the arrival of additional staff. The Rev. Paul Behn arrived in 1968 to serve as Friendly Counselor. He had previously served the Apache Mission both as missionary and as member of the Apache Executive Committee. The Voice of Salvation broadcast brought requests for help from the neighboring island of Taiwan, and two seminary students began work there. A student from Bali, Dipa Pandji Tisna, began his studies at the Hong Kong seminary. A "holding company" was activated by the WELS Board of Trustees to keep all properties of the Chinese Evangelical Lutheran Church (CELC), as the Hong Kong church was now called, in trust. Finally, the growing need for a central church and worker training building in Kowloon was recognized when the WELS Board of Trustees approved the sum of $40,000 for the purchase of land.

But again, just when it appeared that the Hong Kong situation was beginning to take shape, disagreements with Peter Chang arose from various quarters. He had opened another school in downtown Kowloon, this time a private school called the Christian International English College, raising questions about his using subsidy grants for private purposes. Serious differences arose in connection with the running of the seminary as well as with determining the membership of the CELC Board of Directors. Then, rather abruptly, in 1971 Chang announced that he would be resigning as a pastor of CELC. Although marriage problems were mentioned as a reason, it finally became clear that he wished to become a businessman in the United States rather than to continue serving the church he had founded.

Thus the "Chang Era," as labeled by some, had ended. A WELS missionary serving the field at that time puts it this way: "There would be echoes of Chang's voice and methods impacting the field for many years. But for better or for worse, a period of transition had begun."

From CELC To SALEM

Following Peter Chang's departure and the disappearance of his one-man type of leadership from the scene, it became necessary for the operation of CELC to integrate the WELS missionaries more effectively into the work. A mission council made up of American staff was organized to make recommendations to the national church. Its aim, as one missionary expressed it, was "to change the church from a vest-pocket operation to one in which there was grass-roots representation."

Behn, Seim, and Festerling conducted the seminary classes. Missionary Gerald Lange drew up a Bible school curriculum and began preaching in Cantonese, something previously not expected of the WELS missionaries. Statistics of CELC were drastically revised to reflect its actual membership rather than a listing of all who had at one time or other been baptized, but who for some reason were no longer seen in church. In general a more concerted effort was made to carry out the *Guidelines for Cooperative Work in Hong Kong* adopted at the 1965 WELS convention.

The mission's building on Broadcast Drive provides a worship area for Grace Lutheran Church, space for the seminary, and living quarters for missionaries and their families.

Some of the patterns for ministry that had somehow arisen in the minds of ministerial candidates were difficult to erase. Seminary graduates seemed to view the completion of a worker training program as an automatic guarantee of a salaried position for life, the salary assured by the "mother church" in America. One observer remarked, "They wanted a bigger slice of the good life than the WELS missionaries were willing to allow." A record of the appeals of national workers to the Mission Council reflects dissatisfaction with salary subsidies and benefits. Closely connected to this was an unwillingness on the part of nationals to teach stewardship in the congregations.

This friction between national church and mission broke out into the open when Spirit of Love Primary School and Church, the oldest of the CELC congregations and schools, filed a formal protest in May 1972, indicating that the people had rejected the missionary sent to work with them. The CELC school supervisor also refused to register the schools' board of managers with the government. Serious questions were raised at this time by the mission staff as to the viability of continuing to do effective mission work through the schools.

In spite of these vexing problems the educational programs continued. A much needed three-storied church/seminary/residence facility, complete with three apartments for missionary families, was dedicated in Kowloon in 1973. The Immanuel Lutheran English Middle School's facilities and standards were upgraded. The WELS continued to send dedicated teachers, willing to serve the Lord in this crowded city and its unfamiliar language and culture. Among these we mention Kenric and Karen Peterson, Gerald Heckmann, Paul and Janine Swain, Sherwood and Beth Wessel, Steve and Cheryl Grosinske, and Lois and Linda Festerling. Sharon Fischer and Stacy Mosher served for a time as volunteers.

Because of the faithful work of these teachers as well as others who went before them, the school's reputation with the Hong Kong education department steadily improved. Eventually, due in part to this improved reputation, the mission was offered a new and much larger school in the New Territories, one which would be able to contribute more in the way of prospects for the church's outreach program.

Within five years of Chang's departure, all the WELS-trained staff involved in the transition years had left the Hong Kong scene. The Festerlings returned to the United States, Howard on leave of absence to begin his seminary training. Lange left to accept a call to a stateside Lutheran high school. Behn retired that same year, 1974, and, after twelve years in Hong Kong, Seim accepted a call to a congregation in Wisconsin.

Friendly Counselor John Chworowsky (right) visits with Howard Festerling during a conference break. Kenric Peterson and G. Heckmann are in the rear.

In early 1974 Rev. John Chworowsky arrived on the field to become Friendly Counselor for Southeast Asia. In addition to Hong Kong, his responsibilities included Indonesia, Taiwan, and India, new fields which had come into being in that part of the world. Chworowsky was joined in 1975 by the Gary Schroeders and in 1976 by the Gary Kirschkes. Both of these couples gave high priority to intensive study of Cantonese and a thorough understanding of Chinese culture.

This new team of workers became increasingly convinced that the field was in danger of becoming all too dependent on outside support, especially in the light of the 1997 deadline of Hong Kong's lease and its threat of a Communist China takeover. They felt that subsidy to national workers and congregations would have to be drastically reduced if the mission could ever hope to grow into maturity. The executive committee in America through Chairman Koeninger expressed sympathy with this plan, yet cautioned that "any change in program must be done with the knowledge and planning of all the national clergy and laity."

After much consultation and prayerful consideration, it was decided to cut off all direct subsidy (except to Taiwan and to Hong Kong's Immanuel School) as of April 30, 1977. National evangelists were given six months of financial assistance, during which time they were encouraged "to develop a membership which will support your ministerial efforts or prepare yourself for some other type of employment." This directive came with the support of the Board of World Missions as well as the executive committee in America. It was official!

Needless to say, this news was not greeted with enthusiasm by CELC and its national workers. Its Board of Directors responded with an appeal that was more in the form of an ultimatum—WELS missionaries must work at the invitation and under the direction of CELC or go home. Instead of "going home," both mission board and missionaries decided to reorganize the WELS work in Hong Kong independent of CELC. A constitution was drawn up bringing into existence the Southeast Asian Lutheran Mission (SALEM). Chworowsky was to care for the day-to-day administration of the mission; Schroeder was to focus on mission development and Kirschke on worker training. As of January 1978, WELS and CELC were no longer involved in cooperative work in Hong Kong.

Radical Surgery

The above steps, of course, brought on a major shake-up in Hong Kong. A new era had begun. Some referred to it as "radical surgery," in other words, a pulling out of many former roots and starting all over again. Naturally, many soul-searching questions were asked concerning the past. What about the many years of teaching, preaching, and nurturing? What could, perhaps, have been done differently so that such a drastic step might have been prevented? Would the new principles and policies work? Only time would tell.

A field self-evaluation ten years later declared:

> The termination of direct subsidy generally had a good effect on the development of a self-supporting church and congregations. . . . But on the other hand we lost some older evangelists/pastors at that time, who under better circumstances may have been able to provide some stability and maturity to a national church.

Certainly no one could find fault with the objectives of SALEM's mission strategy statement:

> We are to present Jesus Christ by the power of the Holy Spirit that people shall put their trust in God through him, to receive him as their Savior, and to serve him as their King in the fellowship of his church.

On the home front the executive committee, now designated as the Executive Committee for Southeast Asian Missions, also experienced a change in ranks as well as constituency. After eight years of service, lay member Carroll Dummann was replaced by James Haag; Rev. Kurt Koeplin became chairman of the executive committee; Koeninger continued as a member of the committee, a service which ended in 1983 after 18 continuous years. Koeninger had seen the Hong Kong mission through its infancy and teen-age years. It was now on the way to maturity, and he felt that the day had come to turn over the work to others. After expressing its deep appreciation for the faithful service he had given, the 1983 convention elected Rev. Daniel Koelpin to take his place.

Changes in Mission Outreach

During the 1980s a major development in the Hong Kong government's education policies had its effect upon our mission outreach as carried on through the schools. Up to this time, the Immanuel English Middle School (ILEMS) founded by Peter Chang, had been used as an agency for reaching into homes through the Christian education of children. The Hong Kong government, however, had now reached the point where it could provide free education to children through the ninth grade. Parents were no longer attracted to small private, tuition-paying schools like the ILEMS in order to have their children receive an education. As a result, the time came for the ILEMS to be closed, a major step on the part of the mission and one that was taken reluctantly. This move ended the twenty-year practice of calling WELS-trained teachers to serve in the Hong Kong classrooms. Steven and Cheryl Grosinski were the last of a long line of teachers who gave themselves unstintingly to the cause of Christian education at Immanuel.

Another major development, however, took place to counter the other. Because of the church's outstanding record in the field of education, the government offered SALEM the opportunity for the total management of a brand new secondary school with a potential enrollment of 1,200 students. The school was located in a new "housing estate," a term that we shall explain later. Through the sale of the old ILEMS building, enough money was provided to furnish the new school without affecting the budget whatsoever. Teacher Mark Sprengeler was added to the mission staff as a "Director of Outreach through Education," called primarily to develop the evangelism potential offered by the college.

The "housing estate" mentioned above requires some explanation. These "estates" are huge housing complexes dotting the Hong Kong landscape. Each estate has anywhere from 18,000 to 150,000 residents. In these estates are so-called "study cen-

Each family occupies about 130 square feet of space in Hong Kong's massive housing estates.

ters"—quiet areas furnished with tables, chairs, a small library, and all the accoutrements conducive for study by young people of late high school through college age. Participants are charged a nominal fee. An evangelist and supervisor is on duty at all times, prepared to witness for Christ and ready to answer questions about why Lutheran Christians provide this service to the community. On weekends the center can be used as a pleasant chapel for conducting worship services.

SALEM has been granted the opportunity of supervising six such centers. These have not only proved to be effective vehicles for witnessing for Christ but also offer places for the development of Christian congregations. They show promise of being a bright spot in the few years that remain before 1997, when China resumes the sovereignty of Hong Kong, and possibly beyond. In the meantime SALEM is training as many Chinese people as possible to become effective witnesses for Christ.

Study centers are a means of reaching young people of late high school through college age with the gospel.

While these ways of reaching out with the gospel may vary according to the opportunities offered in a particular field, the more familiar methods of developing congregations and training workers continue. Missionaries and national workers keep on serving the congregations and preaching stations that have been established in strategic areas. The Bible institute established earlier for the training of national evangelists was in 1984 extended to include a seminary for the training of national pastors.

In this work, the "two Garys," Schroeder and Kirschke, deserve special mention. Both arrived in Hong Kong in the mid 1970s. They began immediately to study the Cantonese language and to become acquainted with Chinese culture. They have worked tirelessly toward the development of a national church that will serve as a powerful witness to the saving gospel of Jesus Christ among the millions of people who are so desperately in need of it.

The two Garys, Gary Schroeder and Gary Kirschke, did much to shape the development of a national church in Hong Kong.

An Increased Sense Of Urgency

There is a definite sense of urgency in this field in view of 1997, the year when the People's Republic of China exercises full sovereignty over Hong Kong. Reports by the executive committee indicate that as a result of this impending development "the exodus of talent from Hong Kong has hit our churches as well. We've lost evangelists, teachers, and members to Canada, the States, and the United Kingdom." The report quickly adds, "However, this may be used by God to plant new churches elsewhere on this earth."

In fact, executive committee reports continue to be positive. Increasing participation of nationals in the work made it possible in 1989 to scale back the number of WELS missionaries to four. Congregations are growing; worker training programs are progressing; study centers are being opened; opportunities for outreach are beckoning.

Beyond all this lies the Chinese mainland, which always hovers in the background of any considerations relating to Hong Kong. President Nixon's surprise visit to China in 1972 gave some hope, at least, that one day the gospel might again be taken to the one billion or more people who to a great extent

Every three years the entire Southeast Asia team meets with its executive committee and participating guests at some location in East Asia, as did this group in 1982.

have been cut off from Christianity since 1949. What will the future bring? Will Hong Kong serve as a stepping stone for the multitudes lying beyond? Will evangelists being trained like Yeung Wai Shing, Raymond Lai, Tse Tat Chie, and Charles Lee labor where an underground church has long been the only possibility of spreading the gospel?

Anything is possible in a world of change. A full and free gospel message has been proclaimed by the WELS in Hong Kong for nearly three decades. Good seed has been planted. Some seeds have sprouted. Some have grown strong. A few have blossomed and borne fruit. A much stronger national church exists today than in 1965. Dedicated teams of missionaries, teachers, committees, and nationals have not toiled in vain. It remains for the future—including times of testing—to reveal the true glory of the work, namely a church that stands, a church that grows, a church that goes forward with the gospel it has received.

INDONESIA

From Exploration To Appeal

We have seen how the answer to an appeal gave impetus to our synod's involvement in Hong Kong, leading to the forming of an Executive Committee for Chinese Missions. Perhaps some of the early problems in Hong Kong moved this committee to try finding another way of expanding the work in Southeast Asia. In any case, in 1968 the committee, hearing about Indonesia being described as "the greatest area of revival of Christianity in missionary history," traveled there in hopes of finding a place where the WELS could initiate outreach.

The Republic of Indonesia comprises more than 3,000 islands stretching along the equator from the Malaysian mainland to New Guinea. Its main islands are Java, Borneo, Celebes, Bali, Timor, the Molaccas, and Irian Jaya (West New Guinea). The capital city is Jakarta on the island of Java. The islands' resources are among the richest in the world. Islam is the predominant religion. At one time colonized by various European countries, Indonesia was controlled in the years following World War II by a Marxist nationalist named Sukarno. Anti-Communist forces under General Suharto took control in 1965, allowing greater opportunity for Christian missions to work there.

The 1968 visitation committee of our synod consisted of Rev. Marlyn Schroeder, Rev. Leonard Koeninger, and Mr. Adolph Froehlke. They found that getting missionaries into this island nation, however, was easier said than done. They left Indonesia with the disappointing news that "entry is gained only by invitation from another church body or from the Council of Churches." Since there was no church body of our fellowship in Indonesia, there would be no entry into the country. Or so it seemed.

On May 16, 1968, the very day that the above committee was leaving the country, a young national pastor from Sukabumi, West Java, was writing letters to the presidents of Lutheran Free Churches in France, Belgium, and Germany. He was looking for a church body with which to affiliate and which could lend support. The pastor's name was Martinus Adam.

Adam became a "Lutheran" in a sort of roundabout way. His religious background was mixed. Born and raised Anglican, educated in a Bible college of Reformed affiliation, he became attracted to the Lutheran church through a German Lutheran doctor who had saved his life as a child. Various factors, such as a Lutheran teacher at the Reformed Bible College; the film *Martin Luther*, seen at the college; and a book called *Lutheran Symbolics*, found in the school library, all added to his curiosity about the Lutheran Church. Several times he read the book containing Lutheran confessional statements. Later he said of it, "It depicted for me the excellence of the Lutheran Church." He tried to find such a church in Java, to no avail.

Working as an evangelist in the Christian Chinese Church, Adam continued to pursue his love affair with Lutheranism. In 1963 he obtained copies of a Chinese Lutheran hymnal and a translation of Luther's Small Catechism from the Lutheran Literature Society of Hong Kong. This led to the beginning of what Adam later called his "venture on the Lutheran movement."

Teaching Lutheran doctrine at the home of his friend, Max Jacobus, Adam gathered a group that formally organized as the *Geredja Lutheran L'tirafi di Indonesia* (Confessional Lutheran Church of Indonesia). This was on April 27, 1964. At that occasion, each member signed his name on the back cover of a copy of the Lutheran Book of Concord.

To begin with, the little Lutheran group held services in a YMCA chapel and in Adam's house. A need for help caused the fledgling body to reach out to the Lutheran Free Churches in Europe for support. Hence Adam's aforementioned letters. At a meeting in Oberursel, Germany, Acting President Gottfried Hoffmann handed Adam's letter to Rev. Edgar Hoenecke, Executive Secretary of our synod's Board for World Missions. About the same time, President Kreiss of the Lutheran Free Church of France and Belgium, who had also received Adam's letter, sent a copy to WELS President O. J. Naumann with the note, "I would by far prefer that these people establish contact with you."

Thus, from various sources and in a rather roundabout way, contact was established between a Lutheran body in Indonesia and the WELS, again by way of personal appeal rather than by advance investigation. Hoenecke regarded Adam's appeal as extraordinary, coinciding as it did with the investigation of the committee responsible for mission work in Southeastern Asia. He was also impressed by the amazing "printed" orthodoxy of this infant body, as expressed in its official confession of faith. This confession was submitted to the WELS Doctrinal Commission. Hoenecke wrote to Naumann,

> We have been hoping and praying for a door into Indonesia. . . . And now out of the clear blue comes the unsolicited offer of Martinus Adam that we help him with a man at Bali to spearhead a truly orthodox movement in Indonesia. I cannot imagine that the Lord could speak to us more plainly as to what he expects us to do if we are truly concerned about carrying out our mission obligation.

From Java To Bali

Hoenecke's reference to "a man at Bali" came about as a result of Adam's appeal for aid to that island. Separated from Java by a narrow strait, Bali is a lushly fertile, scenic, and densely populated island of 2,200 square miles with several million people. It is known best, perhaps, for the physical beauty of its people, its ritualistic forms of music, and its attractive architecture. Its religion is predominantly Hindu. Adam's church had a branch preaching station on Bali, headed by a Balinese layman named Anak Agung Dipa Pandji Tisna.

How this son of the ex-King of Bali became a co-worker of Adam, a Chinese pastor from Java, is a story all of its own. It goes back to the waning days of World War II and the Japanese occupation of Indonesia.

Former Balinese prince Anak Agung Dipa Pandji Tisna helped bring the saving word to the people of Indonesia to the time of his death in 1991.

Pandji's father, a widely-traveled and well-educated man, was suspected of spying and relaying radio messages out of the country to Japan's enemies. He was taken from his village and interrogated. In the morning it appeared that he would be killed by a firing squad. In non-Hindu fashion, he folded his hands, resigned to his fate. Perhaps he was praying. A Japanese Christian interpreter asked him if he was a Christian. He replied that he was, even though he had been rejecting the teachings of an area missionary for years.

After some discussion between the interpreter and his superior officer, Pandji's father was released and returned to his village. He confessed his faith in Jesus and was baptized soon afterward. None of his sons (including Pandji) joined him.

After the war, Pandji went to Java to further his education. While living there with a Christian family he came to know Jesus, mostly through their consistent Christian home life, which he observed.

After finishing his schooling, Pandji took employment in Jakarta, the capital city, as a clerk for the Navy department. A Navy chaplain who worked with Pandji invited him to go home with him to Sukabumi. They attended a worship service led by Adam.

The relationship blossomed through repeated visits and frequent correspondence. Eventually, Pandji returned to his home island of Bali. He opened a school and began to reach out with the gospel to his Hindu relatives and neighbors. Pandji had only a minimum of training. He felt inadequate to head up the Balinese church. He, perhaps more than Adam, felt the need for a resident missionary.

Correspondence between Hoenecke, Adam, and Pandji continued until July 1969. This led to a visit by Hoenecke; Paul Behn, the Friendly Counselor of the mission in Hong Kong; and Rev. Peter Chang of the Chinese Evangelical Lutheran Church. The impressions received were favorable enough so that a positive recommendation for fellowship with the WELS could be made at the synod's 1969 convention. The synod so resolved, also providing funding for Pandji to be sent to Hong Kong to attend the seminary there. The Executive Committee for Chinese Missions as a result of its enlarged scope became the Executive Committee for Southeast Asian Missions.

Resident Missionaries Needed

As matters progressed in Indonesia, it became apparent that missionaries were needed for the work there to develop satisfactorily. Now that we had an invitation from a church in Indonesia, it was possible for expatriate missionaries to enter the country. In January 1971 former missionary to Central Africa, Rev. A. B. Habben, accepted the call as "Initiator, Coordinator, and Supervisor of Indonesian Missions."

The veteran missionary's first words sent to the executive committee following his arrival on July 26, 1971, indicated that this "promising field of missionary endeavor" left something to be desired from a physical point of view. "What a teeming mass of humanity with all its noise and bustle!" he wrote.

Nevertheless, Habben continued, "The field is ripe for harvest. We get the same feeling we had in Africa. How can you reach out to so many with so few mouthpieces?"

Within a month, a shocking revelation would affect the manpower situation in this field for some years to come. How the discovery came about, the records do not indicate. Was it during a visitation to Bandung, a city where it was hoped the WELS missionary could do some German work? Was it during the trip to Bali a week later? Was it during long discussions in Sukabumi with Adam and his members? Was it while Habben and others shopped for a home that could be converted into a church and parsonage? Whatever the case, just a week after requesting funds to purchase a home in Sukabumi, the "bombshell" dropped. Adam confessed that he had another woman in his life besides his wife. He was not about to forsake this relationship— or repent of it.

With Adam's suspension went Habben's legal sponsor! The unhappy upshot of all this was Habben's return to the States and release from his call. Pandji returned to Hong Kong for the time being to complete his seminary studies there. A lay evangelist, Mr. J. E. Epiphanius, was enlisted to keep the operation in Sukabumi going. He received guidance and further training by means of a correspondence course from Dr. Martin Luther College.

Evangelist J. E. Epiphanius "held the fort" at Sukabumi waiting for the day when WELS would again send missionaries to Indonesia.

After graduating from the Hong Kong seminary in 1973, Pandji returned to Jakarta, where he and his wife found teaching opportunities at a primary school, reaching out with the gospel as best he could. Thus the work continued after a fashion. For the most part, it would be nothing more than a holding action for the next seven years.

Bold Moves

Prior to the 1977 WELS synod convention, Rev. John Chworowsky, the Friendly Counselor to Hong Kong, had made an in-depth study of mission opportunities in Indonesia and Taiwan. During the years of the "holding action" in these areas he had managed to keep in touch with the workers there and encourage them. In his report to the Executive Committee for Southeast Asian Missions he highly recommended Indonesia as "the field with the greatest potential for harvesting souls."

The 1977 convention responded by taking a bold step. It voted to send three missionaries to Taiwan as well as three to Indonesia. One of the men sent to Indonesia was Rev. Howard Festerling who after eight years of service as a teacher in Hong Kong had taken a leave of absence to complete his theological studies at Wisconsin Lutheran Seminary. The second member of the team was Rev. Bruce Ahlers. By January 1978 the two families were busy preparing themselves with studies of language and culture for service in Indonesia. In the meantime Rev. Robert Sawall of Lubbock, Texas, a former missionary to Africa, had accepted the call as the third member of the Indonesian team.

The Festerlings and the Ahlers left for Indonesia in January 1979. Little was it known at the time that it would take all of 1,176 days for the Sawalls to be able to join them. Immigration procedures have a way of getting complicated these days, as many a prospective missionary has had to experience. It's an extreme exercise in patience, and the Sawalls were certainly tried to the limit.

Obtaining a visa for Indonesia can be difficult. It took the Sawalls over three years.

The two families that did not have to wait so long continued their language studies in the mountain town of Bandung on the island of Java. Following this schooling, the Festerlings were stationed in Jakarta, and the Ahlers were given responsibility for the work in Sukabumi. Top priority for both men was the production of Indonesian language materials for use in the Indonesian Lutheran Church as well as the strengthening of the Indonesian workers who had held the fort, so to speak, for so many years. People in America often look for immediate results when a mission team goes to a foreign field with the gospel. They forget that often, as in the case of Indonesia, such important tools as instruction materials that agree with our Lutheran confessions must first be developed or translated. This also means that the missionaries must know the language in which they work.

Although the Indonesian language is not as complicated as Chinese and Japanese, it has its difficulties. Both missionaries soon learned that sometimes a misspoken syllable can give a word an entirely different meaning. To the obvious amusement of his congregation, Festerling experienced this when preaching his first Christmas sermon. He spoke about the shepherds coming with haste and finding Mary and the baby—not in the "*kandang*" (manger), but in the "*kandung*" (womb)!

Howard Festerling, Bruce Ahlers, and Robert Sawall formed the first missionary team for Indonesia. Also shown, Judy Festerling and Charlene Sawall.

The Sawalls finally arrived after over three years of waiting! Sawall's previous missionary experience in Africa as well as his parish experience and his radio ministry in Wisconsin and in Texas added a wealth of evangelism know-how to the field. The

Sawall home served as outreach center, attracting a number of dedicated and talented young people to the church.

The Work Progresses

The year 1984 is described by Missionary Festerling as one of those "good news/bad news" years. The good news was the approval and purchase of a church-parsonage facility for Trinity congregation in Jakarta, where Rev. Pandji and his family could live and hold services and where he continued to serve until his death in 1991. The bad news was that the Religion Department of Indonesia would allow expatriate staff only if it was directly involved in worker-training activities. The government also forbade the evangelizing of anyone belonging to a "permitted religion" (Catholic, Buddhist, Islamic, Hindu). This made for an "underlying feeling of uncertainty" concerning the progress of the work, as one missionary described it, since it involved problems with the visa extension of missionaries as well as possible deportation if any misunderstandings should arise. Only a missionary living in a foreign atmosphere can fully appreciate this feeling.

The Festerlings left the field in 1984 after accepting a stateside call. Ahlers and Sawall organized a Bible institute curriculum and began a worker-training program in a rented facility in Jakarta. This served as a dormitory and classroom for the school, a chapel for worship, and a residence for the Sawalls. In America we sometimes find it necessary to house two church needs under one roof. In a foreign mission field it can involve three, which is just fine if it can be counted on as a dependable arrangement. Unfortunately, the three-year contract on this multi-purpose facility could not be renewed.

Another period of reorganizing and relocation of missionaries, evangelists, and programs followed. Rev. Gary Schult completed his language study and filled the vacancy left by Festerling's departure. Schult was assigned the care of worker training. Ahlers served as administrator and Sawall as mission developer. Work was reopened on Bali, and several other mission congregations were begun. With Sawall's return to America in 1989, Gregory Bey arrived to help carry on the work for the next chapter in the story of Indonesian missions.

"Surely, The Islands Look To Me"

The first twenty years of this work have had their share of "highs" as well as "lows." The German poet Goethe speaks of life in terms of soaring in the heights of heaven and sorrowing in the throes of death. In a similar sense, every missionary has such moments. There are clouds and there are depths, days of victory and joy and days of disappointments and problems. Some of these things are beyond the control of executive planners and missionaries. Some can be chalked up to bad advice, inexperience, and misunderstandings. One also has to learn to expect frustrating red tape and delays as well as outright opposition from those who are enemies of the gospel. The Apostle Paul has given us fair warning about all this in his epistles.

Despite it all, the testimony of God's grace, protection, and blessing has been richly experienced in this Moslem land. Six missionary families have been given the opportunity to hold out the word of life. Faithful national workers, a most necessary ingredient, have always been there to help keep things moving, even when problems seemed insurmountable. New congregations have been planted. Christian literature and training materials have been produced in the Indonesian language. A Bible institute and seminary have been established. Increasingly, graduates are assuming the task of reaching out to their fellow Indonesians. The "few mouthpieces" that our first missionary to this land spoke about have been multiplied. With God's blessing, these voices of salvation will continue to proclaim the gospel in the world's fifth most populous country. Already through his prophet Isaiah, the LORD declared: "The wealth of the seas will be brought to you, and the riches of the nations will come. . . . Surely the islands look to me" (Isaiah 60:5,8).

TAIWAN

Taiwan is an island in the Pacific Ocean about one hundred miles directly east of Hong Kong. It has a population of nearly 20 million people, most of whom are ethnic Chinese living in an area of 14,000 square miles.

Howard Festerling broadcasting the "Voice of Salvation" brings the radio message to listeners in both Hong Kong and Taiwan.

The Portuguese explorers called it "Ilha Formosa"— the beautiful island. For the Chinese Nationalists under Chiang Kaishek it became a haven, when in 1949 they had to flee their homeland following the Communist takeover of mainland China.

For the Chinese Evangelical Lutheran Church (CELC) of Hong Kong the island became "a mission field with bright potential," when in 1964 it was able to beam its Voice of Salvation broadcasts to the Taiwanese people. In fact, the Taiwanese government granted daily half-hour broadcasts into the schools of Taipei, Taiwan's capital city, free of charge.

Our synod's mission work in Taiwan began as a follow-up on prospects attracted by these radio broadcasts. In 1967 CELC sent Mr. Wong Siu Han to Taiwan for this purpose. His first service on May 11 of that year (Mothers' Day) was attended by 20 people. In 1968 two graduates from the CELC seminary in Hong Kong were assigned to Taiwan. One of these was Victor Cheung, a brother of Peter Chang, CELC's president. When the other vicar failed to accept the assignment, he was replaced by Rev. Timothy Lee, a 1967 graduate of the Hong Kong seminary. Both of these men played prominent roles in the development of this mission. Unfortunately Mr. Wong discontinued his work a bit later, when he was asked to continue his theological studies in Hong Kong.

Everlasting Happiness Village

In 1970 Mr. Martin Lin, a man trained by the Presbyterian Church, offered his services and free land in his home village in the Changhwa/Taichung area. The village was called "Everlasting Happiness." Mr. Lin agreed to receive training in Lutheran doctrine. His offer was accepted and

The people at Everlasting Happiness Village worship in Holy Trinity Lutheran Church.

plans were made to build a church with an attached parsonage at this place.

When it was reported by Victor Cheung that the donated site was "in poor location," arrangements were made for the purchase of "a more central location" by Rev. Peter Chang. Later it was discovered that the land was purchased in the name of Victor Cheung, and that the church built here was on property for which WELS held no title. The church was dedicated on New Year's Day, 1971, with 450 people in attendance. Although later some rather disturbing events were to take place here, Everlasting Happiness Village now had a place where the everlasting happiness offered in God's Word would be proclaimed.

Problems with Manpower

Peter Chang's resignation from the ministry, reported in the previous section on Hong Kong, produced few visible ripples in Taiwan. Progress toward incorporating the "Taiwan District of the CELC," however, seemed to run into all sorts of problems. Did this have something to do with the land purchase in Everlasting Happiness village? Since at this time none of the WELS missionaries in Hong Kong spoke Mandarin, it was difficult for them and the stateside executive committee to know what really was happening. They were dependent on nationals when dealing in such complicated transactions.

It was at about this time that Timothy Lee, who was heading up the work in Taiwan, resigned and returned to Hong Kong, leaving the work in charge of Victor Cheung. Because of the resultant lack of manpower, Taiwan became pretty much a holding operation. It became clear that the field needed resident supervision, but the only help that could be sent at the time was in the

Pastors Victor Cheung (left) and Timothy Lee compare notes with missionaries Paul Behn (far left) and Gerald Lange at Everlasting Happiness Village.

person of Vicar Daniel Lee, a 1973 graduate of the Hong Kong seminary. Vicar Lee spotted some potential help in the person of a 52-year-old member of Our Savior Lutheran Church in Taipei, Mr. Chen Tung Ke. Lee reported to Friendly Counselor John Chworowsky: "Mr. Chen is so keen on learning the Bible that he comes to the church every morning to listen and to read God's word. . . . Can our church offer him any training program? What I understand is that he can talk about Jesus to strangers far better than I do." As a result of Lee's request, Chen was sent to Everlasting Happiness Village as translator and lay evangelist, a step that would lead to rich blessings for the Taiwan field.

Help from America

When Daniel Lee returned to Hong Kong after his year of vicarage, the field's three widely scattered congregations were again chiefly in the care of one man, Victor Cheung. An in-depth report on the work on the island by Chworowsky strongly recommended that the field receive missionary help. The 1977 WELS convention, which authorized ten new missionaries for our world missions, designated three of them for Taiwan. The first three-man team consisted of Rev. Marcus Manthey, Rev. Robert Meister, and Rev. Charles D. Found, who with their wives arrived on the field in late 1979 and early 1980.

Sending three men to a foreign field is one thing; preparing them for the actual work is quite another. It involves getting situated in strange living quarters, getting acquainted with the exotic environment, and above all learning the culture and language of the people— all this before any real effective organization of the work itself can be undertaken. It was, therefore, a happy day when on May 10, 1981 (Mothers' Day), Missionary Meister preached his first sermon in Mandarin. To the very Sunday, this was exactly 14 years after Mr. Wong Siu Han had gathered together the twenty people for the mission's first service on Taiwan.

Cheung Disappears

As things progressed it became evident that a mission center was needed in Taipei, Taiwan's leading city. A worship/education/office facility was rented. Plans for a more tightly structured church organization were undertaken. When the time came, however, for Victor Cheung to sign over the deed for

Trinity Church of Everlasting Happiness village, he suddenly disappeared from the scene. It was discovered that Cheung had mortgaged the church property to the tune of $16,000 and had engaged in other financial dealings of a more personal nature, leaving behind a total indebtedness of about $25,000! Although in subsequent court proceedings the Holy Trinity congregation was granted the use of its church building, it had to continue negotiations with the "owner" of the land if it wished to make full use of the property on which the church stood. It wasn't until April 1986 that the matter was finally settled.

In the meantime the work continued. Relatively few members defected as a result of Cheung's "disappearance." There were a number of changes in missionary personnel, but by the year 1984 the staff was back to full strength, with the Robert Meister, Ralph Jones, and Robert Siirila families on the field and involved in the work.

Significant Changes

A significant change took place in 1985, when one of the Taipei congregations received its own ordained national pastor. Evangelist Chen Tung Ke finally realized the fulfillment of a dream he had long pursued. It had been more than 11 years since Vicar Lee had "discovered" this man and his ardent desire to serve his Lord. The man who Lee said "can talk about Jesus to strangers far better than I" now could begin doing it as an ordained pastor— at age 63!

Chen's growing congregation in Taipei also came to have its own place of worship after ten years of renting. This came about as a result of a loan made possible by the WELS "Reaching Out" offering. Seven months after Chen Tung Ke's ordination, this congregation was privileged to dedicate its new home. The eighth-floor church and the

Rev. Chen Tung Ke, the first Taiwan national to become a pastor, serves two congregations in the Taipei area.

second-floor parsonage would probably seem unusual to most of the WELS brothers and sisters back in the States, but high land prices dictated that kind of facility in Taiwan. A grant of $90,000 was needed for the facility, of which the congregation agreed to repay one-third over the next eight years. The money repaid is to flow into the Taiwan Church Extension Fund, so that the "Reaching Out" money might continue to reach out in ever widening circles in Taiwan.

An additional blessing for Taiwan from the "Reaching Out" offering was the 1985 acquisition of a building for a Bible institute, a seminary, and a permanent home for Fountain of Grace Lutheran Church. Missionary Siirila became the congregation's pastor as well as administrator and instructor for the Bible institute program. He was assisted by the other missionaries, each of whom took an active part in teaching at the new facility.

Most of the classes were offered on weekends and evenings, making it possible for students to keep their regular jobs and still get the theological training they desired. Besides Pastor Chen, four graduates of the Bible institute—Tan Hwei-Lin, Chen Ywe-De, Chen Ywe-Min, and Tsai Ming, Jr.—have gone on to serve the church as evangelists. The church hopes to open a seminary in Taipei in the 1990s.

Mission Established

In 1986 Missionary Siirila completed his language study, another milestone event for the Taiwan church. It had taken nine years for the three-man missionary team authorized by the 1977 WELS Synod Convention to become a functioning three-man, Chinese-speaking missionary team. Missionary personnel changes have a way of delaying the achievement of this world mission policy goal. It is a real joy when the expatriates can work together with the nationals in the languages of the country.

In the same year, 1986, it became possible for the Taiwan church to be legally incorporated and recognized by the government. This, too, is an important step in a mission's development and takes more time and effort than is often realized. The leaders chose the name "Christian Lutheran Evangelical Church" (CLEC) for the new church body. Its board of directors is made up of seven men, four Chinese and three expatriate missionaries. This board of directors immediately set about planning a work program for the coming years. Its strategy included the formation of a CLEC Church Extension Fund with the policy "that all new expansion work be funded by the national church." In addition, there was a stated goal of reaching freedom from direct WELS subsidy by 1993.

The establishment of an experienced mission staff together with the organization of a national church body meant that mission outreach could go forward in full gear. Missionary Meister was authorized to begin work in a new outreach facility in the Taichung area, located a hundred miles to the south of Taipei. It is called "The Lutheran Gospel Center." This outreach augments the work done in nearby Everlasting Happiness Village. The responsibilities are shared by Meister and two part-time evangelists in the English, Taiwanese, and Mandarin languages.

Another outreach opportunity was located in Fusying, where a preaching station was begun in the heart of the most traditionally religious area in all of Taiwan. Here the goddess Ma Tsu, guardian of fisherfolk and their craft, is highly esteemed. The area as a result has fewer churches per capita than any other in Taiwan. Yet even here the work of CLEC is spreading the good news and gaining a foothold!

More Beautiful Every Day

Thus after years of frustrating language studies, legal hassles, and organizational problems, the work was finally going forward in Taiwan at a more encouraging pace. Rev. Kurt Koeplin, chairman of the Executive Committee for Southeast Asian Missions, ended his 1987 report to the synod with an urgent plea for more missionaries, missionaries that had already been authorized by the 1985 convention. He declared,

> Number four was needed last year and number five is needed now! The work load, the waiting harvest field, the isolation of the Meister family from the balance of the team, all impel us toward finding an immediate solution to the fiscal problems of our synodical budget which would allow us to call missionary number four!

By August 1988 "number four" was in Taiwan with the arrival of Rev. David Kriehn and family. Unlike the missionaries who went before him, the Kriehns did not set up housekeeping in Taipei and start studying the Mandarin dialect. Instead, they settled in Taichung where the Meisters lived and began learning Taiwanese, the language of the native people of the island. Bible institute work was also extended to this area, offering training for those unable to travel to the capital city.

An important goal was reached when the fifth missionary was added to the Taiwan team. Its members: R. Meister, R. Siirila, D. Kriehn, R. Jones, T. Meier.

In Taipei itself the work continues to progress. The Chinese pastor there is a man of 67 who "can talk to strangers." His love for his Savior continues to inspire his members and his missionary colleagues. The newest of these is Rev. Timothy Meier, who arrived with his wife Mary on February 19, 1990. Like the Kriehns before them they are living, studying, and working in the Taichung area. Taiwanese is spoken by 75 percent of Taiwan's citizens, and the work is being carried on more and more in that language.

The horizon looks promising. The harvest is plentiful. The hands to serve have been provided. A gracious God has brought the ever widening circle of the gospel to Ilha Formosa. And the "beautiful island" is getting more beautiful every day because of it.

INDIA

India occupies most of the south Asian subcontinent, jutting out into the mighty Indian Ocean. One-third the size of the United States, it has over three times as many people. Most of these are villagers, many of whom live far below what we would consider poverty level. Urban India, by way of contrast, is one of the most highly industrialized areas in the world. After many years of nonviolent resistance under Mahatma Gandhi, India finally achieved its independence from British colonial rule in 1947.

India has always captured the fancy of Christian missionaries. Earliest evidences of civilization date back to the third and second millenniums B.C. Christianity may have come there as early as the first century A.D. Tradition has it that the apostle Thomas suffered martyrdom as a missionary to India. Francis Xavier, the famous Jesuit missionary, began work in India in 1542 and is credited with phenomenal mass conversions there. Protestant missionary work was initiated in 1706 by the German Lutheran pietist Bartholomaeus Ziegenbalg. The British Baptist William Carey went to India in 1793. Although originally a shoemaker by trade, Carey's zeal for foreign missions and his abilities as Bible translator in India have won for him the reputation as "Father of Modern Missions." In spite of these efforts Hinduism still controls 85 percent of India's 800,000 people. Another ten percent is Moslem, and Christianity, after centuries of difficult work, has had to content itself with two and one-half percent of India's population.

An Unexpected Appeal

India was not high on the list of countries WELS considered entering as the 1960s drew to a close. The Executive Committee for Chinese Missions didn't even make a stop there on its 1968 exploratory trip. There were other countries where it was felt the limited mission dollars would be put to better use.

Before the 1960s were over, however, India came to our synod's attention by way of an unusual appeal. A man named T. Paul Mitra, a lay-evangelist and leading light of the India Rural Gospel Mission, had received some Bibles from a Scripture distribution society in England. One of the books received contained the name of Mrs. Edward Zacharias, wife of the pastor of Grace Lutheran Church in Flint, Michigan. Before her local Lutheran Women's Missionary So-

Pastor T. Paul Mitra and his wife Sugunam were the first to serve as WELS messengers of the gospel in India.

ciety sent a shipment of Bibles off to England, Mrs. Zacharias had put her name and address in each of them. One of these ended up in Madras, India, where T. Paul Mitra lived. Madras is the capital city of Tamil State on the Bay of Bengal, and is an industrial center of nearly four million people.

Mitra clearly wanted assistance, and he wrote to the Zachariases' address. His earliest letters requested help in gaining "the necessary Bible study and evangelical training in America." Not long after this he also expressed the need for "a headquarters and a place for 200 to meet . . . and a van for camping equipment."

A period of correspondence between Mitra and WELS leaders ensued. Many searching questions were asked. Generally, Mitra's requests gave the impression of modesty, dedication, and conservative Lutheran confessionalism. After receiving a letter from Mitra, Rev. Edgar Hoenecke, Executive Secretary of the synod's Board for World Missions, wrote to President O. J. Naumann, "I am trembling at the thought of the responsibility and the opportunity for Christ which this Christian letter unfolds to us. . . . May I urge that at our next opportunity we confer to take steps to respond to this humble confessor's request."

How those two words "responsibility" and "opportunity" would cause a spiritual tug-of-war in Hoenecke for the next few years! Here was an opening to millions. But how should the matter be handled? Should a visit be made to India? Should Mitra come for an interview? Could something be done through correspondence courses? Or seminary training at Lusaka or Hong Kong or Mequon? It became clear that Mitra wanted nothing less than to study in America.

The Executive Committee for Southeast Asian Missions visited India in November 1969. Chairman Marlyn Schroeder wrote: "We have had 15 hours of meetings with Mitra and wife. A remarkable couple with dedication very seldom seen in our day. Our stop was worth every dollar."

Within eight months, permission was granted for the eventual trip of Mitra and his wife to the United States. Early in January 1970 Mitra began five months of special classes arranged for him at Wisconsin Lutheran Seminary. He was ordained and commissioned to return to India to serve the few fellow believers he had gathered there and to extend the work.

Unfortunately, the years that follow tell a rather depressing story. Reports of unreceptive people, political unrest, destructive storms, illness, lack of proper facilities, etc. consistently occupy the spot designated "India" in our synod convention *Proceedings*. Little if any progress was indicated. Even the van that Mitra had so long desired and had been provided through many individual gifts of WELS' members failed to change matters. Efforts were made to encourage Mitra through visits of the Friendly Counselor from Hong Kong. In 1982 the Executive Committee for Southeast Asian Missions visited the field. Nothing much ever happened. In one of its last reports to the synod this committee stated, "Unless and until we can get expatriates into the country (prohibited on a permanent basis by the government of India), it appears we will have to content ourselves with a marginal presence."

In 1988 it was decided by the Board for World Missions that because India as yet had no expatriate missionary, the responsibility for the work in that country be turned over to the Committee for Interim Missions of the Board for World Missions. This committee has been reorganized and renamed the "Committee for Mission Expansion." Presently this committee is undertaking a restudy of the work. Contacts are being pursued with a Pastor Devabhushanam, who is working among Telugu-speaking people in several villages about 50 miles north of Madras. Other appeals are being investigated.

It is hard to know whether this chapter of WELS mission history is slowly being closed or just beginning to unfold. So far our experiences have been disheartening. Perhaps we need to be reminded that it was possibly India where Thomas, yes, doubting-Thomas, served his Lord. Perhaps we need once again to dare trust that there is a rich harvest field in India, committing our faith and resources to bringing this harvest into the Master's storehouse.

MISSION CURRENTS SEVEN
CHANGING SCENES

Mission work never remains static. Mission fields experience this. Mission boards know this. Missionaries are constantly aware of this. Personnel changes; stages of development change; areas of activity change; the status quo changes. To remain at a standstill means to go backwards. That's what makes the work so alive, so exciting, and perhaps sometimes so painstaking. Edgar Hoenecke has quoted the old German *"Feldmarschall"* Bluecher in support of this: "Our battle cry must always be '*Vorwaerts!*' Advance!"

President Oscar Naumann set this kind of mission emphasis for the 1971 Synod Convention when he chose as theme Paul's quotation from the Psalms in First Corinthians: "We also believe and therefore speak." The synod responded, as we shall see later, by unanimously resolving to enter another continent, namely South America.

Other changes followed. We have already seen that the synod voted in 1975 to enter Cameroon. In Europe the center of interest was changing from West Germany to Sweden. Christ the King Lutheran Synod in Nigeria was requesting our help. With work developing on five continents, the various executive committees of the Board for World Missions were being constantly pressured for additional manpower. From the early exploratory stage, the fields were becoming increasingly involved in worker training programs, development of Christian literature in national languages, mass communication, expansion efforts, and building projects. These positive developments, of course, caused some natural growing pains. In 1979 the Board for World Missions announced the addition, within one biennium, of eight missionaries to its various far-flung fields.

The 1979 roster of the Wisconsin Synod saw two significant personnel changes. Because of President Oscar Naumann's unexpected death, First Vice-President Carl Mischke replaced him in the chair. Pastor Theodore Sauer had begun serving as executive secretary of the Board for World Missions, replacing Edgar Hoenecke, who had retired in 1978. In view of the influence of both Naumann and Hoenecke on the development of world missions in our synod, these changes could be looked upon as considerable. The Lord, however, has his own way of finding the right replacements at the right time.

Mischke's reemphasis on strengthening the home base became necessary because of fiscal problems affecting the entire country as well as the synod in 1981. A situation had arisen whereby the synod treasurer had to pay an effective rate of interest up to 24 percent on money he had to borrow to keep the synod's work going. Some serious regrouping of forces needed attention. Under Carl Mischke's calm and capable leadership the crisis passed, and the synod was again able to place more emphasis on its wider work. The synod can rest assured that this balance will be maintained as long as he has anything to say about it. The synod will continue to "Lift High the Cross" both at home and abroad.

The synod continues to "Lift High the Cross" under Carl Mischke's leadership.

Our historical survey is already replete with Hoenecke's activities. He was truly a pioneer, an organizer, an innovator, and all this flowing out of a deep Scripture-based conviction that the mission of the church is primarily mission work. Not only was he involved in matters directly connected with the work of the board itself, he also spearheaded any number of ancillary programs, such as the world mission seminars at the Wisconsin Lutheran Seminary, which help our men preparing for the ministry get an idea of what it is like out on the mission fields; the World Seminary Exchange Program, whereby the Mequon professors get a taste of the actual work on the mission fields; the World Seminary and World Mission Conferences, which bring missionaries together for an interchange of ideas; and the Medical Mission Program, which he and his wife Meta blueprinted and helped get started in Central Africa. To go into detail on any of these items would fill another volume. Each one of them has helped support the work of world missions perhaps more than one can say.

Missionaries out on the field also knew that they had someone at home to back them up. This writer recalls vividly a visit of Pastor Hoenecke to Central Africa in 1967. Our work there was progressing on all fronts. Opportunities were beckoning everywhere, but we just didn't seem to have the men and the means to reach out adequately. Somehow it didn't take long after Hoenecke's visit for mission logistics from the home base to supply the needs on the battlefront! Hoenecke had once firmly believed that Africa would "soon stretch out her hands unto

The 1977 Board for World Missions Executive Committee, Clarence Krause, William Meier, and Raymond Zimmermann with Executive Secretary Edgar Hoenecke

God." Having seen it actually taking place, he wasn't about to see the work falter for lack of support.

If this writer regards Pastor Hoenecke as a mentor, he considers Pastor Sauer, Hoenecke's successor, as a brother. Our mutual assignments in Zambia, Malawi, Cameroon, Nigeria, and South America give ample evidence of that. Many a sticky situation was encountered that needed his ever patient, diplomatic treatment. One could certainly not wish for a more compatible partner. Hoenecke and Sauer had varied gifts. Each fit into his time, and the time had come under Sauer that the office of executive secretary with its burgeoning fiscal and operational complications be brought to Milwaukee. Coordinating the business of a world board with six executive committees, each involved with varied world situations, plus dealing with the various other departments of the synod, can get pretty intricate, especially when concerned with budgets and projections. We may not especially like all these complications, but it seems that in this modern world of ours they are as inescapable as death and taxes. From his varied background as synod secretary, district president, missionary superintendent, and world board member, Pastor Sauer was not only the ideal coordinator but one with a heart for missions born out of personal experience.

Duane Tomhave became world mission administrator in 1984.

Another change rates special mention during this period of history. After 39 years of world mission board service in one capacity or another, Chairman Raymond Zimmermann retired in 1981. His concise reports to the synod and his direction of world board affairs always reflected a world vision. These were truly men who could say with Isaiah, "My eyes have seen the King, the Lord."

Changes, of course, are inevitable. A William Meier replaces a Raymond Zimmermann in 1981. A Duane Tomhave replaces a Theodore Sauer as executive secretary in 1984. A worker-training counselor, John Kurth, is added as a called worker to the world mission staff in 1985. Although the contributions of these men still lie very much with the present and toward the future, one can only be encouraged by the fresh zeal and efficiency with which they have taken hold of their difficult tasks. Somehow we learn from these changes that no person is indispensable. The work goes ahead, and marvelously so!

World Mission John Kurth was added to the synod's world mission staff in 1985.

No doubt the most extensive and far-reaching changes during our synod's world mission development over the past several decades have to do with its work among Latin Americans. We have already observed how this work leapfrogged, one might say, from Tucson, Arizona (1948) to Puerto Rico (1963) to El Paso, Texas (1966) and to Mexico (1968). But what about South America? What actually preceded the synod's unanimous vote to enter that vast continent? Then, having entered one part of it, what led to the synod's involvement in another part of South America far away, where Portuguese was spoken instead of Spanish?

To follow this development we must again return to the assignment facing the synod's Executive Committee for Latin American Missions.

THE SLEEPING GIANT TO THE SOUTH
SOUTH AMERICA

We Begin in Colombia

"001" — That's how he introduced himself. The Executive Committee for Latin America, composed of Pastors Harold Essmann and Richard Lauersdorf and lay member, Robert Grebe, (all of whom were to serve for 20 years or more) was making its first field visit to Colombia, South America. Standing before them and broadly beaming was the first confirmand in our mission. Reinaldo Gomez was his name, and he worked as an official at one of the large banks in the city of Medellin. But to the committee he introduced himself joyously as "001," the first member of what was to become the Confessional Lutheran Church of Colombia (ILCC).

How did the WELS come to enter that sleeping giant to the south that we know as the continent of South America? Not by a direct route nor very quickly, but at the time and in a way that experienced the Lord's blessing. Already in the *Proceedings* of the 1963 convention, we read the statement:

> All of Latin America is being considered by our Board as our next large mission expansion area. It is the only large

inhabited continent in which our Synod is not now active. All reports agree that the pure Gospel is needed.

That was 1963. Five years later in the 1968 *Report to the Nine Districts*, Executive Secretary Hoenecke of the Board for World Missions could report that Theodore Sauer, on authorization by the board, had carried out a six-week survey of South America, financed by a special gift given especially for this purpose. This survey had indicated many areas where mission work in Spanish, German, and Portuguese could be carried out.

Two more years passed before the Board for World Missions authorized the Latin American Committee to make a second survey of that "sleeping giant to the south." Missioners Eggert and Zimdars were chosen and, after an intensive three-month survey, recommended three areas, any of which could well serve as a starting base for a mission thrust into South America.

In its report to the 1971 convention, the Latin American Committee recommended sending a three-man team of missioners to one of these areas, namely, to Medellin, Colombia. This city offered opportunity for work in a heavily populated area, among people of all classes, especially among a higher than average middle class population. This location also gave promise of expansion into other areas of Colombia. The theme of that convention was "We Believe . . . and Therefore Speak." The delegates showed it was a fitting theme when they unanimously resolved to send a team of two pastors and one male teacher "to go in Jesus' name and proclaim the Gospel in South America."

The convention had passed a resolution, but there was no money for expanding the work into South America until the Lord provided in a most generous way. In September 1972 the synod received a gift of $144,000 from a corporation owned by a WELS family. This gift was to cover costs for opening our mission in that sleeping giant to our south. And it did. That amount, with the interest it would earn and with other gifts from concerned people, underwrote the South American mission budget for its first four years.

It was also up to the Lord to provide the men for the mission team. Again he did. Normally just to land a missioner on the field takes at least twelve months—six months for the calling process and another six for language training. Consider that three missioners were to be called, and you can see how easily months can fly by. But on August 14, 1973, only two years after the resolution to enter South America, the New Ulm synod convention in its closing service had the joy of commissioning Pastors Roger Sprain and Ernest Zimdars, both veterans in our Spanish work, and Teacher Francis Warner to be our first team to the sleeping giant.

Francis Warner, Roger Sprain, and Ernest Zimdars were the first team of missioners to serve in Colombia.

Another important part of foreign mission work is obtaining visas, permits, and proper documents. Form after form, all in Spanish, were filled out and properly stamped at the Colombian consulate. Still, our missioners were told they could not be given resident visas since the synod was not incorporated in Colombia. Again the Lord provided. Provisional residence visas were granted when the synod's Board of Trustees assured the Colombian government that we would incorporate as soon as possible after the men reached the field.

Another vital ingredient in foreign mission work, or any kingdom work, is prayer. On Sunday, January 20, 1974, a synod-wide day of prayer was held for the missioners, one of whom was already on his way, with the other two shortly to follow.

In an article in *The Northwestern Lutheran*, Missioner Sprain requested:

> The Lord is not sending us to build churches or imposing organizations. His purpose with us is to win all those whom God has ordained to salvation with the gospel call. We cannot begin to do this in our own strength; we will need God's abundant grace in our planning, our surveys, and our outreach. He must show us in which area of Medellin, a city of over a million, we are to begin. He must guide us to those whom He wants us to reach. How indispensable it is that God's will be done in these very first steps! For this we would ask you to join us in praying. . . . Let the petition, "Thy kingdom come!" now also include the new South

American mission at Medellin, Colombia, as you come before the Lord daily in the prayer He has taught us!

God's people responded to the missioner's request, and a gracious God in turn responded to their fervent prayers.

Arrival on the Field

Two weeks later, on February 3, 1974, the first WELS service was conducted in Medellin in the home of one of the missioners. Only the team members and their families were present, but by May the missioners reported an average of five Colombians in the Sunday services. In mid-March an instruction class was started with Reinaldo Gomez and his family, and on August 25, just seven months after the missioners had arrived on South American soil, Señor Gomez became "001!" Moreover, on that same memorable day "The Message of Salvation" was broadcast for the first time on Colombian airwaves.

Señor Reinaldo Gomez became the first member of the church in Medellin.

Just one year after setting foot on the soil of the sleeping giant, our missioners could joyously write about a congregation being organized in a Medellin residential area under the name of Santa Trinidad (Holy Trinity). They could tell of a Sunday attendance averaging around 50, of seven adults and two teenagers already confirmed and seven more interested persons enrolled in classes.

They also reported the establishment of a preaching station in Envigado, a large suburb of Medellin. Here a small group was enrolled in Sunday school and five in instruction class. The other preaching station of which they spoke was located in Versalles, a large *barrio* or ward far up the hillside in the eastern part of the city. There, fifty children were attending Sunday school and twelve adults the Bible-study group. The missioners were working hard, and God was blessing their efforts.

Preparing National Workers

The objective for our work in Colombia was not just to gather souls but to help establish an indigenous church. One vital ingredient in such a church is a supply of national pastors, properly instructed for the public ministry. That commodity is often hard to come by. Frequently, years go by before there are any students to train.

La Santa Trinidad, the first congregation to be organized in Medellin

But not in Colombia. Already during the first year of the mission's existence something happened that was to have an impact on the work into the future. A young man, Omar Ortiz, who had been studying for the Roman priesthood, had changed his mind. Then, rejected by his family and excommunicated by his church, he had walked into the study of a Presbyterian pastor in Medellin and poured out his heart. "Omar," that pastor responded after listening and recognizing that the young man was more Lutheran than Presbyterian, "I have good news for you. There are Lutherans in Medellin."

That was Omar's introduction to our mission, and with it our missioners had thrust upon them the need to provide theological training. After his confirmation in the Lutheran faith, Omar still wanted to serve his Lord in the public ministry. Who would teach him, what courses should he have, what Spanish materials were available? His training involved a four-year Bible study program followed by a two-year preseminary program in a Bible institute, then two years of supervised work as an evangelist in one or more of the congregations, and finally a four-year seminary program. Can we even begin to imagine the hours the missioners invested in planning the program, preparing the materials, and instructing Omar and another young man who had come one year later?

Finally on November 28, 1982, graduation came and Pastor Ortiz was called to serve Santisima Trinidad (Most Holy Trinity) Congregation in Medellin. Here was the first Colombian pastor, one of their own and one whom they would support on their own. God had granted this progress much sooner than we had dared hope or expect.

Organizing the National Church

Planting an indigenous church also means consulting with and involving the people as soon as possible. This process is slow, but necessary, so that the nationals will eventually take over from the missioners. In Colombia the first fruits were seen in July 1979, when the Colombian church officially organized itself as the *Iglesia Luterana Confesional de Colombia*. Its Articles of Incorporation were accepted by the government, and the small church body formed itself into the necessary boards for carrying out its work. The learning and growing process takes time but eventually leads to an independent church body, one that will stand at the side of WELS as a sister.

Meanwhile other changes had been occurring. The work continued in Santa Trinidad, which by now had its own chapel. The Versalles group also had its own chapel, while the Envigado group, fraught with difficulties, had been forced to move several times. Work also had expanded into the new area of Belen Las Playas, a subdivision of the city.

In 1982 a shift in strategy led to the formation of a downtown central congregation. Though work continued in the various outlying areas, this central group of over a hundred members was established for worship and fellowship purposes. This was Santisima Trinidad and was the group that called Omar Ortiz as its pastor. Their first worship facility was a hotel conference room. Later, aided by funds from the WELS Reaching Out offering, this group purchased a funeral home in a choice location and remodeled it into their house of worship.

The missioner staff also changed. As the work progressed, the fourth and fifth missioners were allocated by the synod. Larry Schlomer came as theological director for the emerging program and was later replaced by James Connell. Lawrence Retberg became field counselor in place of Roger Sprain, who had accepted a call to a stateside congregation. Later, James Kuehl was called to this post. Other names were Mark Goeglein, who subsequently moved to El Paso, and Thomas Heyn, who was called to stateside Spanish work after one tour of duty in Colombia. As of this writing, Philip Strackbein, Stuart Freese, and Carl Leyrer serve as our missioners in Colombia.

The Move to Bogota

With the change in strategy resulting in the formation of Santisima Trinidad Congregation, and with Omar Ortiz called to serve this consolidated group, two of our missioners were freed to start work in another city of Colombia.

In 1978 the goal of a five-man missioner team for Colombia was realized. The five men were Larry Schlomer, Roger Sprain, Mark Goeglein, Lawrence Retberg, and Ernest Zimdars.

In June 1983 Strackbein and Goeglein moved with their families to Bogota, the capital of Colombia, with a population of well over four million. At first, services were held in the missioner's home. Then a conference room was rented in a downtown hotel. In that rented room, the missioners planned to show the Martin Luther film in commemoration of the great Reformer's 500th birthday and then the following Sunday to hold a worship service. Newspaper advertisements invited the public to come free of charge.

Imagine the joy of the two missioners when on Sunday, August 21, they showed the film twice to a total of 235 people and turned another 100 away because of lack of room. The following Sunday they marveled again as God filled that room with a capacity crowd of 109 for their first worship service. From these events came a list of 40 people who indicated their desire to learn more about the word. At least one of the first confirmands in Bogota would come from that list.

"What blessings the Lord has bestowed on this mission field," the Latin American Committee reported to the synod in 1983, "so that in such a short time, less than ten years, we now have a national pastor, a church that can support that pastor, and additional students in our theological studies program as well as a new area in which to do mission work in Colombia!"

Obstacles

Another factor in foreign mission work, again as in all kingdom work, is the obstacles to overcome. The unbelieving world and the father of lies, who is behind it, often get in the way. Missioner Sprain reported in 1980:

> The task is herculean, not just because there are over two million people in Medellin, but because of the family and social pressures and also because the people have known only one church for centuries. A clear example of this is what happened when several of our Lutheran young people, ages 17 to 22, joined the church. They were either disowned and told to move out of their homes or were verbally and even physically abused. One missionary in the middle of his class was called a liar and worse. Another had several month's work totally undone when one afternoon the local religious leader told the people that they couldn't listen to the foreigner.

For a time, due to governmental restrictions, the granting of visas for our missioners to enter the country slowed down and even stopped completely. These delays in filling vacancies and new positions on the field did not help the growth or stability of the field.

A natural phenomenon observed in other fields occurred in Colombia, too. After an initial surge, a mission field levels off and sometimes even goes backward as the gospel seed wilts on shallow ground or is choked in weedy soil.

One of the most distressing events, however, was the resignation for personal reasons of Pastor Omar Ortiz, the only Colombian pastor. His resignation along with the suspension of a final-year student forced our missioners in Medellin to remain there, serving Santisima Trinidad Congregation instead of being able to carry out their plans to expand the base for the Colombian church by moving to a new area.

The Work Goes On

The work goes on under the direction and with the blessing of a gracious Lord. Changing circumstances dictate changing strategy. The most recent emphasis is again on evangelism, both by our missioners and by the Colombians. In Bogota, the first of several Christian information centers has been opened. These centers are designed to attract people who might want to learn more about the Bible without attending formal worship services. Here they can take a sixteen-unit Bible information course via a rear-screen projector. Such a center has also been opened in Medellin.

Recently one of our missionaries moved to a third major city in Columbia, namely Cali. The work there has already begun.

With this we close our look at our synod's first venture into the Sleeping Giant to the south. By way of summary, Pastor Sprain said it well back in 1980. He wrote:

> Despite the large tasks ahead, we are convinced that the Lord who caused this church to be born through His Word will also see to it that it is nourished and grows. Of that we are confident, for He established the Wisconsin Evangelical Lutheran Synod in the same way. Once you were just a few small groups here and there in WISCONSIN. So are we—in Colombia. Once you took the name EVANGELICAL because you had and loved the Gospel. So do we. You had your problems, but you remained firm in the LUTHERAN doctrine. So we. Now you are a large SYNOD. And, by God's grace, we too will be, for we are but a retouched photo of you 130 years ago.

On Sunday, January 20, 1974, a synod-wide day of prayer had been held for our missioners on the way to the promising new field on the great continent to our south. Our prayers and support are no less necessary today!

BRAZIL

A Persistent Appeal

In the "sleeping giant to the south," besides Colombia, the WELS has another mission, our newest field. In October 1987 we began our work among the 154 million people of Brazil. Again, the account of how we arrived there is intriguing, and it is a tribute to God's grace.

Already in 1976 a native-born Brazilian had traveled from his home in Porto Alegre, a coastal city in the far south of Brazil, to Medellin, Colombia, to meet with the Executive Committee for Latin America during its visit there. Later he would travel also to Milwaukee, Wisconsin, to plead his cause with President Naumann, who was always interested in world missions. The man's name was Luiz Rauter, a business man who headed a firm manufacturing petrochemicals.

Earlier in 1972 Rauter and his family had left the Evangelical Lutheran Church of Brazil (IELB) because it had been tainted with the liberalism that was affecting its parent, the Lutheran Church-Missouri Synod. Senhor Rauter had been active in the IELB as a member of its doctrine committee and also in his home congregation in Porto Alegre, but more than anything else he wanted to remain true to the word.

Senhor Luiz Rauter and his son, Ronaldo

With no place to turn, he formed his own church, registered it with the government (a fact which will appear later as most important), asked an ex-pastor formerly affiliated with the IELB to conduct Sunday services, and started looking for another church body that taught and practiced God's word in its truth and purity. This search led Senhor Rauter to Medellin and later to Milwaukee.

WELS, however, was busy with its two-year-old mission in Colombia and with its efforts elsewhere in the world. Yet Rauter's plea was heard, and a 1978 Wisconsin Lutheran Seminary graduate was assigned to Brazil for one year. He was to test the possibility of working there and to serve the *Igreja Luterana Ortodoxa Brasileira Da Consolacão* (Brazilian Orthodox Lutheran Church of Comfort), which Rauter had founded.

This effort did not work out as planned, but Brazil was not forgotten. In March 1979 Board for World Missions Executive Secretary Sauer and Professor E. H. Wendland visited the country to investigate more closely its potential as a mission field. Their report led the synod to pass a resolution "to send a two- or three-man team to Brazil to explore the mission possibilities in this third most populous nation of Latin America."

But budget stringencies forestalled carrying out the resolution. Not until the 1983 WELS convention was the message stressed again about the "extreme urgency to go into the open door of the field before it is closed." The delegates responded with a resolution to send "an exploratory team to Brazil to report back to the 1985 synod convention with their recommendations."

Before the Board for World Missions, through its Interim Committee, could carry out this resolution, another request came from Brazil. Dr. Paul Oserow, a former pastor of the IELB, now a lawyer living in Dourados, joined Rauter in appealing for aid. In February 1984 the BWM then appointed Pastors Martin Janke and Richard Lauersdorf and Professor E. H. Wendland to make the exploratory trip to Brazil during the month of July. This team was to meet with the Rauter and Oserow families, explore further the country's potential as a mission field, and obtain the necessary information regarding Brazil's requirements for foreigners to do mission work within the country.

A Unanimous Decision

The three men returned with a favorable report. As a result, the Board for World Missions, through its Interim Committee, urged the 1985 convention to enter Brazil with a team of five men. The convention adopted the recommendation without a dissenting vote. "Don't be surprised if I remind you of this resolution in the days ahead," commented President Carl Mischke, referring to the funds that would be needed to carry out this resolution, funds that were not available in the synod's budget.

It was the Lord's work, and again he provided. In the May 15, 1986, issue, *The Northwestern Lutheran* printed this brief notice: "At its meeting on April 11, the Coordinating Council authorized the calling of three missionaries for Brazil as soon as possible." The report further stated: "The first two-year costs will be carried by the Brazil Development Fund, which has received a number of special gifts to cover start-up costs. The fund presently totals about $200,000."

On May 17 Charles Flunker, veteran missionary to Puerto Rico, was commissioned as the first member of the team for Brazil. On June 28 in Columbus, Ohio, and New London, Wisconsin, Pastors Richard Starr and Bruce Marggraf took leave of their stateside congregations as they, too, were commissioned for Brazil. During the first week of October 1987, these three WELS missionaries with their families stepped onto Brazilian soil.

The Country

What kind of country did they set foot on? A large one, fifth largest in the world by area. A populated one, sixth largest in the world, with 70 percent of its population under the age of 30 and with three million more added annually. More than one-third of all Latin Americans are Brazilians. An industrious one, second in the world in agricultural exports and eighteenth in overall exports. A fertile mission field, with less than ten percent of its supposedly Catholic population practicing its faith and with Protestantism multiplying in recent decades.

It was a country WELS could not enter on its own. A law, passed in 1981, permits missionaries to enter the country only when invited by a Brazilian church body registered with the government. Upon such invitation, foreign church workers can apply for temporary visas for entry. These visas then are periodically renewable until a permanent one is issued. In other words, as in so many countries, we needed a bridge to enter. No bridge meant no entry to a country of 154 million people, redeemed by Christ's blood, but knowing so little about that precious gift. It was most fortunate that Senhor Rauter had registered his church with the government nearly ten years before. Thank God for giving WELS that vital bridge and the courage to cross it into Brazil!

Bruce Marggraf, Richard Starr, and Charles Flunker were the first three missioners to begin working in Brazil.

The Work

Our three missionaries had landed in Porto Alegre, a city of two million, but settling into a new country without any previous experience was hardly an easy task. They reported:

There have been many obstacles to overcome. One of the first was obtaining a CIC number, needed by each missioner for any major purchase inside the country. Without our CIC numbers, we couldn't own cars or rent homes today. Ronald Rauter, now president of our sponsor church and son of Luiz, led us through the maze of government bureaucracy to receive these precious numbers. In fact, Ronald spent the better part of our first several weeks here helping us find homes to rent, bank accounts, and cars to buy and just plain making us feel welcome. That's dedication to the Lord from a man who has his own petrochemical business to run. . . . Besides getting our families settled, learning the language is our most important job during our first year here. It's not hard to explain why. Few would argue that the best way to deliver the gospel to people is by speaking in their own language.

For Brazilians that language is Portuguese. The five missionaries, including the newest ones to the field, Kenneth Cherney, Jr. and Charles Gumm, are well into the task of learning how to speak and read and write in another tongue. They are preaching and conducting classes in Portuguese.

Even for Spanish-speaking people such as Missionary Flunker and his family, there are new things to learn. Though many Spanish words are nearly identical to words of the same meaning in Portuguese, the pronunciation often is distinctly different.

Our work in Brazil is in its infancy. The starting place was Gravatai. Here the Rauter family had purchased a house and remodeled it into a chapel for their congregation. Located just outside of Porto Alegre, Gravatai is a rapidly expanding housing area where workers at the main industrial plants are settling. Its population currently numbers 140,000.

Unfortunately, the leadership of the Gravatai congregation found itself increasingly at odds with the aims and goals of our mission, particularly as these related to expansion into other areas. Other matters became an issue as well, and the Gravatai congregation decided to go its separate way.

This has led our mission team to concentrate its efforts on Porto Alegre itself. By the beginning of 1992, Missionaries Starr, Margraf, Cherney, and Gumm had developed and were using a method of outreach similar to that used in Colombia. They have opened an information center in central Porto Alegre and are investigating new areas for similar mission outreach. Several people have become communicant members and gather regularly for study and worship.

A New Frontier

Some 800 miles northwest from Gravatai, on the western frontier of Brazil, lies the city of Dourados. Twenty years ago this was a town with 20,000 people. Today it numbers 150,000. An economic center in this rapidly growing frontier of Brazil, Dourados is the home city of Dr. Paul Oserow, a prominent lawyer and a natural evangelist. Missionary Flunker and his family, in the summer of 1989, moved to Dourados in order to serve the nucleus of believers the Spirit has been gathering there. The missionary writes:

> We hold the services in our home right now, because we have the largest open area in the dining room and living room. There are some 20 people from four families that are the beginning of this church. They meet in each other's homes on Thursday evenings for Bible study and try to invite their friends and neighbors. On Saturdays we have a children's class in one of the homes. Yesterday there were ten children, six of them from families who are not yet part of the group. There is also a Catechism class for young people. This week the men of the group will meet to make more plans. Already they have mentioned various ways they want to reach out to the town with the word of God.

Contacts have been made in other areas of this massive country. What will come of them remains to be seen. The work in Brazil lies before us as an open book in which the Lord of the Church will do the writing.

From Tucson to Dourados and Beyond

There you have it—the story of our Latin American mission work begun so humbly back in 1948, briefly in Phoenix and then in Tucson. Statistics are only one-dimensional figures on equally flat pieces of paper and cannot even begin to measure the effort expended and the results achieved. But the following figure does excite us. At the beginning of 1989, for the first time, the total number of souls served by the gospel in all our Latin American fields surpassed the 1,000 mark.

Praise God, for only he can give such blessings. Pray God, for only he can number these souls among those of "every nation, tribe, language and people" who will stand before the throne in heaven.

Conclusion
LOOKING TO THE PAST, PRESENT, AND FUTURE

A story has been told. It has spanned a century of world mission history in the Wisconsin Synod. It shows how from modest beginnings a hundred years ago this church body has become ever more involved in proclaiming the eternal gospel "to every nation, tribe, language, and people" (Revelation 14:6). Hence the title of this book.

Our story is, therefore, a "people story." Our Savior God has seen fit to use people to reach out to people. He through his Spirit has empowered "jars of clay," as the Apostle Paul expressed it, to carry out the primary mission of his church, which is the rescue of fallen mankind. Most of the names of these people do not appear in the record of this book. Yet they have had a part in the greatest work in the world.

It is a story about *missionaries.* Many of them never dreamed that they would one day be a part of the teeming masses of Hong Kong, or walk the streets of Tokyo, or drive through the African bush to carry out their daily tasks. They never thought they would be speaking Cantonese or Portuguese or Chinyanja

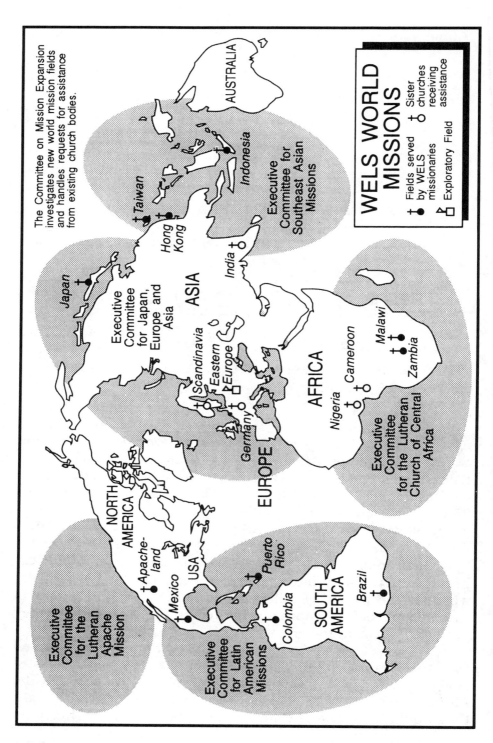

in order to bring a message from the Lord. They couldn't possibly have anticipated some of the unusual situations they would be called upon to face in the course of their ministry, as well as in their personal lives. One has to read between the lines of this story and imagine what it must be like to bring the message of Christ to those who have never heard it before, to work in an entirely foreign atmosphere, to have a vital part in the development of a church body from its beginning. In the isolated circumstances of transcultural service, both the worries as well as the joys have a way of becoming exaggerated and intensified. We call it "the agony and the ecstacy" of missionary life. It has to be lived over a period of years to be appreciated.

It is a story about *missionaries' wives.* They haven't received much special attention in our account. Nevertheless, many a missionary will readily tell you how much his wife's contribution has meant to him in his work. The day-to-day existence in another country often requires more ingenuity, also more patience and forbearance than one might imagine. Meals, shopping, recreation, social activities are all included. The pangs of family separation are hard to describe— such as a teenage son or daughter sent the long distance back to the United States to receive an education, or the news of the sudden death of a loved one thousands of miles away. There ought to be a special niche in our listings of centennial thanksgivings for those who have had to cope with such situations.

It's a story about *national Christians* and their vital role in the development from mission to church on foreign soil. Missionaries will unanimously agree that without men like Salimo Hachibamba or Ryuichi Igarashi or Chen Tung Ke their work could never be properly indigenized. Training such men to become church workers is of the essence. What a joy to see their talents developed and used in ways better adapted than those of foreigners to serve the needs of their own people! What a thrill to see that first love of the gospel bring forth fruit in miracles wrought by the Spirit of God! Our world mission outreach today rests more on the number of national Christians reaching out to their own people than on the amount of missionaries sent from America.

It's a story about people who have served on *mission boards and committees* here in America. They, too, have received little mention on these pages by way of special acknowledgment. It takes special effort for a busy layman to spend days in meetings and weeks in field visits while serving on an executive

The Board for World Missions cares for the "logistics" of God's mission army.

committee. It takes special effort for busy parish pastors to do the same, also for their congregations to share the time and talents of their pastors. These men care for the logistics of God's mission army, wrestling with problems like supply of manpower, and budgeting limited funds for the field. According to synod policy, our church still relies more on the services of pastors and laymen elected from its "grassroots" than on those of full-time executives. How important this voluntary service!

**LWMS conventions are arranged nationwide so that
the women of our synod can be informed about its mission.**

When thinking of voluntary service to missions let's not overlook the contributions of *women's organizations and others* throughout the synod, especially those connected with the Lutheran Women's Missionary Society and the Central African Medical Mission. LWMS conventions have been arranged nationwide so that the women of our synod can be informed about its mission, and their meetings have been an inspiration to many. A church paper in Latin America continues to be published because of their help. In Scandinavia a confessional church body has found much of its financial support coming from women's groups in our synod. The medical mission, having sent teams of nurses to Central Africa for over thirty years, looks to the women's groups in our congregations for financial aid totaling some 150,000 dollars annually. A missionary recently declared, "This has undoubtedly become the greatest outlet for charitable service in our entire church."

Not only have the women of our synod joined in this support of world mission programs. More recently, the men have organized as the Kingdom Workers, who among other things are supporting much needed lay missionaries in Central Africa. Add to this the programs that from time to time have become possible through the substantial special donations of individuals whom the Lord has blessed both with material means and with a deep love for world missions. The early world seminary conferences, the first years of operation in Colombia, the current work in Germany, and the thrust into eastern Europe come to mind. The Nigerian story tells of the gift from a WELS couple for the Eket hospital. There are, no doubt, many others.

We should also mention those *in our synod's headquarters* at 2929 Mayfair Road, Milwaukee, who labor faithfully and unobtrusively to keep the entire

Gloria Hermanson and Kaye Eckert provide able assistance to World Mission Counselor John Kurth and Administrator Duane Tomhave.

world mission operation on target. Mission outreach has become a day-to-day operation. Whether we like it or not, synodical business has grown into big business, and world missions is an integral part of it. It means a great deal to have administrators and a secretarial staff with a heart for missions! It also helps to have a fiscal department in the same building with an understanding for world mission problems. Moreover, without the efforts of those in our synod who are called upon to deal with publicity and stewardship matters, our people would not be adequately informed about the magnitude of the worldwide task that lies before us, and how much is needed for its support.

The Northwestern Lutheran with its editorial policy and through its capable staff has consistently given top billing with attractive graphic art work to world mission articles, and *Northwestern Publishing House* has gone out of its way to fit mission publications into its busy printing schedule.

Our "people story," finally, must include *the rank and file of those throughout the synod* who have placed the work of world missions prominently in their thoughts and prayers. Their support shows itself in so many ways. A missionary in Puerto Rico will receive a greeting on his birthday from somebody previously unknown to him. A mission family in Malawi will unexpectedly received a packet of "goodies." A check will arrive in a Christmas greeting to Tsuchiura, Japan, to which are attached the words, "thinking of you" or "our prayers are with you" or "thank you for what you are doing for us." Little things? Perhaps so. But they mean so much. Missionaries and their families have no reason to feel that their work in the Lord is unappreciated, or that it is without the prayers of many, many people.

So much for the past. The Lord has blessed our humble, often stumbling efforts far beyond anything we can say or think. The tiny mustard seed has become a tree, "so that the birds of the air come and perch in its branches" (Mt 13:32). Those who have been involved in this process of growth have experienced again and again how God's power is made perfect in spite of human weakness (2 Co 12:9). They have learned what it means to praise God for the fulfillment of his prophecy: "So is my word that goes out from my mouth: it will not return to me empty, but will accomplish what I desire and achieve the purpose for which I sent it" (Is 55:11). Indeed, we need to exclaim with Paul, "All this is from God, who reconciled us to himself through Christ and gave us the ministry of reconciliation" (2 Co 5:18).

When in 1975 our synod celebrated its 125th anniversary, Pastor Karl Krauss wrote in the Wisconsin Lutheran Quarterly: "We have grown from a body whose interest in world missions was spasmodic and sporadic into a body which is set on a course of continuing and expanding world mission endeavors." Krauss also pointed out that this growth in sharing the truth "began in earnest at the same time that we were involved in a trying doctrinal struggle." We believed—and therefore we spoke!

* * * * * * * *

The past brings us to the present, a present rich in mission opportunities all over the world. While one hundred years ago we as a church body could look to a tribe of Native Americans within our own country as our sole outlet for "work among the heathen," we today are blessed with a global vision.

Africa still calls. The Dark Continent has become a center of Christian growth. Malawi is so rich in opportunities that, according to a recent report, "the typical missionary is responsible for an average of ten congregations and 1,780 souls." Men serving with a full schedule of classes at the Lusaka Lutheran Seminary throughout the week are carrying on a full load of congregational services on weekends. The report continues, "Still God has given the missionaries the zeal to think in terms of expansion." Not only are other areas within Zambia and Malawi pleading for "the Lutheran Church to come to them," but neighboring Zaire and Mozambique are doing the same. To the west lie Nigeria and Cameroon, two of Africa's most densely populated countries, each with a young confessional church body that looks to us for help.

Latin America with South America, its "Sleeping Giant," has finally been penetrated. Teams of missionaries and nationals are at work in Mexico, Puerto Rico, Colombia, and Brazil. And it all started with one pastor, Venus Winter, as the only person present for 16 consecutive Sundays, in a rented building in Tucson, Arizona! Brazil with its 154 million people is regarded as one of the most promising Protestant mission fields in the world today.

Four beachheads have been established in *Southeast Asia*— Hong Kong, Taiwan, Indonesia and India—not without many an anxious moment along the way. On three of them, missionaries have learned the difficult oriental languages of the country. They have established worker training programs and founded congregations. After many years of frustration, the

1989 report of the executive committee in charge of this area could state, "The words excitement, progress, and change are fitting to describe what is happening in Taiwan, Hong Kong, and Indonesia. . . . It is heartening to see and read about scores of new souls being won for Christ."

Repeatedly reports from this area look to the millions, yes, billions of Christless people who live beyond these beachheads. The Lord has placed these open doors before us, doors that no one can shut. Will the same spiritual awakening happen in the Far East as in Africa, where a century ago the beginnings were so painfully slow?

Work in the islands of *Japan*, too, requires much patience and perseverance. *One at a Time* is the title of a video depicting evangelism work in the Land of the Rising Sun. Nevertheless, the Lutheran Evangelical Christian Church which has been established there has developed to a point where Japanese nationals are actively involved in every phase of the church's program.

Europe, of course, remains a spiritual enigma. Apparently the "local shower" of the gospel, as Luther put it, has moved with greater effect to other places. The tumbling down of the Berlin wall, however, which inaugurated the collapse of communistic, anti-Christian rule in Eastern Europe, has surely opened up new possibilities for greater outreach in this vast area of the world. And we certainly would not want to refuse lending our support to confessional groups that are still there and looking to us for help.

Finally, *Apacheland*. Admittedly our beginnings there a hundred years ago were inexperienced, possibly even somewhat naive. But a beginning was made. We learned from experience. And for many years the reports from Arizona were all that our people had to assure them that something, at least, was being done for people of another culture. The fascinating novels of Gustav Harders, the interesting accounts in *The Apache Scout*, the opportunity to help with the East Fork Orphanage—all helped to keep alive the interest of our people in missions.

Even today we marvel as we hear about the experiences of those veteran missionaries in Arizona who labored so long "with patience and persistence." And let's not forget that the urgent call to reach out elsewhere in the world with the gospel came to our synod in 1945 from the executive committee that was working among the Apaches. God has richly blessed this century of mission activity on the reservations, especially in the area of Christian education. The Lord is not letting this work return to him empty (Isaiah 55:11). Praise him for letting us be there for one hundred years with word and sacrament!

* * * * * * * * *

Both past and present are important in a practical way only to the extent that one has learned from the past and looks positively and energetically to the future.

As world missions in general go, one hundred years is a relatively short period of time. In fact, most of our synod's beginnings in outreach have taken place only within the latter part of this twentieth century. Our own experience tells us that often it takes years just to get a foothold in a new venture. One must become acquainted with people, learn their language and their customs. One needs to develop a strategy, to prepare materials in accordance with our Lutheran confessions. There is the business of training nationals with whom we can work in partnership before the real work can get underway. One lays foundations for a church body that is to govern, support, extend, and discipline itself. In many of our foreign fields, these things are just beginning to take shape. Often a synodical constituency will send a team of missionaries to a new area and after a few years wonder how many hundreds of souls have been saved. It just doesn't work out that way. What we are trying to say is that a hundredth or fiftieth anniversary is not a time to rest on our laurels.

It is in the future, therefore, where the real work still lies. Our mission call from God is just as urgent and in many ways even more compelling and important than ever. We in our synod should be especially aware of this. We are among the few church bodies that stand unequivocally upon the Holy Scriptures as the sole foundation of our mission. We teach the *total* depravity of mankind's nature because of sin. We proclaim God's eternal will of grace to *all* people. We center our teaching in the fact that God has justified, declared righteous, *every* sinner in the death and resurrection of Christ.

Ours is an unconditional gospel, no strings attached. We give assurance of the sanctifying power of the Holy Spirit through the precious *means of grace,* which we still have in truth and purity and administer as the sole power of God unto salvation. We stress the *urgency* of the church's mission in the light of Christ's second coming. As we hold fast to these sacred, eternal truths God has so graciously entrusted into our hands, should we who are so signally blessed not be impelled to share them with all who are still without Christ and on the way to eternal destruction?

Our uncompromising confession to these truths as expressed in our Lutheran Book of Concord is also a rich legacy we would not want to see buried. Instead of broadcasting a vague and watered-down gospel, as do so many mission movements of today, it is the goal of our missionaries to bear witness to the "full counsel of God." It is our purpose to help develop churches that can stand side by side with us confessionally in every respect, whether they are in Lusaka, Zambia; in Mito, Japan; or in Sukabumi, Indonesia. What a privilege to share with our national churches a confessional heritage which goes back to the time of the Reformation!

How beautifully these doctrinal and confessional principles are stated in our synod's *Handbook for World Missions,* adopted by the WELS 1957 convention. We hear much these days in our synod about "spiritual renewal." It would be good if during this centennial observance of world mission work we could take another look at the "Primary Objectives" and "Underlying Principles" as stated in this handbook. Surely a restudy of them together with the Scripture passages on which they are based will remind us again of our primary mission as a church of Jesus Christ, which is to "preach the good news to all creation" (Mk 16:15).

Our primary mission as a church of Jesus Christ is to "preach the good news to all creation." (Mark 16:15)

It is by happy coincidence that the theme of our centennial mission history is taken from Revelation 14:6,7. This Scripture happens to be the standard epistle text for the Festival of the Reformation. It is thus a part of our Lutheran heritage that the eternal gospel be proclaimed "to those who live on the earth— to every nation, tribe, language and people" (v 6). By God's grace our church body has become involved in the fulfillment of that prophecy.

Let us remember that to these words of prophecy this text adds, "Fear God and give him glory, because the hour of his judgment has come" (v 7). Appropriately, our synod's *Handbook for World Missions* closes its "underlying principles" with the words:

> Our King's business requires haste. The time for doing the Lord's bidding in an intensive mission program is running out. The Lord, who has placed the sacred trust of His Word into our hands, has also blessed us with religious freedom, peace, and material blessings. His faithful followers will heed His warning and redouble their efforts to preach the Gospel in all the world before it is too late.

May our Wisconsin Evangelical Lutheran Synod face its second century of world mission activity with these thoughts in mind.

CHRONOLOGY WELS WORLD MISSION HISTORY

1850 The German Evangelical Lutheran Ministerium of Wisconsin is organized on May 26 in Granville, Wisconsin.

1860 The Michigan and Minnesota Synods are organized.

Pastor John Bading succeeds Pastor John Muehlhaeuser as president of the Wisconsin Synod.

1868 The Wisconsin Synod breaks off its relations with the unionistic mission societies of Europe.

1872 The Wisconsin and Missouri Synods become charter members of the Synodical Conference (The Evangelical Lutheran Synodical Conference of North America).

1883 The Wisconsin Synod resolves to seek out and support an orthodox mission society as it celebrates the 400th birth year of Luther.

1884 When the committee appointed to find an orthodox mission society cannot find one to meet specifications, it is instructed to look for a potential mission field and for young men within our own synod to serve a mission among the heathen.

1889 John Plocher, George Adascheck, and Paul Mayerhoff are enlisted as trainees for mission service.

1892 The Federation of the Joint Synod of Wisconsin, Minnesota, Michigan, and Other States is founded.

The decision is made to begin heathen work among the American Indians. Pastors Theodore Hartwig and O. H. Koch explore Arizona and recommend Apacheland as the place to begin.

1893 Missionaries John Plocher and George Adascheck come to Apacheland and begin work at Peridot in the San Carlos Reservation.

1896 Missionary Paul Mayerhoff begins work at East Fork in the Fort Apache Reservation.

1907 Pastor Gustav Harders accepts the call to serve as superintendent of the Apache Mission at Globe, Arizona.

1908 Pastor G. E. Bergemann is elected president of the Federation of the Joint Synod of Wisconsin, Minnesota, Michigan, and Other States.

1911 Missionary E. Edgar Guenther and his bride, Minnie, begin 50 years of service at East Fork on the Fort Apache Reservation.

1917 The federated synods become the corporate Joint Synod of Wisconsin, Minnesota, Michigan, and Other States.

Missionaries Alfred Uplegger and Henry Rosin are assigned to work in Apacheland, both beginning 50 years of service there.

Missionary E. Guenther is appointed superintendent of the Apache mission field, serving until 1936 in that capacity.

1919 Missionary Francis J. Uplegger begins service in the Apache field at San Carlos, later succeeding Guenther as superintendent of the field in 1936, serving 20 years in that capacity.

1919 As the Wisconsin Synod remembers 25 years of work in Apacheland, Prof. August Pieper of the Wisconsin Lutheran Seminary presents an inspiring paper at the convention on *The True Reconstruction of the Church.*

1922 Chief Alchesay is baptized by Missionary Guenther on April 22 at the dedication of the church at Whiteriver, Arizona.

An orphanage is established on the Apache Reservation at East Fork.

Pastor Otto Engel of the Wisconsin Synod meets with evangelist Gustav Maliszewski in Lodz, Poland, in answer to a request for help in supporting Lutheranism in that country.

1923 The Wisconsin Synod resolves to assist confessional Lutherans in Poland.

The Apache Scout (later the *Apache Lutheran*) begins publication.

1924 Pastor Otto Engel is called to superintend work among confessional Lutherans in Poland. St. Paul's Evangelical Lutheran Free Church is organized in Lodz on May 11.

1925 Pastor Adolf Dasler succeeds Engel as the director of work in Poland.

1927 The Synodical Conference celebrates its 50th anniversary. During this year a conference of black congregations in the South collects $7,000 "to carry the gospel to Africa."

1930 The Wisconsin Synod's debt through various building projects totals $752,649.

1933 Synod President G. E. Bergemann is succeeded by Pastor John Brenner.

1934 An appeal from the Ibesikpo clan of the Ibibio tribe of Nigeria, Africa, is received by the Synodical Conference Mission Board. The conference votes to send a delegation to investigate.

1935 Pastor Immanuel Albrecht, Pastor O. Boecler, and Dr. Henry Nau are sent to Nigeria to investigate the appeal of the Ibesikpos. Synodical Conference President Ludwig Fuerbringer instructs its mission board to call missionaries to Nigeria upon receiving an urgent appeal from the investigating committee.

The Wisconsin Synod resolves "to retire its debt without delay." The "Michigan Plan" for increased information and stewardship is introduced on a synodwide basis.

1936 Dr. Henry Nau returns to Nigeria to help organize the Ibesikpo Lutheran Church.

1937 The Evangelical Lutheran Free Church of Poland is organized. Pastor Maliszewski is elected president.

Missionaries William Schweppe and Vernon Koeper, and Nurse Helen Kluck arrive at Port Harcourt, Nigeria, on April 27.

1939 Germany invades Poland on September 1. Bodamer is refused a visa to reenter the country. The mission's "responsibility list" grows to 8,000 souls despite the anti-church policies of the Nazis.

1945 The Board of Trustees announces at Wisconsin Synod's "Happy Convention" that the synodical debt is retired. The convention resolves that a committee be appointed "to gather information regarding foreign fields."

The Russians invade Poland. The pastors from the Polish Free Church regroup in Zwickau, Germany.

1946 The pastors from the Polish Free Church meet at Memmingen, Germany, to organize as The Evangelical Lutheran Refugee Mission. Six pastors from Poland are deployed to various zones of Allied occupation of Germany.

1947 The Wisconsin Synod authorizes "the expansion of mission work in foreign mission fields."

Pastor Alfred Maas becomes non-resident director of Germany Refugee Mission.

1948 A ninth grade is added to the Apache mission school at East Fork, the beginning of what later becomes East Fork Lutheran High School.

Pastor Venus Winter conducts the first Spanish service at Phoenix, Arizona, on December 5. (The work is later shifted to Tucson.)

1949 Pastors Arthur Wacker and Edgar Hoenecke begin exploration of fields in Africa on April 29. After 4,000 miles of bush travel from Capetown, South Africa, they end their trip in Lusaka, Northern Rhodesia. They report the area to be a promising field.

The Diaspora Circuit of our mission in Germany is formed in the Russian Zone of occupation, supported by our synod through the Saxon Free Church in the East.

The seminary of the Evangelical Lutheran Church in Nigeria is established.

1950 The official church paper of our mission in Germany, *Durch Kreuz zur Krone* (*Through the Cross to the Crown*) begins publication in January.

1951 The "Hook of the Kafue" report is presented to the Wisconsin Synod convention. The synod votes to send two missionaries to Northern Rhodesia, Africa. It also resolves to ask the Spiritual Welfare Commission to place a man in Japan to care for people in the armed services as well as "to investigate mission opportunities there."

The Lutheran refugee Mission in Germany reports 3,000 souls in the Russian Zone and 18,000 souls in the three western zones.

1952 The Lutheran Refugee Mission is reconstituted as the Evangelical Lutheran Confessional Church in the Dispersion at Blomberg, Germany.

Missionary Fred Tiefel arrives in Japan.

1953 Pastor Oscar Naumann succeeds Brenner as president of the Wisconsin Synod.

The Wisconsin Synod's General Mission Board is divided into a General Board for Home Missions and a General Board for Foreign and Heathen Missions.

The synod resolves that two men be called as missionaries to Japan.

Pastor and Mrs. A. B. Habben and Mr. Paul Ziegler arrive in Lusaka, Northern Rhodesia, in June. Pastor and Mrs. Otto Drevlow arrive in August with Ziegler's family. The African mission's first English service is held in Lusaka on June 28 and the first African service in Matero on December 6.

1954 In April a mission station is established on a native reserve land grant at Lumano (Mwembezhi) in the Sala area of Northern Rhodesia.

1955 Pastor Edgar Hoenecke is elected chairman of the General Board for Foreign and Heathen Missions.

1956 The Northern Rhodesian mission takes on the management of schools in the Sala Reserve, with Missionary Harold Essmann serving as Manager of Schools. (This management is relinquished in 1965.)

1957 The East Fork Nursery and Child Placing Agency begins its care on the Apache Reservation replacing the orphanage established in 1922.

The general policies, underlying scriptural principles, and primary objectives of the Board for Foreign Missions are adopted by the synod.

The WELS convention approves setting up a medical mission in Central Africa, with support to come from women's groups throughout the synod.

Missionary Fred Tiefel of Japan resigns from the synod. Missionary Richard Seeger arrives in Japan on April 26.

1958 Missionary Richard Poetter begins work in the Ibaragi Prefecture of Japan.

1960 Peter Chang requests financial assistance from the Wisconsin Synod for work in Hong Kong.

Missionary Richard Mueller begins a mailing program in Central Africa. This later leads to requests for missionaries to come to Malawi.

Students at Wisconsin Lutheran Seminary conduct their first annual world mission seminar.

1961 The Wisconsin Synod breaks fellowship relations with the Lutheran Church-Missouri Synod.

The WELS convention adopts the "Christian Missioners' Corps" concept.

Missionary Theodore Sauer begins service as superintendent of the mission in Central Africa.

The Lumano Lutheran Dispensary is dedicated in Central Africa on November 26. (Medical mission work is later extended to the Salima Settlement Scheme on Lake Malawi in 1970.)

1962 The Wisconsin Synod's participation in the work of the Evangelical Lutheran Church in Nigeria ceases as a result of the breakup of the Synodical Conference.

Pastor Karl Krauss succeeds Alfred Maas as non-resident director of the mission in Germany.

Pastor Ernst H. Wendland is called to initiate a worker training program for the Lutheran Church of Central Africa.

1963 The Wisconsin Synod resolves to establish the office of Executive Secretary of the Board for World Missions. Pastor Edgar Hoenecke is called and accepts the office. Pastor Raymond Zimmermann is appointed as board chairman, replacing Hoenecke.

The synod authorizes the calling of two missioners to Puerto Rico.

Missionaries Richard Mueller and Raymond Cox arrive in Blantyre, Malawi, to extend the Central African work to that country.

The first representative meeting of congregations from the Lutheran Church of Central Africa is held at Matero Lutheran Church, Lusaka, Zambia.

1964 A committee consisting of Executive Secretary E. Hoenecke, President O. Naumann, and Pastor L. Koeninger of the synod's Relief Committee meet with Peter Chang in Hong Kong and agree to supply limited support to the Chinese Lutheran Christian Mission.

The first convention of the Lutheran Women's Missionary Society is held in St. Matthew's Church, Winona, Minnesota.

Professor Conrad Frey receives a year's leave of absence to serve as resident seminary advisor for the Chinese Christian Lutheran Mission.

The Lutheran Bible Institute of the Lutheran Church of Central Africa begins at Chelston, near Lusaka, with eight students.

Missioners Rupert Eggert and Roger Sprain arrive in San Juan, Puerto Rico, later beginning work in Guayama and Humacao.

Pastor Martinus Adam organizes the Confessional Lutheran Church of Indonesia on April 27 in Sukabumi, Java.

1965 Lutheran services are held in Kumba, Cameroon, for the first time, begun by former members of the Nigerian Lutheran Church who had come there as refugees as a result of the Biafra crisis in Nigeria.

Pastor Marlyn Schroeder replaces Frey as interim counselor in Hong Kong.

Articles of Organization are adopted by the Lutheran Church of Central Africa in a meeting held at the Lutheran Bible Institute, Chelston, Lusaka, Africa.

1966 Missionary Ernest Zimdars is commissioned to work in El Paso, Texas, and in Ciudad Juarez, Mexico, among Latin Americans.

After nine years in Japan, Missionary Richard Seeger begins work as Friendly Counselor in Hong Kong.

Mr. Elmer Schneider arrives in Lusaka, Zambia, in September to work as Publications Director of the Central African mission.

1967 The first worship service is held in Taiwan on May 11 at the home of Mrs. Wong Liu Pik Yee. The service is conducted by Mr. Wong Siu Hun, sent as a follow-up of the Voice of Salvation broadcasts in Hong Kong.

Pastor and Mrs. Theodore Sauer make a survey of South America. His report is given to the Board for World Missions at its October meeting.

1968 Rev. Timothy Lee, a graduate of the Hong Kong Lutheran Seminary, is sent to Taiwan.

Pastor Karl Wengenroth replaces Pastor Armin Schlender as president of the Evangelical Lutheran Church of the Confession in Germany.

The Institute of Biblical Research (Biblicum) is founded in Uppsala, Sweden. Later served by Dr. Seth Erlandsson, this institute becomes the starting point of confessional Lutheran work in Sweden.

The Wisconsin Synod begins funding confessional Lutherans in Mexico.

Pastor Martinus Adam in Indonesia appeals to the Lutheran Free Churches of Europe for aid. His appeal is referred to the Wisconsin Synod. Anak Agung Dipa Pandji Tisna, a Balinese layman, requests aid from the synod.

Missionary William Schweppe dies in a tragic auto accident in Zambia.

1969 Christ the King Lutheran Synod in Nigeria is organized by nine congregations and three pastors who seceded from the Evangelical Lutheran Church of Nigeria.

Dr. Orea Luna and Pastor Chichia Gonzales are found to be in confessional agreement with us. The Wisconsin Synod decides to support these confessional Lutherans in Mexico.

The Wisconsin Synod resolves to declare fellowship with the Confessional Lutheran Church in Indonesia following a visit by Rev. Paul Behn, Peter Chang and Executive Secretary E. Hoenecke.

Evangelist T. Paul Mitra, living in Madras, India, appeals for help for his Rural Gospel Mission.

1970 A congregation is begun at Everlasting Happiness Village on the island of Taiwan. (Its church is dedicated on New Year's Day, 1971. Victor Cheung, the brother of Peter Chang, is ordained as pastor.)

Paul Chonason, the head of a group of Lutherans meeting in Kumba, Cameroon, appeals for help.

The Confessional Evangelical Lutheran Church of Mexico (IELC) is formally organized with Dr. Luna as its first president. Its official church paper, *El Amanacer* (*The Dawning*), again appears in print.

T. Paul Mitra arrives with his wife in the United States and studies at Wisconsin Lutheran Seminary. (He is ordained and returns to India the following year.)

1971 Professor E. H. Wendland is asked to investigate the appeal from the Lutherans in Cameroon. He recommends a further close look at this field and interim assistance.

Rupert Eggert is called to El Paso to serve as Friendly Counselor of the Mexican mission and director of the seminary in El Paso.

Dr. E. R. Wendland is called as Language Coordinator of the Lutheran Church of Central Africa.

A church center, including seminary building, printshop and missionary dwelling, is dedicated in Tsuchiura, Japan.

Peter Chang resigns as head of the Hong Kong mission. Teacher Howard Festerling is chosen as chairman of the Chinese Evangelical Lutheran Church Board of Directors.

The Wisconsin Synod Convention unanimously approves the recommendation of the Latin American Committee to send a three-man team of missioners to Medellin, Colombia, South America.

The first World Seminary Conference is held at Kowloon, Hong Kong, with representatives from Mequon, Wisconsin, as well as from world mission fields.

1972 The Wisconsin Synod receives a gift of $144,000 from a WELS family to enable it to begin work in South America.

The Board for World Missions decides to support the Lutherans in Cameroon following favorable reports from a visit by Executive Secretary Hoenecke and Missionaries Sauer and Wendland from Zambia.

The Independent Evangelical Lutheran Church (SELK) is organized as a union of free churches in Germany on June 25. The union does not include the free church supported by our synod, but does include the Saxon Free Church and the Breslau Synod.

Dr. Orea Luna, head of the Confessional Evangelical Lutheran Church in Mexico, dies unexpectedly.

Pastor A. B. Habben, formerly missionary in Africa, is called as the first resident missionary in Indonesia. Unforeseen circumstances result in his early return from the field and release from his call.

1973 Missioners Roger Sprain, Ernest Zimdars, and Francis Warner are commissioned to begin work in Medellin, Colombia.

A three-storied building containing church, seminary, and residence facilities is dedicated in Hong Kong.

A meeting of representatives of the various Lutheran free churches of Germany is held in Mequon, apparently with favorable results. (Unfortunately some of the delegates present do not speak with complete authority for their respective church bodies.)

Dr. Siegbert Becker and Executive Secretary Edgar Hoenecke meet with leaders of the Lutheran free church movement in Uppsala, Sweden, to explain the doctrinal position of the Wisconsin Synod.

Dipa Pandji Tisna, a Balinese student, graduates from the Hong Kong seminary and is stationed in Jakarta on the island of Java, Indonesia.

Missionary Douglas Weiser is sent as the first resident missionary on the Copperbelt of Zambia.

1974 The first service of the Wisconsin Synod's mission to Colombia, South America, is held in Medellin. Reinaldo Gomez becomes the first Colombian confirmand ("001") on August 15.

Rev. Bruno Njume replaces Paul Chonason as head of the Cameroon Lutherans.

The Lutheran Confessional Church in Sweden is organized in Uppsala with six pastors, three congregations, and 68 souls.

The Lutheran Church of Central Africa adopts its first formal constitution. Three seminary graduates are ordained.

Salimo Hachibamba is called to serve as instructor at the Bible Institute and Seminary of the Lutheran Church of Central Africa.

1975 Missionary Gary Schroeder arrives in Hong Kong to bolster congregational activities there. He is joined a year later by Gary Kirschke, who is placed in charge of worker training.

The Wisconsin Synod Convention resolves to give the Lutheran Church in Cameroon guidance and financial support and to call two resident missionaries to that field when permission is granted by the Cameroon government to send expatriates.

The Lutheran Confessional Church of Sweden formally establishes fellowship ties with the Wisconsin Synod.

The first World Mission Conference is held at West Allis, Wisconsin, with representation from each world mission field.

1976 Luiz Rauter, a Brazilian manufacturer, appeals to the Wisconsin Synod to help begin a confessional Lutheran church in Porto Alegre.

The Evangelical Lutheran Church of the Confession in West Germany, heretofore supported by the Wisconsin Synod, merges with the union of free churches in Germany (SELK), not in fellowship with us.

Pastor Lars Engquist of Råneå, Sweden, leaves the Church of Sweden and joins the Lutheran Confessional Church of Sweden in fellowship with us.

1977 Pastors Arnold Mennicke, Richard Lauersdorf, and Theodore Sauer visit Nigeria in answer to an appeal from Pastor Edet U. Eshiett of Christ the King Lutheran Synod. The Wisconsin Synod at its convention in August decides "to explore the best possible way of standing at the side" of this church body.

The Japan Mission begins work near Yokohama in Kanagawa Prefecture.

The Synod Convention approves the sending of ten new missionaries, three of them to Taiwan and two to Indonesia.

1978 A Mequon seminary graduate is assigned to Brazil for one year.

Work in Hong Kong is reorganized as the Southeast Asian Lutheran Evangelical Mission (SALEM).

Pastor Ole Brandal of Stavanger, Norway, leaves the Church of Norway and joins the Lutheran Confessional Church of Scandinavia.

Pastor Theodore Sauer replaces Edgar Hoenecke as executive secretary of the Board for World Missions.

1979 Executive Secretary Theodore Sauer and Prof. E. H. Wendland travel to Porto Alegre and Gravatai, Brazil, to investigate further the mission possibilities in that country.

Regular worker-training seminars are inaugurated in Cameroon when permission to send expatriate missionaries to the field is not granted by the government.

The Iglesia Luterana Confessional de Colombia is officially organized.

Pastor Carl Mischke replaces the deceased Oscar Naumann as president of the Wisconsin Evangelical Lutheran Synod.

1981 Fellowship relations are declared between the Wisconsin Synod and Christ the King Lutheran Synod in Nigeria.

Church fellowship between the Lutheran Evangelical Christian Church of Japan and the WELS is formalized.

Pastor William Meier is elected as chairman of the Board for World Missions, replacing Raymond Zimmermann who served in that office since 1963. Pastor Arnold Mennicke ends 31 years of service on the Executive Committee of the Lutheran Church of Central Africa.

A Lutheran Bible institute is opened at Lilongwe, Malawi, under the headship of Missionary Walter Westphal.

1982 Pastor Victor Cheung disappears from Taiwan, leaving supervision of the work entirely in the hands of the expatriate missionaries.

Seminary graduate Omar Ortiz is ordained as the first Colombian pastor on November 28.

1983 Pastor Leonard Koeninger steps down after 18 years of service on the Executive Committee for Southeast Asian Missions.

On August 21 Missionaries Philip Strackbein and Mark Goeglein begin new work in Bogota, Colombia, South America.

1984 A seminary program is opened in Hong Kong under Missionary G. Kirschke.

Pastor Duane Tomhave replaces Theodore Sauer as executive secretary of the Board for World Missions.

The Lutheran Confessional Church of Scandinavia celebrates its tenth anniversary, four days after the death of Dr. Siegbert Becker.

Pastors Martin Janke and Richard Lauersdorf and Prof. E. H. Wendland meet with the Rauter and Oserow families in Brazil.

1985 Study centers are opened in large housing estates in Hong Kong as a new approach to mission work in that field.

Pastor John Kurth accepts the call as Worker Training Counselor on the world mission staff.

Chen Tung Ke is ordained as pastor of Jiang Chuey Church in Taipei at the age of 63, after 11 years of service to the church as evangelist.

A Bible institute program is initiated in Jakarta by Missionaries R. Sawall and B. Ahlers.

The Synod convention resolves to enter Brazil with a five-man team.

1986 Missionaries Charles Flunker, Richard Starr, and Bruce Marggraf are sent to Brazil. (Missionaries Kenneth Cherney Jr. and Charles Gumm follow a year later.)

A Theological Study Centre is built near Uruk Uso village in Nigeria for Christ the King Lutheran Synod. It is to serve the training of church workers as well as provide housing for visiting missionaries.

The Christian Lutheran Evangelical Church is legally incorporated in Taiwan. A church-parsonage facility is dedicated in

Taipei at a cost of $90,000 through a loan made possible by funds from the Reaching Out Offering.

East Fork Lutheran High School is gutted by fire. Increased interest and participation by the Apaches hasten plans for rebuilding.

1987 Dr. Seth Erlandsson resigns his positions in the Lutheran Confessional Church of Scandinavia. President Per Jonsson resigns and leaves the fellowship with 75 souls. The remaining six pastors, seven congregations, and 277 souls reorganize.

Pastor Salimo Hachibamba becomes principal of the Lutheran Bible Institute and Seminary in Chelston, Lusaka, Zambia.

1988 Pastor Peter Chikatala is elected as the first national chairman of the Lutheran Church of Central Africa.

1989 In East Germany ELF, including the Diaspora District, suspends fellowship with SELK as it continues to favor ties with the Wisconsin Synod.

Missionary Charles Flunker takes up residence in Dourados, a new frontier area in Brazil.

1990 Deacon Ryuichi Igarashi, seminary instructor, literary editor, and translator in Japan, is called to his eternal rest.

1991 Missionary and field administrator Richard A. Poetter retires after 33 years of service to the Japan Mission.

Pastor Kirby Spevacek is commissioned to explore the possibilities for mission work and radio and television outreach in the countries of the former USSR and in other parts of eastern Europe and Asia.

1992 Raymond G. Cox accepts call to be Mission Coordinator for the Apache mission field, bringing to a close nearly 28 years of service to the Central Africa Mission and the Lutheran Church of Central Africa.

BIBLIOGRAPHY

Books

Erlandsson, Seth, and Johansson, Sten, *Biblicum's Battle for Biblical Faith*, Tr. by S. W. Becker. Uppsala: Biblicum Institute, 1974.

Ferg, Alan, Ed., *Western Apache Material Collection, The Goodwin and Guenther Collection*, University of Arizona Press, 1987.

Herrmann, Gottfried, *Lutherische Freikirche in Sachsen: Geschichte und Gegenwart einer lutherischen Bekenntnis Kirche*, Berlin, ca.1985.

Kiessling, Elmer, *Centennial Memoir*, Milwaukee: Northwestern Publishing House, 1979.

Koehler, J. P., *The History of the Wisconsin Synod*, Protes'tant Conference, Tr. by Leigh D. Jordahl.

Kowalke, E. E., *You and Your Synod*, Milwaukee: Northwestern Publishing House, 1972.

Nau, Henry, *We Move into Africa*, St. Louis: Concordia Publishing House, 1936.

Tomhave, Duane E., Ed., *World Mission Handbook*, Board for World Missions, WELS, 1989.

Uko, M. N., Editor, Golden Jubilee Edition, *A Short History of the Lutheran Church of Nigeria, 1936-1986*, Obot Idim: The Lutheran Press.

Vicedom, George F., *The Mission of God*, St. Louis: Concordia Publishing House, 1965.

Voss, Arthur P., Ed., *Continuing in His Word*, Milwaukee: Northwestern Publishing House, 1951.

Wendland, Ernst H., *Ibibio*, Milwaukee: Northwestern Publishing House.

Wendland, Ernst H., and Sauer, Theodore A., *A Nigerian Safari*, Grand Junction, CO: Wilson & Young Printers.

Periodicals

Deye, Armin, Ed., *The Lutheran Journal*, Edina, MN: Outlook Publications, Vol. 55, No. 2, 1988.

Durch Kreuz zur Krone, Publication of the Evangelical Lutheran Confessional Church, Germany, 1950-1975.

Engel, Otto, "The Wisconsin Synod Mission in Poland," *WELS Historical Institute Journal*, Vol. 4, No. 2, 1988.

Gemeinde Blatt, Official Publication of the Joint Synod of Wisconsin and Other States, 1965.

Guenther, E. E., Ed., *The Apache Scout*, a.k.a. *The Apache Lutheran*, Whiteriver, AZ, April 1923 ff.

Hoenecke, Edgar H., "The End of an Epoch in the Apache Indian Mission," *WELS Historical Institute Journal*, Vol. 2, No. 2, 1986.

Hoenecke, Edgar H., "Report from Barrancas," *The Northwestern Lutheran*, November 16, 1975, page 365.

Hoenecke, Edgar H., "The Lord Calls Us into Mexico," *The Northwestern Lutheran*, June 9, 1968, pages 186-187.

Hoenecke, Edgar H., "The WELS Forty-niners," *WELS Historical Institute Journal*, Vol. 3, No. 1, 1985.

Krauss, Karl F., "Our World Missions," *Wisconsin Lutheran Quarterly*, 1975, pages 274-293.

Marggraf, Bruce, "Settling in Brazil," *The Northwestern Lutheran*, September 15, 1988, pages 310-311.

Martens, Ralph, "*Firmes y Adelante*," *The Northwestern Lutheran*, November 1, 1989, page 368.

Sprain, Roger, "A Sunday of Prayer," *The Northwestern Lutheran*, January 13, 1974, page 5.

The Northwestern Lutheran, Official Publication of the Wisconsin Evangelical Lutheran Synod.

Warner, Francis, "Report from South America," *The Northwestern Lutheran*, June 2, 1974, pages 165-166.

Warner, Francis, "Our First Confirmation in Colombia," *The Northwestern Lutheran*, November 3, 1974, pages 348-349.

Wendland, Ernst H., "Brazil: A Country on the Move," *The Northwestern Lutheran*, February 1, 1985, pages 40-41.

Wendland, Ernst H., "Our Synod's First Mission Overseas," *WELS Historical Institute Journal*, Vol. 2, No. 1.

Convention Reports

Book of Reports and Memorials for conventions of the Wisconsin Evangelical Lutheran Synod.

Proceedings of the conventions of the Wisconsin Evangelical Lutheran Synod.

Proceedings of the Evangelical Lutheran Synodical Conference of North America, 1934, 1936.

Reports to the Districts of the Wisconsin Evangelical Lutheran Synod.

Pieper, August, "The True Reconstruction of the Church," *WELS Convention Proceedings*, 1919.

Sauer, Theodore A., "God's Word, a Heritage to Share," *WELS Convention Proceedings*, 1985.

References

Annual Mission Booklets, Board for World Missions, Wisconsin Evangelical Lutheran Synod.

Lutheran Cyclopedia, Erwin L. Lueker, Ed. St. Louis: Concordia Publishing House, 1951.

World Almanac, Scripps Howard, 1989.

World Book Encyclopedia, Field Enterprises, U.S.A., 1965.

Unpublished Materials

Bernhardt, William F., *The History of our WELS Mission in Japan with Historical and Cultural Background*, Library, Wisconsin Lutheran Seminary.

Becker, Bruce, Mark R. Freier, Mark P. Henke, David R. Clark, David A. Nolting, William E. Runke, Michael K. Biedenbender, Kevin R. Hastings, Lloyd C. Schlomer, *The History of the Wisconsin Synod in Japan*, Library, Wisconsin Lutheran Seminary.

Drevlow, Elaine, *Diary*.

Eggert, Rupert, Essay, *The Lutheran Church in Mexico*, September 10, 1981.

Files, Executive Committee for the Lutheran Evangelical Christian Church in Japan, WELS Archives.

Hoenecke, Edgar H., *Correspondence Relative to the German Mission*, WELS Archives.

Hoenecke, Edgar H., *Reflections on the Inter-relationships between the Theological Seminary and World Missions*, 1988.

Hoenecke, Edgar H., *Development of WELS into a Mission Church*, Essay delivered at El Paso World Seminary Conference, 1978.

Hoenecke, Edgar H., Letter, to E. H. Wendland, November 22, 1988.

Interviews with various individuals. Notes and tapes in WELS archives.

Kurth, John H., *Focus on Nigeria*, Report to WELS Board for World Missions, January 24, 1989.

Maas, Alfred, Complete Official Correspondence, WELS Archives

Martens, Ralph, Essay, *Christian Missioner Corps in Puerto Rico*, November 1979.

Martens, Ralph, Essay, *Focus on Puerto Rico*, February 24, 1988.

Mennicke, Arnold L., Correspondence, Reports.

Minutes of the Board for World Missions and its Executive Committees.

Minutes of Joint Meeting of Foreign Mission Board with E. Hoenecke and A. Wacker, Milwaukee, WI, December 8, 1949.

Minutes and Reports, Executive Committee for the Lutheran Church of Central Africa.

Naumann, Oscar J., Correspondence, WELS archives.

Poetter, Richard A., *Notes*, a year-by-year listing on the Japan mission field, WELS archives.

Report of the Executive Committee for the Lutheran Apache Mission, April 28, 1987.

Wacker, Arthur, and Hoenecke, Edgar H. *Report of Exploratory Mission in Africa*, 1949.

Video

Hoenecke, Edgar H., *Inashood*, VCR video from 16mm. motion pictures of Missionary E. Edgar Guenther. Commentary by E. Hoenecke.

INDEX OF SUBJECTS, PERSONS, AND PLACES

A

Abak 128
Adam, Martinus 243,260-264,315, 316,
Adascheck, George 20,26-28,33,310,311
Africa Still Calls 170
Ahlers, Bruce E. 265-267,320
Aid to Sister Synods Fund 130
Akagami, Wakichi 160
Akpakpan, Edet 129,133
Albrecht, C. J. 15
Albrecht, Immanuel 121,312
Albuquerque, New Mexico 38
Alchesay, Chief 40,42-45,52,311
Allen, Roland 225
Allgemeine Zeitung 57
American Zone of Occupation 78
Andrespol 70,71
Angerstein, W. P. 69
Angola 170,177
Apache Lutheran, The 52,311
Apache Scout, The 39,49,51,52,306, 311,323
Apache Mission 23-62,306
    East Fork Lutheran High School 49-51,313,321
    East Fork Nursery 37,47,48,314
    East Fork Orphanage 46,306
    Lutheran Elementary Schools 49
    San Carlos Church 36,51,55,61

Apacheland 14,20,21,23-61,241, 306,311
Apostle Paul 18,23,30,56,225,236, 268,279,299,304
Apostle Thomas 276,278
Arizona Lutheran Academy 50
Ashikaga, Japan 159
Avaldsnes, Norway 104

B

Bading, John 15,17,19,20,65,310
Baer, E. J. 125
Baer, George 125
Baerbock Ronald 240
Balge, Richard 11
Bali 251,260,261-264,267,316,318
Balovale, Zambia 204
Baltic Countries 76
Bandung 264,265
Bantu People 178,186
Baptist Mission, Gwelo 205
Barrancas 238,323
Basel Missionary Society 14,15
Baumler, Gary 11
Becker, Siegbert 99-101,104,106, 107,109,318,320,322
Behn, Paul 36,58,250,252,253,263, 270,316
Belen Las Playas 290
Belgian Congo 170
Bergemann, G. E. 65,111,114,222, 311,312

Berlin-Zehlendorf 69,71,81
Bessarabia 76
Bey, Gregory 267
Biafra, Nigeria 128,135,315
Bibel og Bekjennelse (Scripture and Confession) 104
Bibeltrogna Vaenner (Bible Believing Friends) 103
Biegalke, K. 73,75
Black Light 202
Black River 26,38
Blantyre 178,195,201,207-209,215, 315
Blomberg 83,86,313
Blondet 239
Bodamer, William 72-74,76-79,83, 85,312
Boecler, Otto 121,312
Bogota, Colombia 291,292,320
Bowman, Cylice 208
Brandal, Ole 104,319
Brazil Mission 293-298
Brazil 82,240,293-298,305,319, 320
Brazilian Orthodox Lutheran Church of Comfort 294
Brenner, John W. 85,114,115,143, 144,171,222,223,312,313
Breslau Synod 81,90,91,317
British Society for the Propagation of the Gospel 15
Brudnowo, Poland 73,75
Buchholz, Reinhold 89
Buddhism 149,267
Burkhardt, Alvin 143
Burma Road, Lusaka 206
Bylas, Arizona 27,49,58

C

Cairo Road, Lusaka 179
Calabar, Nigeria 128,133,134
Cameroon 117,119,128,135-140, 243,279,282,305,315,317-319
Canto Plain 155
Canyon Day, Arizona 27,44,59
Capetown 170,177,313
CARE Packages 78
Carey, William 15,276
Carrizo 47,58
Central African Federation 178,207

Central African Medical Mission 191,192,197,198,303,314
Chang, Peter 243,247-251,253,270, 314-317
Changhwa 269
Chelston 202,206,208,216-218,220, 315,321
Chemnitz 96
Chen Tung Ke 271,272,275,301,320
Chen Ywe-De 273
Chen Ywe-Min 273
Cherney, Kenneth Jr. 297,321
Cheung, Victor 269-272,316,320
Chiang Kaishek 269
Chiba, Japan 160
Chichia, David 232,235,316
Chie, Tse Tat 259
Chihuahua 231
Chikatala, Peter 218,321
China 31,105,149,244,245,249,254, 257,258,266,269
Chinese Evangelical Lutheran Church (CELC) 249-254,269, 270
  Board of Directors 254,317
  Immanuel Lutheran English Middle School (ILEMS) 249,255, 256
  Seminary 252,264,269,270,316, 318
  Taiwan District of the CELC 270
Chipata, Zambia 177,201,215
Chipoya, Lawrence 204
Chiradzulu, Malawi 195,196,208, 209
Chiricahua 41
Chiyaba, Zambia 182
Chizera, Zambia 205
Chonason, Paul 135-137,317,318
Christ the King Lutheran Church of Nigeria (CKLCN) 128-134, 279
  Board of Directors 131,133
  Theological Study Centre 133,320
Christian Information Centers 293,297
Christian Lutheran Evangelical Church (CLEC), Taiwan 270, 272-274

Bible Institute and Seminary 273, 274
Board of Directors 273
Fountain of Grace Lutheran Church 273
Holy Trinity Congregation 272
Lutheran Gospel Center 274
Taiwan Church Extension Fund 273
Christian Chinese Church, Indonesia 261
Christian Indian, The 54
Christian International English College 251
Christian Chinese Lutheran Mission (CCLM) 243,247,249,250
Grace Lutheran Bible Institute 249
Guidelines for Cooperative Work in Hong Kong 250,252
Immanuel Lutheran English Middle School (ILEMS) 249,254-256
Spirit of Love Primary School and Church 252
Voice of Salvation Radio Broadcast 248,251,268,269,316
Christian Missioners' Corps 226,236,240,314
Christian Dogmatics 109
Christianson, Ruben and Hannah 101,108
Chu, Stephen 250
Chunga Line, Zambia 181
Church of Sweden 97,99,100,103, 105,109,319
Church of Norway 104,319
Chworowsky, John 253,254,265,271, 318
Cibecue, Arizona 27,51,54,58,59
Ciudad Juarez, Mexico 213,234,235, 315
Civil War 24
Cochise, Chief 25
Colombia 235,240,284-293,294,297, 303,305,317-320,323
Confessional Lutheran Church of Indonesia 243,261,315
Bible Institute and Seminary 267,268
Confessional Lutheran Church of Colombia (ILCC) 284-293

Bible Institute and Seminary 289
The Message of Salvation Broadcast 288
Confessional Evangelical Lutheran Church of Mexico (IELC) 233-236,317
Cristo Redenter Congregation 231
Cristo Resuscitado Congregation 233
Martin Luther Theological Institute 234
Mass Communications Director 235
Message of Salvation Broadcast 233
El Paso Seminary 231,234,317
Confucianism 149
Connell, James 235,240,290
Continuing In His Word 32,60,323
Cook, Dr. 20,23,55,56
Coolidge Dam 26,55,56
Copperbelt 206,207,215,318
Coronado 24
Cox, Lois 201
Cox, Raymond G. 138,187,195,199, 201,206-209,213,214,216,217, 220,315
Crimmitschau, Germany 95
Crook, General 25,40,42
Cross River State, Nigeria 128
Czechoslovakia 76

D

Danell, Gustav Adolf 97,99,100
Danowiec 75
Dasler, Adolf 71,72,312
Deming, Arizona 38
Denmark 33
Devabhushanam, Pastor 278
Dorado Subdivision, Puerto Rico 239
Douala, Cameroon 136
Dourados, Brazil 295,298,321
Dreves, Pastor 19
Drevlow, Elaine 176,177,179,190, 313,324
Drevlow, Otto 172,176,177,180,181, 313
Drum Beat 202
Dummann, Carroll 255

Durch Kreuz zur Krone 82,83,313,323
Dutch Protestants 150

E

East Fork, Arizona 26-28,32,37,38, 40, 46,47-51,58,306,311,313, 314,321
East Germany 77,90,92-97,321
Eastern Front 76
Eastern Province, Zambia 177,181, 182,215
Eberhardt, Christoph 14
Education and Social Services Ministry, Northern Rhodesia 184
Eduok, Isaac 135
Edwardsson, Gunnar 109
Eggert, Rupert 234,235,237,240, 286, 315,317,324
Einigungssaetze (Union Theses of 1947) 90
Eket, Nigeria 193
Ekong, Jonathan Udo 120,121,129
Ekpo, Jonah U. 129
El Amanacer 234,236,317
El Mensajaro Luterano 234,235
El Paso, Texas 231,234,240,283,290, 315,317,324
Engel, Otto 66,69-71,74,311,312, 323
Engquist, Lars 97,100,103,105,319
Envigado, Colombia 288,290
Epiphanius, J. E. 264
Erlandsson, Seth 99,101-104,109, 316,321,322
Ernst, Dr. A. F. 63,64
Eshiett, Edet U. 129,130,133,319
Essmann, Harold A. 185,189,284, 314
Essmann, Ruth 185
Etim, Frank Udo 133
Europe 14,15,16,18,20,66,67-110, 120,150,243,306,321
Evangelical Augsburg Church of Poland 69,74,75
Evangelical Lutheran Confessional Church in the Dispersion (ELCC) 83,89-92,313
 Diaspora Circuit 90,94
 Ebenezer Congregation, Blomberg 86
Evangelical Lutheran Church of Brazil (IELB) 294,295
Evangelical Lutheran Church of Nigeria (ELCN) 119,125,127-130
 Eket Hospital,126,193,195,303, Lutheran Seminary 125,126,200,204,313
Evangelical Lutheran Free Church, East Germany (ELF) 92-97
 Diaspora District 90,94,95,321
 Leipzig Seminary 95
Evangelical Lutheran Free Church in Poland, The 63,74
Evangelical Lutheran Free Church of Saxony (ELFC). See Saxon Free Church
Evangelical Lutheran (Old-Lutheran) Church. See Breslau Synod
Evangelical Lutheran Synod (ELS) 248
 Bethany Seminary 248
Everlasting Happiness Village, Taiwan 269-272,274,316

F

Falk, Roger 159
Fastenau, Don 133
Federal Republic of Germany 96
Festerling, Howard 11,250,252,253, 265-268,317
Festerling, Linda 253
Festerling, Lois 253
Fiedler, Johannes 83
Fischer, Sharon 253
Flunker, Charles 238-240,295-298, 320,321
Forchheim, Johannes 38
Formosa 269,275
Fort Apache Reservation 26-28,38, 45,311
Fort Jameson, Zambia 178. *See also* Chipata
Fort Apache 26,41,44,56
Found, Charles D. 271
Frankfurt, Germany 81,96
Fredrich, Edward 65
Freese, Stuart 291
French Zone of Occupation 79
Frey, Conrad 172,250,315

329

Froehlke, Adolph 260
Fromm, Elwood 160
Fuerbringer, Ludwig 121,312
Furberg, Ingemar 104,109
Fusying, Taiwan 274

G

G'ad N'schahi 53,54. *See also* Old Cedar
Gandhi, Mahatma 275
Gausewitz, C. 15
Gawrisch, Wilbert 95
Gemeinde Blatt 17-19,323
General Council 18
German Mission Societies 19
German Democratic Republic 92,94
Germany 77-97
Geronimo, Chief 25,41
Gila River 26,55
Gisselsson, Gideon 104
Globe, Arizona 31-33,37,38,311
Goeglein, Mark 235,290,291,320
Gomez, Reinaldo 284,288,318
Gospel Light Mission 172
Göteborg, Sweden 104
Gran Stan Bran, Puerto Rico 237,238
Granville, Wisconsin 14,310
Gravatai, Brazil 297,298,319
Great Century of Missions 120
Great Depression 114
Great Rift Valley 177,178
Grebe, Robert 284
Greve, Edgar 125,126,188-190,193
Greve, Helen 125,190
Grosinske, Steven and Cheryl 253, 256
Grothe, Walter 49
Guadalajara 234,235
Guayama 237-239,315
Guenther, Arthur 27,29,30,39,44, 45,47,56-58,60
Guenther, Carl 30
Guenther, E. Edgar 29,32,39-46,48-50,52-56,311,323,325
Guenther, Minnie 29,38-43,45,46,48,61,62,311
Guenther, Wenonah 41
Guenther, Winifred 49,57
Guenther Indian Collection 48,322
Guillen, Vincente 235
Gumm, Charles 297,320

H

Haag, James 255
Habben, Kermit 160,161
Habben, A. B. 172,176,177,180-184, 187-191,493,199,202,219,263, 264,313,317
Haberkorn, David 158
Hachibamba, Salimo 133,196,205, 211-213,218,301,318,321
Hadler, Willis 58
Handbook for World Missions 308, 309,322
Happy Convention 141,143,226,227, 312
Harders, Gustav 29-33,39,44,306, 311
Harders, Hilda 31
Harders, Irmgard 31
Hartman, Paul 235,240
Hartwig, Theodore 20,23,311
Hartzell, Eric 50
Hartzell, Eugene 50
Heckmann, Gerald 253
Hedegard, David 97,99
Helimissions 139
Henry, DeAlva Rainbow 51
Hering, John 161
Hermannsburg Mission Society 19
Herrnhut 15
Heyer, Johann 15
Heyn, Thomas 290
Hinduism 262,263,267,276
Hintz, Michael 138
Hiroshima, Japan 143,227
History of the Wisconsin Synod 20, 30,322
History of the Lutheran Church of Nigeria, Golden Jubilee Edition 125,322
Hitachi, Japan 159,160
Hoenecke, Adolf 17,21,322
Hoenecke, Edgar 3,11,33,34,37,82, 86-88,99,101,107,115,129,136-138,143-145,153,169-171,183, 189-193,195,224-226,233,249, 261-263,277,279-282,286,313-319, 323-325
Hoenecke, Heinz, M.D. 162
Hoenecke, Meta, R.N. 191-193,195, 225,281

Hoenecke, Otto J. R. 64
Hoenecke's Dogmatik 81
Hoffmann, Gottfried 261
Holbrook, Arizona 38
Hong Kong 160,241,243,244,245-259,261,263,264,265,268,270, 271,278,299,305,306,314-319 See note at end of Index, page 339.
Hong Kong—An Open Door 249
Hook of the Kafue 169,171,172,313
Hotel Authentique 136
Hoyer, Waldemar 207
Humacao, Puerto Rico 237,239,315

I

Ibaragi Prefecture 154-156,159-161,314
Ibesikpo Clan 119-121,312
Ibesikpo United Church 120
Ibibio Tribe 119,312,122,323
Ibibio 122,123
Igarashi, Ryuichi 153,164,301,321
Inashood 27,56,325
Inashood Hastihn 34
Inashood N'daesn 43,45,46
Independent Evangelical Lutheran Church (SELK) 89,91,92,94, 95,317,319,321
Independent Evangelical Lutheran Free Church in Germany (IELC) 90
India Mission 254,275-278
India Rural Gospel Mission 276
India 15,149,243,244,254,275-278, 305,316-318
Indigenous Church Policy 87,122, 164,184,186-188,204,210,211, 219,224,226,289,290
Indonesia 243,244,254,259-268,305,306,308,315-319
Ishioka, Japan 156
Islam 120,140,260,267

J

Jaalahn 321
Jacobus, Max 261
Jakarta, Indonesia 260,263-267,318, 320
Janke, Martin 95,109,295,320

Janosek, John 195,209,214
Japan 20,106,143,145,146,147-167, 172,226,227,250,262,266,304, 306,308,313,314,316,317,319, 321,324,325
Java 201,243,260-263,266,315,318
Jesaias II 81
Johansson, Sten 100-102,106,322
Johne, Harold 11,157,159
Jones, Ralph 272,275
Jonsson, Kjerstin 100
Jonsson, Per 99,102,103,109,110, 321
Jos, Nigeria 126
Josefa, Doña 237,238
Juarez, Mexico 231,234,235,315
Junior Northwestern 52

K

Kabile, Zambia 185
Kabompo, Zambia 204
Kaesmeyer, Harris 96
Kafue River 169,171,172,313
Kaluwa, Zambia 181
Kanagawa Prefecture, Japan 161, 319
Kananga, Zambia 216
Karl Marx Stadt 96
Kasumigaura, Lake 155
Katinti, Zambia 182,185
Kawiliza, Benford 179,211,212,215
Kessel, William 39
Kingdom Workers 303
Kinshasa, Zaire 136
Kirschke, Gary A. 254,257,258,318, 320
Kitwe, Zambia 215
Klingmann, Stephen 14
Kluck, Helen 122,312
Knoop, Arnold 47,48
Knoop, Frieda 47,48
Knoop, Arthur 43
Koch, Dr. Henry 74,81,83
Koch, O. H. 20,23,311
Koehler, J. P. 20,21,30,59,63,64,66, 70,201,322
Koelpin, Winfred 11
Koeninger, Leonard J. 249,250,254, 255,260,315,320
Koeper, Vernon 122,125,312,

331

Koeplin, Kurt 255,274
Koffi, Elijah 277
Kohl, John 181,182
Konde, Jim 204
Korea 145,151
Korean War 151
Kowalke, E. E. 64,115,322
Kowloon 249,251,253
Krause, Clarence 281
Krauss, Karl 78,88,305,315,323
Kreiss, President 261
Kretzmann, Justus 125
Kretzmann, Theodore 196
Kriehn, David 274,275
Krueger, Mark 138,217
Kuehl, James 290
Kujath, Mentor 11
Kumba, Cameroon 136-139,315,317
Kurth, John 132,133,138,214,283, 303,320,325
Kutz, Louise 47,48

L

La Paloma 32
Lai, Raymond 259
Lake Malawi 178,196,314
Lambarene, Gabon 193
Landskrona, Sweden 99,102
Lange, Gerald 252,253,270
Langenberg Mission Society 14
Langfield, Irving 11
Languages
    Apache 28,35-37
    Bantu 178
    Bemba 213
    Cantonese 252,254,257,299
    Chewa 213
    Chinyanja 178,182,202,213,299
    Danish 36
    Efik 127
    German 111,286
    Greek 36,111,157
    Hebrew 36,111
    Indonesian 265,266,268
    Japanese 154,161-163
    Lala 213
    Latin 36
    Lenje 213
    Lunda 213
    Luvale 213
    Mandarin 270,271,273,274,
    Mbunda 213
    Navajo 36
    Nkoya 213
    Portuguese 283,286,297,299
    Spanish 36,229,286,287,289,297
    Swahili 178
    Taiwanese 274,275
    Telugu 278
    Tonga 213
    Tumbuka 213
Latin American Lay Delegate Conference 235
Lauersdorf, Richard 11,130,284,295, 319,320
Lawrenz, Carl 91,127
Lawrenz, Dr. John 11
Lee, Charles 259
Lee, Daniel 271,272
Lee, Timothy 250,269,270,316
Lelke, Eduard 71,73
Leningrad 96
Lerle, August 71,77,79,80,92,94
Lesschaft, Jack 196
Leyrer, Carl 240,291
Lilanda Convalescent Hospital 181
Lilongwe, Malawi 195,197,206,216, 320
Lin, Martin 269
Little Rock, Arkansas 115
Livingstone, Zambia 177
Livingstone, David 170
Ljungby, Sweden 104
Lodz, Poland 67,69-71,73,92,311
Loe, Dr. Fred 42,43
Lubaba, Lot 211,212
Lumano, Zambia 180,182,185,190, 193,204,314
Lumano, Headman 182
Lumano Lutheran Dispensary 195,198,314. *See also* Mwembezhi Lutheran Dispensary
Lusaka, Zambia 105,172,173,176-181,184,188,190,199,200,202, 206-208,215,219,277,305,308, 313-316,321
Luther, Martin 20
Lutheran Christian, The 202
Lutheran Church-Missouri Synod (LCMS) 18,70,115,117,121,

122,127,128,151,152,154,158, 160,196,225,236,247,294,310, 314
Concordia Theological Seminary 33,35,123
Lutheran Church of Central Africa (LCCA) 175-221
Articles of Organization 211,315
Bible Institute, Malawi 216-218
Bible Institute, Zambia 202,203, 205,206,208,210-213,217,218, 315, 318,321
Chairman's Advisory Council 212
Language Coordinator for Publications 212,213,317
Lutheran Press 202
Lutheran Seminary 203-206,213, 217,218,220,305,318
Manager of Schools 185,186,314
Martin Lutheran School 186
Mission Council 188,199,201,207, 217
Mwembezhi Lutheran Dispensary 180,183,193,195,197,198,314. See also Lumano Lutheran Dispensary
Lutheran Church of Cameroon, The 128,135-140,315,317-319
Lutheran Church of Hannover 89
Lutheran Churches of the Reformation (LCR) 130
Lutheran Confessional Church in Scandinavia (LCCS) 97-110, 316,318,319
Biblicum 97,99,100,104,106,108, 109,316,322
Evangelical Lutheran Confessional Congregation (Finland) 98, 103
Evangelical Lutheran Mission in Uppsala 101
Lutheran Evangelical Christian Church, Japan (LECC) 147-168,306
Fellowship with WELS Formalized 165
Nozomi Congregation 158
Printshop 157,162,317
Theological Seminary 156-160,164
Lutheran Free Churches in France, Belgium 260,261

Lutheran Hour 155
Lutheran Journal, The 51,323
Lutheran Laymen's Mission (Norway) 104
Lutheran Literature Society of Hong Kong 261
Lutheran Symbolics 260
Lutheran Synod of Mexico 236
Lutheran Synodical Conference 18,19, 65,115,117,119-121,127-129, 131,135,151,193,310,312,314, 324
Missionary Board 119,121,312
Lutheran Women's Missionary Society (LWMS) 107,131,276,303, 315
Lutheran World Federation 129,219
Luthersk Sandebrev (Lutheran Dispatch) 102

M

Maas, Alfred 73,74,78-83,85-88,94, 143,313,315,325
Mabedi, Daison 213,216,218
Macedonian Call 70,115,144
Madras,India 243,277,278,316
Malawi 175-221,241,282,304,305, 314,315,320
Maldonado, Mrs. 239
Maliszewski (Malschner), Gustav 69-71,73,74,76-79,82-84,92,311, 312
Malschner. See Maliszewski
Manthey, Marcus 271
Marggraf, Bruce 295-297,320,323
Martens, Ralph 240,323
Martin Luther Film 260,291
Martin Luther Theological Institute, Mexico 234
Matero, Zambia 178-182,187-189, 207,212,215,314,315
Maverick, Arizona 44
Mavika, Benson 212
Mayerhoff, Paul 20,28,36,59,310,311
McNary, Arizona 44,45,
Medellin, Colombia 284,286-290,292-294,317,318
Medical Mission Program 190-198,281,303,314
Meier, Arthur 50

333

Meier, Norbert 160
Meier, Timothy 275
Meier, William 8,11,50,281,283,319
Meiji Restoration 155
Meister, Robert 240,271,272,274,275
Memmingen, Germany 78,82,312
Mennicke, Arnold 130,172,186,188, 192,200,207,221,320,325
Mennicke, Mrs. Arnold 197,221
Mexico 26,227,231-236,243,283,305, 315-317,323,324
Mexico City 233-235
Meyer, John 113
Miami, Arizona 31
Michigan Plan 141,312
Michigan Synod 14,63,64
Midima Road 195
Miles, General Nelson 25
Milwaukee Lutheran High School 30,33
Ministry of Public Worship and Instructions (Warsaw) 70
Minnesota Synod 15,64,310
Miracle Church 60
Mischke, Carl H. 280,295,319
Missions at the Crossroads 225
Missionary Lutheran, The 54
Missionary Methods: St. Paul's or Ours 225
Mito, Japan 155-157,160,161,308
Mitra, T. Paul 243,276-278,316,317
Mitteilungen 83
Mkandawire, Alfred 195
Moffat, Sir John 171
Monze, Zambia 182
Moody Bible Institute Monthly, The 54
Moravian Brethren 15
Moscow, Russia 96
Mosher, Stacey 253
Moslem 209,268,276
Mount Tsukuba 155,158
Mozambique 305
Muehlhaueser, John 17,65,310
Mueller, Heinrich 71,73,77
Mueller, Irene 201
Mueller, Richard W. 187,189,199, 201,206-209,314,315
Munali Secondary School 180,181, 202,204

Muyangana, Albert 181,182,204,215
Mwambula, Joseph 178,179,181,182
Mwembezhi, Zambia 180,189,193, 195-197,199,209,314
Mwepeta, Kalungu 209
Mzuzu, Malawi 216

N

Nachuma, Malawi 209
Nakamoto, Menuhide 158
Nantan Mountains 38,55
Napp, Arthur 71
National Christian Council of Nigeria 129
Nau, Henry 121-123,312,322
Naumann, Oscar 127,129,130,153, 223,225,231,232,249,261,277, 279,280,293,313,315,319,325
Naumann, Mrs. Oscar 225
Navajo 36
Ndola, Zambia 215
Nelson, Gordon 201
Nidaira, Takeshi 164
Nigeria 117-134,305
Nigerian Safari, A 132,323
Nitz, Fred 58
Nitz, Henry 58,145
Njume, Bruno 135,137,139,318
Nkufulu-Lutulu, Babungi 216
North Fork River 26,42
Northern Rhodesia 145,170-172,178, 191,192,313,314. *See also* Zambia
Secretary for Native Affairs 171
Northern Rhodesia Gazette 184
Northwestern Lutheran 50,52,73,107, 139,287,295,304,323
Norway 103,104,106,108,319
Ntambo, Deverson 208,209,212,216, 218
Nyandong, Cameroon 137
Nyasaland 178,207. *See also* Malawi

O

Oberursel Seminary 81,86,96,261
Obot Idim 120,123,125,127,322
Ogoja Province 126
Ojibway Indians 14
Old Cedar 27,28,54. *See also* G'ad N'schahi

Old San Carlos, Arizona 27,37,54
Oldenburg, Germany 92
Orea Luna, David 232-236,316,317
Ortiz, Omar 289-292,320
Oserow, Paul 295,298,320
Oshino, Fukuichi 259

P

Pandji-Tisna, A. A. Dipa 251,262-264,267,316,318
Papagos 24
Patillas, Puerto Rico 239
Patzer, Karl 71
People's Bible, The 235
People's Republic of China 245 258
Perez, Daniel 235
Perez, Jose Lorenzo 235
Peridot, Arizona 27,30,33,36-38,55,59,311
Perry, Admiral Matthew 150
Petauke, Zambia 178,182
Peterson, Kenric and Karen 253
Pettersson, Erland 102
Phelps (Golembiewski), Linda, R.N. 197
Phoenix, Arizona 50,52,228,298,313
Pieper, August 63-66,81,311,324
Pieper, Franz 33,109
Pima Indians 23,24,55,56
Plocher, John 20,26-28,33,48,60,310,311
Poetter, Richard 153-156,160,161,164,314,321,325
Poland 66,67-77,78,80,84-86,89,92,96,104,107,311,312, 323
Polish National Catholic Church 69
Popular Symbolics 232
Port Harcourt, Nigeria 123,312
Porto Alegre, Brazil 293,294,296,297,319
Private Hospital Association of Malawi (PHAM) 196
Protes'tants 112
Prussian Union 90
Public Health Services, Whiteriver 43
Puebla, Mexico 234,235
Puerto de Jobos, Puerto Rico 239
Puerto Rico 226,227,234,235,236-240,241,283,295,304,305,315, 325

Q

Qua Iboe Mission 120,121

R

Rachner, Pastor 94
Råneå, Sweden 103,105,108,319
Rapier, Christine 125
Rauter, Luiz 294-297,319,320
Rauter, Ronaldo 294,297,320
Reaching Out Offering 133,139,272,273,290,321
Refugee Mission Church, Germany 82,83. See also Evangelical Lutheran Confessional Church
Reim, G. 15
Reim, Norbert 125,126
Reit, Alfred 71,76
Report to the Nine Districts 286
Retberg, Lawrence 290,291
Retzlaff, Frank 115
Rice, Arizona 33
Rijicho 156
Rogers, Rankin 58
Rogers, Will 56
Rosin, Henry 30,32,33,36,37,38,55,311
Rosin, Johanna nee Uplegger 33,36-38
Roslund, Bror 104
Rostock, Germany 33
Ruege, Ruth 149
Russian Zone of Occupation 79,80,94,313

S

Sacaton, Arizona 23
Sala Native Reserve 180
Sala Tribal Council 180,190
Salima Settlement Scheme 196,314
Salt River 26,31
Salt River Canyon 26,37
San Carlos, Arizona 20,30,31,33,37,56,59,311
San Carlos Desert 34
San Carlos Lake 26
San Carlos Reservation 26,30,31,33,37,56,311
San Carlos River 26
San Juan, Puerto Rico 237,239,315

San Pablo Spanish Mission 228,229
Sasse, Hermann 18
Satorius, Timothy 240
Sauer, Althea, R.N. 197,199,316
Sauer, Theodore 11,130-133,136,137, 188,195,198-200, 204,205,207, 210-213,220,241,243,280,282, 283,286,294,314,316,317,319, 320,323,324
Sawall, Robert 185,186,193,195,199, 200,265-267,320
Saxon Free Church 69,70,73,77,81, 90-95,313,317
Schaller, John 39,64
Schaller, Loren 11
Schlender, Armin 71,75-79,83,84,87, 88,89,316
Schlender, Helmuth 71,77,79,94
Schlomer, Larry 290,291
Schmid, Friedrich 14
Schneider (Hintz), Edith, R.N. 196, 197
Schneider, Elmer 202,316
Schoenberg, O. P. 58
Schroeder, Gary 254,257,258,318
Schroeder, Marlyn 250,260,277,315
Schult, Gary 267
Schweitzer, Albert 193
Schweppe, Leola 122,123
Schweppe, William, D.D. 122-126, 185,188,193,199-202,207,312, 316
Schwertfeger, John 248
Seeger, Richard 152-155,159,160, 314,316
Seim, Kenneth 249,252,253
Sena People 214
Senga Bay, Malawi 196,197
Shabasonje, Zambia 182,185
Shakumbila, Chief 179,180,188,190, 195
Shamanism 61
Shamwete, Zambia 185
Shiley, Harry 153
Shima 41
Shimodate, Japan 158
Shing, Yeung Wai 259
Shinto 147,149,151
Shire Highlands, Malawi 178
Shire River 178,214

Siegler, Oscar 127
Siirila, Robert 272,273
Simon, Gertrude 247,248
Sitz, E. Arnold 58
Skrypkowo, Poland 75
Soltau, Stanley 225
South China 245
Southeast Asian Lutheran Mission (SALEM) 251,254-257,319
    Bible Institute and Seminary 252, 257,320
    Director of Outreach through Education 256
    Immanuel Lutheran College 256
    Immanuel Lutheran English Middle School (ILEMS) 249,255,256
    Study Centers 257,258
Southern Rhodesia 178,205 (See also Zimbabwe)
Southern Pacific 23
Southwest Africa 170
Spangenberg, R. A. 125
Spanish Conquistador 24
Spanish-Mexican Government 24
Speckin, Erna 197
Spevacek, Kirby 96,133,136,321
Sprain, Roger 237,240,287,290-293, 315,318,323
Sprengeler, Ernest 58
Sprengeler, Mark 256
Spurgeon, C. H. 54
St. Chrischona Mission Society 15
Starr, Richard D. 295-297,320
Starr, Sadie 49
Stavanger, Norway 104,319
Steeden, Germany 96
Stoeckhardt, George 33
Strackbein, John T. 240
Strackbein, Philip B. 240,291,320
Suharto, General 260
Sukabumi, Indonesia 260,263-266, 308,315
Sukarno, President 260
Sullivan, John 96
Sun Rise Dance 60
Svensson, Alvar 102
Svensson, Arne 102
Swain, Paul and Janice 253
Sweden 97-110,279,316,318,319

Sweden Conference and Aid Fund 107
Swedish Mission in China 105
Swedish Mission, Mnene, Zimbabwe 205

T

Tacke, Arthur, M.D. 172,192
Taichung, Taiwan 269,274,275
Taipei, Taiwan 269-275,321
Taiwan 240,241,244,251,254,265, 268-275,305,306,316,318-320
Takahashi, Keiichi 159
Tamil State, India 277
Tan Hwei-Lin 273
The American Lutheran Church (TALC) 231
Theological Education by Extension (TEE) 217
This We Believe 100
Thyolo District, Malawi 195,196,208, 209
Tidskrift Biblicum (Magazine for Bible Research) 99
Tiefel, Frederick 146,152,153,313, 314
Tochigi Prefecture, Japan 155,158, 159,162
Tokyo, Japan 145,146,154-156,160, 161,299
Tomhave, Duane 11,282,283,303, 320,322
Tonga, Akimu 181,215
Tonga, Timothy 181
Tonga, Yona 181,215
Tri-Parish Monthly Caller, The 54
Tsai Ming, Jr. 273
Tsuchiura, Japan 156-158,160,161, 162,304,317
Tsukuba Science City, Japan 155,158
Tucson, Arizona 24,39,45,48,226- 231,233,234,283,298,305,313

U

Udofia, E. E. 135,137
Udofia, Ikpe 129
Uko, M. N. 125,322
Ukpong, Ebong 133
Union Theses of 1947 (Einigunssaetze) 90

United Bible Societies in Central Africa 213
University of Arizona 39
University of Uppsala 99
Uplegger, Alfred 29,32,33,36-38,311
Uplegger, Dorothea 36,48
Uplegger, Emma 36
Uplegger, Francis 30,33,36-38,52,53, 311
Uplegger, Gertrude 36,55
Uplegger, Irma nee Ruge 33,36-38
Uplegger, Johanna 33,36-38
Uplegger, Karl 37
Upprop (Proclamation) 102
Uppsala 97,99-104,107-110,316,318, 322
Uruk Uso, Nigeria 133,320
Utsunomiya, Japan 158,159

V

Valleskey, David 109
Valleskey, Stephen 11
Varel, Germany 87
Versalles, Colombia 288
Victoria Falls 177
Viet Nam 245
Volker, Ervin 206

W

Wachler, Gottfried 95
Wacker, Arthur 144,145,169-172, 181-183,187,188,191,193,313, 325
Wacker, Hilda 191,193
Wagner, Alfons 71,77-79,81
Waljö, Paul 104
Walther, C. F. W. 33,69
Warner, Francis 287,318,323
Warsaw, Poland 69,70,75
Warthegau, Germany 76
Wauwatosa Seminary 63,70,71,113
Wauwatosa Theology 63
Weindorf, Luther T. 161
Weinmann, John 14
Welch (Thalin), Barbara, R.N. 193,195
WELS Forty-niners, The 170,183,323
WELS Historical Institute Journal 33, 323,324
WELS Kingdom Workers 303
We Move into Africa 121,122,322

337

Wendland, Betty 210
Wendland, Ernst H. 11,86-88,122, 131,132,136-139,186,188,198-200,204,205,210-212,294,295, 315,317,319,320,323-325
Wendland, Ernst R., Ph. D. 133,212, 213,317
Wendland, Paul 133,138
Wengenroth, Karl 83,88,89,91,92,316
Werre, Alvin 125
Wessel, Sherwood and Beth 253
Westphal, Walter 216,320
White River 26,42
Whiteriver, Arizona 27,29,37,39,41-47,49,51,61,311,323
Wilberforce SS 123
Wilde, Gerhard 95
Wille Wider Wille 32
Wilson, Chief 136
Winter, Venus,228,229,233,305,313
Winter, William 125
Wisconsin Evangelical Lutheran Synod (WELS)
  African Exploratory Commission 171
  Board for Foreign and Heathen Missions 153,223,224,313,314
  Board for Home Missions 223,313
  Board for World Missions 8,11,50, 61,86,88,95,96,99,100,130-132,134,136,137,183,187,218, 219,224,226,231,236,241,243, 249,250,261,277-280,286,294, 295,315-320,324,325
  Board of Trustees 141,144,251, 287,312
  Commission on Doctrinal Matters 91,92,130
  Commission on Inter-church Relations 95,130
  Committee for Mission Expansion 278
  Committee on Interim Missions 109,130,278,295
  Committee on Relief 78
  Convention Proceedings 74,278, 324
  Dakota-Montana District 65
  Dr. Martin Luther College 64,112, 264
  Executive Committee for Japan, Europe, Asia 156,162,324
  Executive Committee for Latin American Missions 226,234, 283,284,293
  Executive Committee for Southeast Asian Missions 250,254, 255,258,259,263,265,270,274, 276-278,305,320
  Executive Committee for the German Mission 87,88
  Executive Committee for the Lutheran Apache Mission 33,58, 143,251,306,325
  Executive Committee for the Lutheran Church of Central Africa 137,172,176,181-183,185-189, 191,192,196,199,200,204-207, 210,212,218,221,320,325
  Executive of Indian Missions 39
  General Mission Board 31,87,144, 145,172,313
  General Synodical Committee 143, 144,172
  German Evangelical Lutheran Ministerium of Wisconsin 14,310
  Home Missions Program 145
  Joint Commission on Missions 70
  Joint Synod of Wisconsin, Minnesota, Michigan and Other States 14,20,65,311,323
  Lutheran Spiritual Welfare Commission 145,151,313
  Michigan District 115,145,249
  Michigan Lutheran Seminary 96, 112,250
  Northwestern College 63,64,71, 112,113,212
  Northwestern Lutheran Academy 112
  Pacific Northwest District 65
  Reaching Out Offering 133,272, 273,290,320
  Special Ministries Board 151
Wisconsin Lutheran High School 212, 253
Wisconsin Lutheran Seminary 32,39, 64-66,95,106,110,113,130,131, 161,240,265,277,281,294,311, 314,317,324
Wong Siu Han 269,271

World Mission Conference 281, 318
World Seminary Conference 303, 324
World War I 56,65,66,67,73,111-114
World War II 37,60,73,75-77,115, 125,143,151,166,178,183 222, 260, 262
Worldwide Evangelist 136
Wrede, H. 14

X

Xavier, Francis 150,276

Y

Yamada, Pastor 158
Yokohama, Japan 153,161,319
Yoshida, Tadashi 160
You and Your Synod 60,322
Yxenhult, Sweden 101,102,108

Z

Zacharius, Mrs. Edward 276,277
Zaire 213,216,305
Zambezi River 171,177,178
Zambia 105,123,136,175-221,241, 282,305,308,315-318,321
Zgierz, Poland 71
Ziegenbalg, Bartholomaeus 15,276
Ziegler, Paul 172,176,177,180,182, 185,219,313
Ziegler, Tilda 176,177,182,313
Zielke, Leopold 71,77,78,79
Zimbabwe 177,178
Zimdars, Ernest 231,286,287,291, 315,318
Zimmermann, Raymond 58,244,281-283,315,319
Zomba, Malawi 195,218
Zushi, Japan 161
Zwickau, Germany 77,312

NOTE: WELS work in Hong Kong has been carried on under the following names:
1. Christian Chinese Lutheran Mission (CCLM), founded in 1956. WELS official support began in 1965.
2. Chinese Evanqelical Lutheran Church (CELC), 1965-1977
3. Southeast Asian Lutheran Mission (SALEM), 1977 to present

MAPS

WELS in the Midwest	12
Lutheran Apache Mission	22
Churches in Germany and Poland, 1924 to Present	68
Evangelical Lutheran Free Church, Germany	93
Lutheran Confessional Church, Sweden, Norway, Finland	98
Christ the King Lutheran Church of Nigeria, The Lutheran Church of Cameroon	118
Lutheran Evangelical Christian Church in Japan	148
1949 Mission Trek	168
Lutheran Church of Central Africa, Zambia	174
Lutheran Church of Central Africa, Malawi	194
Confessional Evangelical Lutheran Church of Mexico	230
Confessional Lutheran Church in India, Christ Evangelical Lutheran Church (India), Indonesian Lutheran Church	242
South Asian Lutheran Evangelical Mission (Hong Kong), Christian Lutheran Evangelical Church (Taiwan)	246
Confessional Lutheran Church of Colombia, Confessional Lutheran Church of Brazil	285
WELS World Missions	300